The Go-To Guide for

ENGINEERING CURRICULA, PreK–5

The Go-To Guide for

ENGINEERING CURRICULA, PreK–5

Choosing and Using the Best Instructional Materials for Your Students

EDITED BY

CARY I. SNEIDER

CORWIN
A SAGE Company

FOR INFORMATION:

Corwin

A SAGE Company

2455 Teller Road

Thousand Oaks, California 91320

(800) 233-9936

www.corwin.com

SAGE Publications Ltd.

1 Oliver's Yard

55 City Road

London EC1Y 1SP

United Kingdom

SAGE Publications India Pvt. Ltd.

B 1/I 1 Mohan Cooperative Industrial Area

Mathura Road, New Delhi 110 044

India

SAGE Publications Asia-Pacific Pte. Ltd.

3 Church Street

#10-04 Samsung Hub

Singapore 049483

Acquisitions Editor: Robin Najar

Associate Editor: Julie Nemer

Editorial Assistant: Ariel Price

Project Editor: Amy Schroller

Copy Editor: Amy Rosenstein

Typesetter: C&M Digitals (P) Ltd.

Proofreader: Rae Ann Goodwin

Indexer: Michael Ferreira

Cover Designer: Gail Buschman

Printed in the United States of America.

A catalog record of this book is available from the Library of Congress.

ISBN 978-1-4833-0736-7

This book is printed on acid-free paper.

14 15 16 17 18 10 9 8 7 6 5 4 3 2 1

Contents

Foreword

I have a dream. Nearly all of our youngsters will graduate high school, and nearly all will be excellent readers, manipulate numbers and estimate easily, be able to argue a point using trustworthy evidence to back it up, make decisions informed by common knowledge, solve complex problems well, understand how scientists and engineers reason and be able to do some of that reasoning themselves, express themselves articulately, work well with others, recognize what they know and when they need to learn more, have passionate opinions backed by knowledge, and appreciate the roles they might take on (and love to engage in) as productive adults.

By middle school, students will begin to have some idea of the kinds of employment they might want to engage in as adults, and as a result of the experiences they are having in school and at home, they will evolve their interests over time and develop mature passions as they move through high school and beyond, imagining what they might be or be doing as adults, working toward aligning themselves with some of these possibilities, deciding they are interested in some and not interested in others, and eventually identifying how they will live their lives and achieve their goals. Some will be scientists or engineers; some will be writers or expressive artists; some will provide services; some will be technicians; but all will be gainfully employed doing something they want to be doing.

Plenty of research on how people learn suggests that engaging learners in achieving engineering challenges that they are personally interested in and capable of solving successfully (with help) can go a long way toward fulfilling my dream, which I hope you share. You can play an essential role in your students' lives by engaging them in design challenges that are relevant to their personal interests and helping them to extract lessons from their work about how to define and solve problems and to imagine themselves as grown-ups who can solve important problems in the real world. A tall order, for sure, but not an impossible one. It won't happen tomorrow, and it won't happen at all if we don't seriously take on the challenge.

There are many reasons to be optimistic about the role design challenges can play in helping our youngsters grow and learn. First, it is not hard to make engineering design challenges fun, and it is not hard to help students see the value of math and science in their everyday lives if they are using disciplinary knowledge to address challenges they recognize as important. Achieving complex design challenges will not be easy fun for students, but if they are interested enough, they will put in the hard work. And if they see the value in what they are doing and learning and experience the success of learning and using science, more might enjoy science; more might see themselves as people who can engage well in thinking scientifically; more might understand the role science plays in our everyday world; more might become scientists, engineers, technicians, or policy makers who use science; and more might engage, during their adult lives, in thinking scientifically at times when that is appropriate.

Second, we know that developing deep understanding and masterful capabilities is hard and requires considerable time, but we also know that when somebody is really interested in what they are learning or in what they are attempting to do, and if the expectations are not so far beyond their capabilities that activities are overly frustrating, then people are willing to put in the time and effort. Learning something well, whether we are gaining understanding or learning how to do something, requires time and patience; it requires that we try our best to understand or achieve a challenge, that we pay attention to results and judge what is successful and not as successful, that we work on explaining when we don't understand something well or when we are not as successful as we want at solving a problem, that we develop new ideas and understandings, and that we have chances to try again (and fail again, and so on).

Achieving engineering design challenges provides opportunities for doing all of these things—trying and not quite getting it right, observing what happens, explaining, developing new understandings, and trying again. When a science class is achieving engineering challenges together, the teacher and class can work as a unit to provide the help everyone in the class needs to engage successfully in all of these processes. Not every student in the class will learn everything in depth or become masterfully adept at all skills and practices, but engaging together as a class in achieving engineering design challenges makes the classroom a place to help all students achieve as well as they can.

Third, engineering design challenges provide opportunities to use science, to engage in carrying out disciplinary practices, to engage in engineering design practices, and to engage in 21st-century skills. When students get excited about achieving a challenge, they will want to develop the necessary skills well enough to be able to achieve the challenge; if they need each other's advice, they will want to learn how to give good advice and take advice well, and if they are working on a challenge that requires several kinds of expertise or perspective, they will want to learn to collaborate well. When a class engages in engineering design together, there are opportunities to reflect on and discuss how to carry out skills and practices well, and when students are eager to achieve the engineering design goal, they will also be eager to know how to do whatever is necessary to achieve that goal; they will take the time to reflect on what they are doing and work on refining the way they carry out processes if time is set aside for that and appropriate help is given.

Fourth, we know that learners become more engaged and interested and willing to work hard when they are able to take on agency, that is, when they are trusted to make choices. There are rarely optimal choices in achieving engineering goals; engineers are constantly involved in making trade-offs, and several engineers working on the same real-world problem might come up with very different designs. The context of achieving engineering design challenges is perfect for allowing learners agency. When different groups suggest different solutions, have a chance to present and justify their solutions for the class, and have a chance to argue with each other using evidence, learning opportunities are enhanced for everybody in the class, as each group gets to experience and think about not only their own ideas but also the ideas of others.

Finally, when learners are allowed to try on the shoes of scientists and engineers, they also can begin to imagine themselves in those shoes. Students who are helped to be successful student scientists and student engineers, as they are asked to do in achieving engineering design challenges, will also begin to develop understandings of the kinds of activities they enjoy and the kinds of work they might want to do later in life. If the set of challenges they attempt is large, encompassing a large variety of disciplines, life situations, and roles they might take on, they will have solid foundations to build on in imagining their futures.

Everything we know about how people learn and how to promote learning suggests that engaging our young people in achieving engineering challenges and solving engineering problems has potential to promote deep science learning and mastery of important disciplinary and life skills. The Next Generation Science Standards (NGSS) (NGSS Lead States, 2013), in encouraging curriculum approaches that foster learning STEM skills and practices along with science content, give school systems and teachers permission to move in that direction.

* * *

This book documents 14 sets of curriculum materials for the elementary years that integrate engineering design as a part of science. Although these materials were developed before publication of the NGSS, the authors of these chapters explain ways that they can be used today to support the NGSS at the middle school level. And nearly all will be fine-tuned in the years to come as developers gain further experience with the NGSS.

Each of the chapters illustrates different ways that engineering design can help achieve my dream, starting with Chapter 1, *Engineering Is Elementary: Engineering for Elementary School Students,* which illustrates how to use engineering as a context to combine science, social studies, and reading. Students use storybooks about children from around the world to learn about different engineering projects and professions, and then engage in related hands-on engineering design projects related to the stories.

In Chapter 2, *Physical Science Comes Alive! Integrating Engineering and Science Through Design and Troubleshooting of Cars and Gadgets* students combine art, science, and engineering design as they create their own vehicles and gadgets that move and light up. The tasks are designed to introduce students to mechanical and electrical principles that they apply to building, troubleshooting, and redesigning their creations.

Chapter 3, *Engineering byDesign TEEMS™: Kindergarten Through Second Grade,* describes three modules organized around environmental contexts and real-world design challenges, including designing a birdhouse, planning a sustainable garden, and cleaning up oil spills, that require students to learn and apply targeted technology, engineering, mathematics, and science concepts.

BSCS Science Tracks: Connecting Science and Literacy, featured in Chapter 4, is a complete K–5 curriculum in which students learn and apply basic science concepts through engaging experiences that involve them both physically and mentally in the processes of scientific inquiry and engineering design. Lessons employ the 5E instructional model, developed by educators at BSCS.

Chapter 5, *A World in Motion: From SAE International,* offers design challenges for students in Grades K–3, 4–6, and 7–8. The materials were developed by SAE International, a professional organization of more than 100,000 engineers in various industries, with a strong commitment to volunteering in the nation's schools. The challenges involve designing, creating, and testing various kinds of vehicles.

Chapter 6, *Engineering Opportunities in FOSS (The Full Option Science System): Third Edition for Upper Elementary Science Students,* summarizes the history of this K–8 curriculum series that has long featured engineering alongside science. The third edition, which is featured in this chapter, was a major reinvention of the curriculum that featured fusion of the STEM fields, consistent with the vision of the *Framework for K–12 Science Education* (NRC, 2012). Featured modules in this chapter include Electricity and Electromagnetism and Motion, Force, and Models.

Chapter 7, *Seeds of Science/Roots of Reading,* engages students in firsthand investigations, student-to-student discussion, reading science texts, and writing. The curriculum is designed to help students develop the specialized skills involved in reading, writing, and talking about science as well as practices of science and engineering.

Computer programming for kindergarteners is the topic of Chapter 8, *Tangible Kindergarten: Learning How to Program Robots in Early Childhood.* The chapter describes how kindergartners work individually, in pairs, and in teams to program a robot's behaviors. In the process they apply knowledge of mathematics, use inquiry and problem-solving skills, and develop their creativity by using the engineering design process.

Educators who teach in afterschool or summer programs will be especially interested in Chapter 9, *Engineering Adventures: Engineering for Out-of-School Time,* which provides several examples to illustrate how setting the context for an engineering challenge by using a realistic scenario helps children connect engineering to the world in which they live and helps them become more invested in the problem.

Chapter 10, *Engineering byDesign TEEMS™ and I³: For Grades 3, 4, 5, and 6,* describes how a fifth-grade teacher helps his students design and build a working wind turbine, develop their ideas into inventions, and solve problems in food safety, structural engineering, transportation, and communication.

Chapter 11, *Design It! Design Engineering Projects for Afterschool,* is about a curriculum that was created for children from traditionally underserved communities who regularly attend afterschool and other nonacademic out-of-school programs. Each *Design It!* project consists of a series of *challenges* that lead toward an engaging endpoint—a rollercoaster, go-cart, bridge, crane, glider, string telephone, pinball machine, trebuchet, top or yo-yo—made out of commonly available, expendable, and inexpensive materials.

Chapter 12, *Engineering for Everyone: 4-H's Junk Drawer Robotics Curriculum,* describes a series of three modules that use common household items such as paperclips, brass brads, toy motors, craft sticks, batteries, aluminum foil, and binder clips in a sequence of activities that enable students to design their own creative electro-mechanical robots. The program is designed for use by 4-H volunteers or other youth program leaders.

Chapter 13, *PictureSTEM,* concerns a series of modules that use high-quality trade books with compelling stories that engage student interest and pose a problem that can be solved by the engineering design process. In the next part of the module, students solve the problem by brainstorming, proposing multiple potential solutions, and evaluating the pros and cons of competing solutions. The students then implement their design by creating and testing a prototype, model, or other product.

Chapter 14, *STEM in Action: Solar House Design,* describes a series of modules for preK through Grade 5 that integrate science and mathematics through engineering design challenges. The developers emphasize the importance of beginning with integrated STEM programs as early as possible. The chapter features a unit for fourth grade on designing and building a model house warmed by the power of sunlight.

* * *

It will not be easy to make traditional classrooms into engineering design classrooms. Some students who are used to reading and answering questions will balk at having to work hard; other students for whom learning comes easy will balk at having to work collaboratively with their classmates. If you are new to engineering education, you will have to learn new ways of interacting with students and facilitating learning. It does not take long to draw students in if challenges are meaningful to them and if they are trusted with agency, but it will take a special effort to develop new ways of interacting with your students.

If this is your first time teaching engineering, you may not be as successful as you want immediately, but don't worry. As you learn to be a better facilitator of the engineering design process, your students will learn more deeply. If possible, work together with other teachers who are also learning to implement engineering or other project-based activities in their classrooms. And just as your students will be learning a new approach by attempting to solve a problem but not quite succeeding, getting help in understanding why their first approach didn't work, then redesigning, and trying again, it is very likely that you will go through a similar sequence of stages in your teaching. It will take time and willingness to work through possibly frustrating attempts to enact very different kinds of activities than you are used to, but it will be worthy and worthwhile work.

* * *

The many chapters in this collection provide advice and resources for using design challenges and problems to promote science learning. I hope that the chapters help readers develop imagination about integrating engineering design and problem-solving experiences into science classes, passion for moving forward to implement engineering design activities in their classrooms, and understanding of the conditions under which integrating such activities into our classrooms will lead to deep learning.

Choosing which of these instructional materials are right for you and your students is, of course, a huge part of the challenge. But it should be possible to identify likely candidates by reading the first three or four pages of each chapter, then reading the complete chapter for those that are most likely to meet your needs. As you do that, you might keep in mind several thoughts:

- Good education is not about "covering the material." Developing deep understanding and masterful capabilities is hard and requires considerable time. It is more important that students spend significant time on a few projects than that they do a lot of brief activities that cover a wide variety of topics.
- In order to sustain your students' interests over time, it is essential for projects to be sufficiently interesting and diverse to maintain your students' attention. Resources will provide some advice about how to do that, but you know your students better than curriculum developers; use your judgment to help problems come alive for your students, and if you see interest waning, figure out how to bring interest back. It's not hard to keep youngsters excited about things that impact their world and that help them experience worlds they've become familiar with, from TV or the movies, but sometimes they need to be reminded why they are doing what they are doing.
- Judging the difficulty of a task will require your best judgment as a teacher. The requirements of a task should not be so difficult that it becomes frustrating so that students give up. Conversely, if what they are asked to do is too easy, students will not have opportunities to develop new skills or gain confidence in their abilities to tackle and solve really challenging problems. Some materials allow you to modify the level of the challenge to meet your students' needs.
- Opportunities for teamwork are evident in every one of these sets of materials. However, some are more explicit than others about how to manage teams and help students learn to work together effectively. What is important to remember is that working in teams should not just be seen as a way of managing the classroom, but rather, it is important for students to come to appreciate the benefits of collaboration and learn how to collaborate well. Help your students identify the understanding

and capabilities they are gaining from teamwork and help them develop collaboration habits that they use and further develop across curriculum units and projects.

- Many of the materials described in this book expose students to the world of technology and a wide variety of career possibilities. Helping students recognize those possibilities provides a way of keeping them engaged and will aim students toward goals that are part of my dream (and I hope yours).
- In choosing materials to use in your classroom, remember that in addition to choosing particular curriculum units for the targeted content they address and the interests of your students, it is important that your students experience and appreciate the big ideas of science and technology. Curriculum materials used over a year or several years of school should build on each other in ways that allow learners to see the connections between topical areas and to exercise and develop their capabilities. Help your students see across curriculum units as well as digging deep into the content and skills targeted in each one.

I offer my best wishes and congratulations to all of your efforts! I will be cheering for all of you and looking forward to meeting your many learned and mature-thinking students and experiencing the success of your endeavors in the decades to come.

Janet L. Kolodner
Georgia Institute of Technology

References

NGSS Lead States. (2013). *Next Generation Science Standards: For states, by states.* Washington, DC: The National Academies Press.

National Research Council. (2012). *A framework for K–12 science education: Practices, crosscutting concepts, and core ideas.* Washington, DC: The National Academies Press.

 **Janet L. Kolodner** is Regents' Professor at Georgia Institute of Technology, where she served as coordinator of the cognitive science program for many years. Dr. Kolodner was founding director of Georgia Tech's EduTech Institute, whose mission is to use what we know about cognition to inform the design of educational technology and learning environments. Professor Kolodner is founding editor in chief of *The Journal of the Learning Sciences,* an interdisciplinary journal that focuses on learning and education. She is also a founder of the International Society for the Learning Sciences, and she served as its first executive officer. Her research has addressed issues in learning, memory, and problem solving, both in computers and in people. Dr. Kolodner's book, *Case-Based Reasoning,* synthesizes work across the field. Dr. Kolodner has focused most of her research using the model of case-based reasoning to design science curricula for middle school, in which students learn science and scientific reasoning in the context of designing working artifacts. More recently, she and her students are applying what they've learned about design-based learning to informal education—afterschool programs, museum programs, and museum exhibits. The goal of these projects is to identify ways of helping children and youth consider who they are as thinkers and to come to value informed decision making and informed production and consumption of evidence.

Acknowledgments

First, I wish to thank the authors of these chapters, not only for taking the time to craft a compelling description of their curriculum, but also for the foresight and persistence that it took to develop instructional materials in engineering, long before there were standards to support their efforts.

Recalling my early education that technology and engineering are allied with science but are also different in important ways, I want to acknowledge my early mentors, Robert Maybury, Harold Foecke, and Alan Friedman, as well as the leaders of the National Center for Technological Literacy at the Museum of Science in Boston, including especially Ioannis Miaoulis, Yvone Spicer, Peter Wong, and Christine Cunningham, and the many teachers and administrators in Massachusetts who were among the early adopters of what we now call Integrated STEM education.

I also appreciate the support of colleagues at Achieve, Inc., including the writers of the NGSS, Stephen Pruitt who led the effort, the brilliant and supportive staff, and the members of the NGSS Lead State Teams, for their steadfast dedication to crafting standards that fully embrace engineering as an equal partner to science. The current leadership of Achieve, Inc. is commended for granting permission to quote extensively from the NGSS.

Thanks also to the extraordinary personnel at the NRC, including the committee members and staff who developed *A Framework for K–12 Science Education: Practices, Crosscutting Concepts, and Core Ideas* and members of the Board on Science Education, especially Helen Quinn, Linda Katehi, and Heidi Schweingruber, who played crucial roles in the development of new science education standards.

Senior staff of the National Academies Press have also contributed to this work and to science education more broadly by making available free of charge the Framework and NGSS, along with many other important science education reports. The Press has given its permission to quote freely from the Framework and has asked us to publicize the availability of both the free downloads and hardcopy versions of the Framework and NGSS at its website (http://www.nap.edu/catalog.php?record_id=13165).

Worthy of special thanks is the generosity of Jan Morrison, president and chief executive officer of Teaching Institute for Excellence in STEM (TIES), whose major gift provided substantial support for this effort, and to the leadership of Corwin, who also provided financial support above and beyond the costs of publishing.

I also want to acknowledge Robin Najar and Julie Nemer, my editors at Corwin, her assistant, Ariel Price, copy editor Amy Rosenstein, and the many other people at Corwin who made this set of volumes possible.

Although it is somewhat unusual for an editor to thank his readers, I also want to acknowledge your courage for being among the first to help bring the new world of STEM learning into being.

Publisher's Acknowledgments

Corwin wishes to acknowledge the following peer reviewers for their editorial insight and guidance.

Joan Baltezore, Science Instructor
West Fargo High School
West Fargo, ND

Arthur H. Camins, Director
Stevens Institute of Technology/CIESE
Charles V. Schaefer School of Engineering
Castle Point on Hudson
Hoboken, NJ

Kelly Cannon, K–12 Science Program Coordinator
Washoe County School District
Reno, NV

Mandy Frantti, Physics/Astronomy/Mathematics Teacher
NASA Astrophysics Educator Ambassador
Munising Middle-High School
Munising, MI

Loukea Kovanis-Wilson, Chemistry Instructor
Clarkston Community Schools
Clarkston, MI

Sara Stewart, Educational Technology Specialist
Washoe County School District
Reno, NV

About the Editor

Cary I. Sneider is an associate research professor in the Center for Science Education at Portland State University in Portland, Oregon, where he teaches research methodology to teachers in a master's degree program. In recent years, he served the NRC as design lead for technology and engineering to help develop *A Framework for K–12 Science Education: Practices, Crosscutting Concepts, and Core Ideas*, which has provided the blueprint for the NGSS. He then played a similar role on the writing team to produce the NGSS, which was released in April 2013. The recognition that teachers would need access to instructional materials to help them meet the new standards led Sneider to develop the current volume, *The Go-To Guide for Engineering Curricula PreK–5.*

Sneider was not always interested in engineering—or at least he didn't know that he was. For as long as he can remember, he was interested in astronomy. He read all he could find about it, and when he was in middle school his father bought him a small telescope. In high school, Sneider built his own telescopes, grinding mirrors, and designing and building mountings. All this time he thought he was doing *science*. Today, he recognizes that like many scientists, he especially enjoyed the *engineering* part of the work.

During his junior year at college, Sneider had an opportunity to teach at an Upward Bound program and found that he enjoyed teaching even more than research in astronomy. In subsequent years, he taught science in Maine, Costa Rica, Coalinga California, and the Federated States of Micronesia. He returned to college, this time to obtain a teaching credential and eventually a Ph.D. in science education from the University of California at Berkeley. He spent nearly 30 years in Berkeley, developing instructional materials and running teacher institutes at the Lawrence Hall of Science. He spent another decade as vice president at the Museum of Science in Boston, where he developed a high school curriculum called Engineering the Future, and finally moved to Portland, Oregon, to be closer to children and grandchildren.

During his career, Sneider directed more than 20 federal, state, and foundation grant projects, mostly involving curriculum development and teacher education. His research and development interests have focused on helping students and museum visitors unravel their misconceptions in science, on new ways to link science centers and schools to promote student inquiry, and on integrating engineering and technology education into the K–12 curriculum. In 1997, he received the Distinguished Informal Science Education award from the National Science Teachers Association and in 2003 was named National Associate of the National Academy of Sciences for his service on several NRC committees.

About the Contributors

Jacqueline Barber is associate director of the Lawrence Hall of Science at the University of California, Berkeley. She is responsible for the Hall's Curriculum Center and also leads The Learning Design Group, a team of talented curriculum designers. The Learning Design Group has a portfolio that includes an award-winning collection of curriculum products supported by a robust curriculum implementation network, with active implementation support sites from Carson City to Cleveland, and from Japan to Jordan. With her long-time collaborator, P. David Pearson, Barber has launched a curriculum and research program, focused on the integration of science and literacy, titled *Seeds of Science/ Roots of Reading.*

Gary Benenson is Professor of Mechanical Engineering at City College, and Project Director of Physical Science Comes Alive! Prof. Benenson has taught engineering and technology for more than 30 years, and has been Project Director of four NSF-funded projects focused on elementary science and engineering.

Marina Umaschi Bers is a professor at the Eliot-Pearson Department of Child Study and Human Development and an adjunct professor in the Computer Science Department at Tufts University. She heads the interdisciplinary Developmental Technologies research group. Her research involves the design and study of innovative learning technologies to promote children's positive development.

Angula Bumbury Camacho has been an educator for the past 32 years, with students both in and out of New York. She is currently a third-grade teacher at Public School 5, in Bedford-Stuyvesant, Brooklyn.

Cherubim Cannon currently teaches pre-K at PS 5 in the Bedford-Stuyvesant section of Brooklyn, where she has also taught both in Special Education, and grades K, 1, 3 and 5 over the past 15 years. She has also led City Technology Professional Development for the NYC DoE.

Diana V. Cantu is assistant director of Professional Development for the STEM Center for Teaching and Learning, a division of the International Technology and Engineering Educators Association. She has been an elementary school teacher, corporate trainer, and Teacher Effectiveness Coach for Engineering byDesignTM. She also works as an adjunct instructor at Old Dominion University in Virginia, where she is finishing her doctoral degree in elementary STEM education. Her passion is working with teachers to promote STEM awareness, engineering education, and integrative practices in primary grades.

Janet Carlson, Ph.D., is currently the executive director of the Center to Support Excellence in Teaching at Stanford University in the Graduate School of Education. Prior to taking this position, she worked at BSCS for 23 years developing curriculum materials, leading professional development, and conducting research. She began her career as a middle and high school science teacher after receiving a B.A. in environmental biology from Carleton College. After leaving the classroom, she went on to earn an M.S. in curriculum and instruction from Kansas State University and a Ph.D. in instruction and curriculum from the University of Colorado.

Christopher Ciuca is *Director of Pre-Professional Programs* at SAE International. As a former classroom teacher, Chris oversees the strategic direction of SAE's pre-professional program portfolio including the *National Science Board Public* Service Award Winning—*A World In Motion* (AWIM) and Collegiate Design Series programs.

Dr. Christine M. Cunningham is an educational researcher who works to make engineering and science more relevant, accessible, and understandable, especially for underserved and underrepresented populations. A vice president at the Museum of Science, Boston, since 2003, she founded and directs Engineering is Elementary™, a groundbreaking project that integrates engineering concepts into elementary curriculum and teacher professional development. Dr. Cunningham previously served as director of research at the Tufts University Center for Engineering Educational Outreach and directed the Women's Experiences in College Engineering project. Dr. Cunningham holds B.A. and M.A. degrees in biology from Yale and a Ph.D. in science education from Cornell University.

Linda De Lucchi is co-director of the Full Optional Science System Project (FOSS K–8) at Lawrence Hall of Science, University of California at Berkeley. She has designed instructional materials in science education (FOSS), environmental education (OBIS), health education (HAP Project), and special education (SAVI/SELPH) for 40 years.

Dr. Barbara diSioudi was educated at Texas A&M University, earning both an undergraduate degree as well as a Ph.D. in toxicology. She spent the first nine years of her career teaching eighth-grade science and eventually taught college-level biology. After leaving the classroom, Dr. diSioudi developed technology curriculum and teacher's editions for Pearson Scott Foresman. In 2007, she joined ETA hand2mind, directing product development. Today, she leads the hand2mind research and development team. Driven to provide exceptional learning experiences for both students and teachers alike, Dr. diSioudi participates in industry groups such as the National Science Teachers Association, the National Council of Teachers of Mathematics, and SIIA's education division.

Saundra Wever Frerichs, Ph.D., is the 4-H science education specialist at the University of Nebraska–Lincoln. Dr. Frerichs's work is focused on informal science education—science learning outside of a traditional classroom setting. This has included work with 4-H, with museums in the United States and the United Kingdom, and other youth development programs. In the area of developing resources for learning, her work includes museum-based programs for youth, adults and educators, science learning kits, museum exhibits, curricula for youth, and professional development for educators. Dr. Frerichs's research examines the impact of these learning resources, the effectiveness of teacher professional development, and interaction between informal and formal educational institutions.

Elizabeth Gajdzik is the assistant director of the Institute for P–12 Engineering Research and Learning (INSPIRE) in the School of Engineering Education at Purdue University. Prior to her work at INSPIRE, Gajdzik was a district curriculum math specialist in San Antonio, Texas, and a middle school math teacher at a Title I school in Waco, Texas. She received both her B.S. in interdisciplinary studies, with a specialization in mathematics education, and M.S.Ed. in curriculum and instruction, with an emphasis in mathematics education from Baylor University. She, her husband, and their two children currently reside in West Lafayette, Indiana.

William Giese is currently a principal at Sam Davey Elementary in Eau Claire, Wisconsin. Prior to becoming an administrator, he had taught in the elementary classroom for 19 years. While teaching, Giese tried to engage all learners in a hands-on, minds-on fashion. STEM education is a way to accomplish this. Giese is a Teacher Effectiveness Coach with the EbD (Engineering byDesignTM) Curriculum through the International Technology and Engineering Education Association. He is married and the proud father of four children.

Melissa Higgins is the director of curriculum development for Engineering is Elementary (EiE). She works to create exciting, hands-on, minds-on engineering challenges that inspire children and educators to engage in and enjoy STEM learning. Upon joining the EiE team in 2004, Higgins helped to create the project's flagship in-school EiE curriculum. Beginning in 2010, Higgins spearheaded the development of engineering curricula for afterschool and camp programs, including the Engineering Adventures and Engineering Everywhere programs. Higgins holds a B.A. in architectural studies from Connecticut College and an M.A. in museum studies from the Harvard University Extension School.

Jody Hilton is currently a 2nd-grade teacher at the Christopher Avenue Community School in Brownsville, Brooklyn. She has taught for 17 years in the NYC Public School system, in grades 2, 3 and 6. She has conducted City Technology workshops at three Environmental Sciences Summer Institutes sponsored by Texas A&M.

Charles Hutchison, Ed.M., senior research scientist at Education Development Center, Inc. in Waltham, Massachusetts, directs the National Partnerships for AfterSchool Science that trains afterschool educators to lead high-quality afterschool science and engineering programs and works to increase the quality and quantity of science available for students from underserved populations. He coauthored the Design It! and Explore It! afterschool science and engineering curriculum series. Hutchison is a former military engineer (U.K.) and elementary and middle school teacher in the United States, with more than 25 years of experience teaching and developing hands-on science and engineering curriculum for school-age children.

Donna Johnson is a Science and Technology Teacher at PS 21, the Crispus Attucks School, in the Bedford-Stuyvesant section of Brooklyn, NY. She has been a teacher for 28 years, and has taught students in Kindergarten through sixth grade.

Janet Kolodner's research addresses learning, memory, and problem solving in computers and people. She pioneered the computer method called case-based reasoning and uses its cognitive model to design formal and informal science curriculum. Learning by

Design, her design-based inquiry-oriented approach to science learning, is a foundation of Project-Based Inquiry Science, a three-year middle school science curriculum. In her informal science education endeavors, middle schoolers learn science through cooking and learn to explain while designing hovercraft. She is founding editor in chief of *Journal of the Learning Sciences* and a founder of the International Society for the Learning Sciences.

Nancy M. Landes, Ph.D., recently retired from BSCS, where she served as a senior science educator. She has a master of arts degree in curriculum and instruction and a Ph.D. in science education from Michigan State University. Dr. Landes joined the BSCS staff as a curriculum developer in 1983. At BSCS, she directed a number of projects, including BSCS Science TRACKS: Connecting Science and Literacy. She was part of the team that developed the BSCS 5E instructional model, and she helped cultivate the organization's use of collaborative learning, formative assessment, inquiry-based strategies, and the inclusion of engineering-based education in the elementary science curriculum.

Richard Mahacek, M.A., is the 4-H youth development advisor, emeritus, at the University of California Agriculture and Natural Resources. During his career, Mahacek placed an emphasis on program development around engaging young people in science and engineering and using youth development models. He used his degrees in industrial arts and technology education in the development of curricula and activities in science processes, robotics, computers, GIS/GPS, and environmental issues, such as watersheds and wildlife habitats. Mahacek was lead author and directed the development of Junk Drawer Robotics, published in 2011.

Larry Malone is co-director of the Full Option Science System Project, and has been on the staff at the Lawrence Hall of Science, University of California at Berkeley for 46 years in curriculum development and teacher preparation. He is the creative designer and lead writer of the FOSS instructional materials.

Barbara Martucci teaches 3rd grade at PS 92, Mary McLeod Bethune, in Central Harlem. She has also taught in grades K, 1, 2 and 6 at the same school, where she has been for 12 years. She entered the system as a NYC Teaching Fellow, and holds two Master's degrees.

Emmy Matias-Leonard has worked as an elementary school teacher for the NYC DoE since 1993. She currently teaches a 4/5 bridge class at the Earth School in lower Manhattan, and also works with 1st and 2nd grades. She has been appointed a Science Teacher for 2014-15.

Tamara J. Moore, Ph.D., is an associate professor of Engineering Education at Purdue University. Dr. Moore's research is centered on the integration of STEM concepts in K–12 and postsecondary classrooms in order to help students make connections among the STEM disciplines and achieve deep understanding. Her work focuses on defining STEM integration and investigating its power for student learning. She is creating and testing innovative, interdisciplinary curricular approaches that engage students in developing models of real-world problems and their solutions. Her research also involves working with educators to shift their expectations and instructional practice to facilitate effective STEM integration.

Janice Porter has taught at Pre-K through College levels, and currently teaches fifth grade at Public School 5, in Brooklyn, NY. She is a native of St. Vincent and the Grenadines, where she served as the Principal of an elementary school.

Travis Sloane has been a teacher in the NYC DoE for the past ten years, the last eight of them as an early childhood science specialist. He is currently teaching science in grades pre-K through 2 at the East Side Elementary School, PS 267.

Dr. Johannes Strobel is director, Educational Outreach Programs, and associate professor, Engineering and Education at Texas A&M, College Station. After studying philosophy and information science in Germany, he received his M.Ed. and Ph.D. in Information Science and Learning Technologies from the University of Missouri. NSF and private foundations fund his research. His research and teaching focus on engineering as an innovation in preK–12 education and preK–12 STEM education policy; how to support teachers and students' academic achievements through engineering, engineering "habits of mind," empathy, and care in engineering; and the use of cyberinfrastructure to provide access to and support learning.

Kristina M. Tank is a Ph.D. candidate in science education, with a supporting field in literacy education at the University of Minnesota. She is a former elementary teacher, and her research interests include improving children's science and engineering learning and increasing teachers' use of effective STEM instruction in the elementary grades. More recently, her research has focused on using literacy to support scientific inquiry, engineering design, and STEM integration.

Tara D.M. Wheeler, M.P.A., is the director of Positive Youth Development Learning Products for the National 4-H Council. Wheeler provides leadership for curriculum and professional development operations, which includes product development, management of contracts with universities, and marketing of 4-H educational materials. She coaches national curriculum development teams through the design process of new products and oversees 4-H's Web-based peer-review system. Wheeler earned her masters of public administration, with a focus on nonprofit leadership, from the University of Delaware.

Steven M. Worker, M.S., is the 4-H Science, Engineering, and Technology coordinator at the University of California Agriculture and Natural Resources. Worker coordinates California 4-H professional development, program planning, evaluation, and curriculum development efforts related to science, engineering, and technology education. His work is focused on strengthening 4-H STEM programs using inquiry-based, experiential education grounded in a positive youth development approach. He is a Ph.D. candidate at the UC Davis School of Education, studying design-based learning integrated into out-of-school time learning environments. He earned a master's degree in community development.

Introduction

The NGSS (NGSS Lead States, 2013) have opened the door for engineering to join science as an equal partner in the classroom. What this will look like is still unfolding, but happily, we are not starting from scratch. Many talented educators have been developing instructional materials in engineering for a long time. That's what this book is all about.

The idea of integrating technology and engineering into science teaching is not new. More than 100 years ago, educators such as John Dewey advocated technology education for all students (Lewis, 2004, p. 22). The call for integrating technology and engineering into science standards began with publication of *Science for All Americans* (AAAS, 1989) and has been featured prominently in standards documents ever since. A case in point is the National Science Education Standards (NRC, 1996), which advocated that all students should learn about the relationship between technology and science as well as develop the abilities of technological design.

Despite the many efforts to infuse science teaching with ideas and activities in technology and engineering, the call has been largely ignored. One of the reasons was simply inertia. Science education has traditionally included only the core disciplines of life science, physical science (including chemistry), and Earth and space sciences, so there has been little room for technology and engineering. A second reason is that although state standards were commonly derived from the National Science Education Standards and Benchmarks for Science Literacy (AAAS, 1993/2008), which also called for engineering and technology, each state crafted its own standards, and most ignored engineering and technology. As of 2012 only 12 states included engineering in their science standards (Carr, Bennet, & Strobel, 2012, p. 552).

A third reason is confusion about the term "technology," which most people only apply to computers, cell phones, or other modern gadgets (Meade & Dugger, 2004). There is even less understanding of the term "engineering." If you've ever had difficulty with plumbing in a hotel room and reported the problem to the front desk, it is likely that they called "engineering" to fix the problem. It's not surprising that most people think of engineers as people who fix things (Lachapelle, Phadnis, Hertel, & Cunningham, 2012).

Today the situation is entirely different. A blue-ribbon panel of the NRC, which included Nobel Prize–winning scientists, engineers, university professors, and educational researchers, created a new blueprint for science—*A Framework for K–12 Science Education: Practices, Core Ideas, and Crosscutting Concepts* (NRC, 2012). The Framework calls for engineering to be included at the same level as Newton's laws and the theory of evolution. Furthermore, the Framework served as the blueprint for the NGSS, which are aimed at replacing the current patchwork of state science standards with a common core, as has already been done in mathematics and English language arts. To emphasize that these standards are not federal, but rather an initiative of the National Governor's Association, the full title of the new standards is *Next Generation Science Standards: For States, By States.*[*]

In the new world of science education that is brought into being by these two documents, engineering is a true partner to science. There are several good reasons why this change may pay off at the classroom level in a big way.

The Value of Engineering to Reduce Declining Interest in Science

Most children love science, but it doesn't last. The majority of research studies have found that interest in science remains strong for most boys and girls throughout the elementary grades but begins to drop off in middle school (Osborne, Simon, & Collins, 2003; Sneider, 2011). A few studies, however, have shown some decline as early as elementary school, and a consistent finding is that at all ages, most girls exhibit less interest than boys and students of most minority ethnic groups tend to be less interested in science than Caucasian and Asian American students.

The introduction of engineering as a continuous thread in the science curriculum has the potential to change that trend and maintain students' interests in science as they transition to high school. There are several reasons why (from Cunningham & Lachapelle 2011):

- While many students who are competent in science view the subject as irrelevant for future careers or everyday life, some of these same students—and especially girls and underrepresented minorities—respond positively to subjects such as environmental and medical engineering since these topics have obvious relevance to people's lives.
- Engineering involves students working together in teams, so design challenges appeal to students who enjoy collaborative activities.
- Engineering design challenges have more than one answer, and creativity is a plus. So the activities themselves tend to be fun and engaging.
- There are many more jobs available for engineers than there are for scientists. NASA, for example, hires 10 engineers for every scientist (NASA.gov, 2013). So students see engineering as offering real future job prospects, especially when they see role models of different genders and racial backgrounds who enjoy their work.
- Failure of a design to work as expected does not mean being "wrong." Failure is a natural part of the design process, leading to improved designs, so students are encouraged to try out their ideas without worry.

In the past, few children were exposed to engineering as a school subject. In rare cases, when children were given engineering activities at school, it was likely to have been called "science," and engineering skills were not made explicit. Even in those cases where children *were* given engineering opportunities, it is likely to have been in the physical sciences, such as robotics or building bridges and towers that boys tend to favor, rather than topics

---

[*]*Next Generation Science Standards (NGSS), For States, By States* is a registered trademark of Achieve, Inc. Neither Achieve, Inc. nor the lead states and partners that developed the Next Generation Science Standards were involved in the production of and do not endorse *The Go-To Guide for Engineering Curricula PreK–5*. However, Achieve, Inc. has granted permission for the authors of this book to quote extensively from the NGSS.

such as medical or environmental engineering that appeal equally to girls (Cunningham & Lachapelle, 2011).

So, now that we have science education standards that call for engineering to be deeply integrated into all science classes, how do we get from here to there? If you are reading this book, it is likely that you are interested in an answer to that question. And not surprisingly, there is more than one answer.

How to Get Started

First, you will need instructional materials. Such materials do exist, and many of them can be found on the Web. A variety of websites with engineering activities are listed in Table 0.1. Each of the chapters in this book references additional websites associated with a particular engineering curriculum.

Second, it will be helpful to have at least one colleague, and hopefully several, who can work with you to comb through instructional materials, consider how your school's curriculum might change to implement the new standards, and perhaps establish a professional learning community to examine your first efforts as you try new approaches.

Third, you might be invited to spend a summer writing new curriculum materials that are fully aligned with the NGSS. Having spent a long career developing instructional materials in science and the related STEM fields, let me caution you to think carefully about how you might undertake such a project. Curriculum development is a labor-intensive process that often takes years, and the assistance of many other teachers, to develop an effective lesson that will engage your students' enthusiasm and that also has clear educational objectives and assessment tools. Nonetheless, I have found curriculum development to be a creative and rewarding experience, and you may too.

Fourth—and now we get to the reason this book has come into being—you will very likely find it to be a valuable and enriching experience to listen to the voices of the pioneers, the people who held the vision of "engineering as a partner to science" long before these documents were written and who have spent decades developing engineering curricula.

In the chapters that follow, you will see how engineering educators build on children's innate interests by presenting them with challenging problems, engaging them in designing creative solutions, and helping them understand how science and mathematics apply in their everyday lives. While many of the curricula do concern physical sciences, as a whole they span the entire spectrum of science disciplines.

How This Book Is Organized

Each chapter describes one set of instructional materials with vivid examples of what the curriculum looks like in the classroom, what learning goals it is intended to accomplish, and how it can help you address the vision of the Framework and the performance expectations in the NGSS.

Perhaps more importantly, the instructional materials described in these chapters do more than spark students' interests. They help students develop skills in defining and solving problems, in working on collaborative teams to brainstorm creative ideas, to build prototypes and use controlled experiments to compare different ideas, to design an optimal solution, and to learn about a wide variety of engineering professions.

Table 0.1 A Selection of K–12 Engineering Education Websites

A Framework for K–12 Science Education—http://www.nap.edu/catalog.php?record_id=13165#

Building Big—http://www.pbs.org/wgbh/buildingbig/

Center for Innovation in Engineering and Science Education—http://www.ciese.org

Design Squad—http://pbskids.org/designsquad/

Discover Engineering—http://www.discovere.org

Dragonfly TV—http://pbskids.org/dragonflytv/show/technologyinvention.html

Engineering Education Service Center—http://www.engineeringedu.com

Engineering Go For It—http://teachers.egfi-k12.org

Engineering Pathway—http://www.engineeringpathway.com

How to Smile: All the Best Science and Math Activities—http://www.howtosmile.org

The Infinity Project—http://www.infinity-project.org

Institute for (P–12) Engineering Research and Learning—http://www.inspire-purdue.org

Intel Design and Discovery—http://educate.intel.com/en/DesignDiscovery/

International Technology and Engineering Education Association—http://www.iteaconnect.org

Materials World Modules—http://www.materialsworldmodules.org

Museum of Science, Boston—http://www.mos.org/nctl/

My NASA Data Lesson Plans—http://mynasadata.larc.nasa.gov/my-nasa-data-lesson-plans/

National Science Digital Library—http://nsdl.org/

Next Generation Science Standards—http://www.nap.edu/ngss/

Oregon Pre-Engineering and Applied Sciences—http://opas.ous.edu/resourcesEngCurricular.php

Project Lead the Way—http://pltw.org

Sally Ride Science Academy—https://sallyridescience.com

Science Buddies—http://sciencebuddies.org

Spark Plug into Science—http://www.gse.upenn.edu/spark/sparkkits.php

Stuff that Works (CCNY)—http://www.citytechnology.org/stuff-that-works/home

Teach Engineering—http://www.teachengineering.org/

Try Engineering—http://www.tryengineering.org/

Women in Engineering ProActive Network—http://www.wepan.org/displaycommon.cfm?an=1&subarticlenbr=39

Zoom—http://pbskids.org/zoom/activities/sci/

All of the materials in the collection have been under development for several years, tested by teachers and their students from a wide range of communities, and revised based on feedback. In many cases, they are also supported by research studies of effectiveness. A listing of all the curriculum materials included in this three-volume sequence can be found in Table 0.2, which illustrates the full range of grade levels for which the curriculum can be used.

Table 0.2. Instructional Materials in the *Go-To Guide for Engineering Curricula* Series

Book	Elementary							Middle School			High School			
Curricula	P	K	1	2	3	4	5	6	7	8	9	10	11	12
E1 Engineering is Elementary			▓	▓	▓	▓	▓							
E2 Physical Science Comes Alive!	▓	▓	▓	▓	▓	▓	▓							
E3 Engineering byDesign TEEMS, K–2		▓	▓	▓										
E4 BSCS Science Tracks		▓	▓	▓	▓	▓	▓							
E5 A World in Motion		▓	▓	▓	▓	▓	▓	▓	▓	▓				
E6 FOSS Full Option Science System		▓	▓	▓	▓	▓	▓	▓	▓	▓				
E7 Seeds of Science/Roots of Reading				▓	▓	▓	▓							
E8 Tangible Kindergarten	▓	▓	▓											
E9 Engineering Adventures (OST)					▓	▓	▓							
E10 Engineering byDesign TEEMS, 3–5 & I³					▓	▓	▓	▓	▓					
E11 Design It! (OST)				▓	▓	▓	▓	▓	▓	▓				
E12 Junk Drawer Robotics					▓	▓	▓	▓	▓	▓				
E13 PictureSTEM		▓	▓	▓										
E14 STEM in Action	▓	▓												
M1 Design Squad (OST)							▓	▓	▓	▓	▓	▓	▓	▓
M2 Models in Technology and Science								▓	▓	▓				

(Continued)

Table 0.2 (Continued)

Book / Curricula	Elementary							Middle School			High School			
	P	K	1	2	3	4	5	6	7	8	9	10	11	12
M3 Everyday Engineering							▓	▓	▓	▓	▓			
M4 SLIDER								▓	▓	▓				
M5 Teaching Engineering Made Easy								▓	▓	▓				
M6 Fender Bender Physics								▓	▓	▓				
M7 Technology in Practice								▓	▓	▓				
M8 IQWST								▓	▓	▓				
M9 Project-Based Inquiry Science								▓	▓	▓				
M10 Issue-Oriented Science								▓	▓	▓				
M11 Techbridge (OST)								▓	▓	▓	▓	▓	▓	▓
M12 Waterbotics (OST)								▓	▓	▓	▓	▓	▓	▓
M13 Engineering Now								▓	▓	▓	▓	▓	▓	▓
M14 Engineering byDesign 6–8								▓	▓	▓	▓	▓	▓	▓
H1 INSPIRES											▓	▓	▓	▓
H2 Active Physics											▓	▓	▓	▓
H3 Active Chemistry											▓	▓	▓	▓
H4 Engineering the Future											▓	▓	▓	▓
H5 Engineer Your World											▓	▓	▓	▓
H6 Global Systems Science											▓	▓	▓	▓
H7 Science and Global Issues											▓	▓	▓	▓
H8 Engineering byDesign											▓	▓	▓	▓
H9 Science by Design											▓	▓	▓	▓
H10 Biology in a Box								▓	▓	▓	▓	▓	▓	▓
H11 Voyage Through Time											▓	▓	▓	▓
H12 EPICS											▓	▓	▓	▓

If you are looking for engineering curricula to try out, you will undoubtedly find something of interest on these pages. If you are part of a group of teachers interested in exploring engineering and science curricula, these chapters could provide stimulating topics for discussion. And if you are challenged with developing new instructional materials, these chapters will help you avoid the need to re-create the wheel.

As you read through these chapters, you may find that several strike you as top candidates for enriching your classroom or school science program. Although too many options is far better than too few, you may need some help in deciding among the top contenders. Happily, a new and very useful tool, with the acronym EQuIP, has popped up on the www.nextgenscience.org website. Educators Evaluating the Quality of Instructional Products (EQuIP) Rubric for Lessons and Units: Science is designed to help you review and select materials based on how well the lessons and units align with the NGSS, and provide instructional and assessment supports.

Before you can use the EQuIP rubric, you will need to have samples of the materials to examine. Contact information is provided at the beginning of each chapter to allow you to do that. You will also need to be familiar with the Framework and the NGSS. The next section provides an overview of engineering in these two important documents, but of course the documents themselves, which can be downloaded free of charge from the National Academies Press website (www.nap.edu), provide much more detail. If you are already familiar with these documents and want to move on to the main business of this book, which is to learn about existing engineering curricula as described by the people who created them, you can get started with Chapter 1, "Design Squad: Inspiring a New Generation of Engineers."

The Framework and the NGSS have the potential to change the face of science education in the country, but only if educators like you embrace the opportunity and begin to imagine what it may mean for the students in your care.

References

American Association for the Advancement of Science. (1989). *Science for all Americans.* New York, NY: Oxford University Press.

American Association for the Advancement of Science. (1993/2008). *Benchmarks for Science Literacy.* New York, NY: Oxford University Press.

Carr, R. L., Bennet, L. D., & Strobel, J. (2012). Engineering in the K–12 STEM standards of the 50 U.S. states: An analysis of presence and extent. *Journal of Engineering Education, 101*(3), 539–564.

Cunningham, C., & Lachapelle, C. (2011). *Designing engineering experiences to engage all students.* Boston, MA: Museum of Science. Retrieved from http://www.eie.org/sites/default/files/2012ip-Cunningham_ Lachapelle_Eng4All.pdf.

Lachapelle, C., Phadnis, P., Hertel, J., & Cunningham, C. (2012). *What is engineering? A survey of elementary students.* Boston, MA: Museum of Science. Retrieved from http://www.eie.org/sites/default/files/ research_article/research_file/2012-03_we_paper_fo_p-12_engineering_conference.pdf.

Lewis, T. (2004). A turn to engineering: The continuing struggle of technology education for legitimization as a school subject. *Journal of Technology Education, 16*(1), 21–39.

Meade, S., & Dugger, W. (2004, September). The second installment of the ITEA/Gallup Poll and what it reveals as to how Americans think about technology. *Technology Teacher, 64*(1), 29–35.

NASA.gov. (2013). *NASA workforce.* Retrieved from http://nasapeople.nasa.gov/workforce/default.htm.

NGSS Lead States. (2013). *Next Generation Science Standards: For states, by states.* Washington, DC: The National Academies Press.

National Research Council. (1996). *National science education standards*. Washington, DC: The National Academies Press.

National Research Council. (2012). *A framework for K–12 science education: Practices, crosscutting concepts, and core ideas*. Washington, DC: The National Academies Press.

Osborne, J., Simon, S., & Collins, S. (2003). Attitudes toward science: A review of the literature and its implications. *International Journal of Science Education, 25*(9), 1049–1097.

Sneider, C. (2011, September 9). *Reversing the swing from science: Implications from a century of research.* Presented at ITEST Convening on Advancing Research on Youth Motivation in STEM. Retrieved from the Noyce Foundation at http://www.noycefdn.org/news.php.

Technology and Engineering in Elementary School Standards

One of the most important contributions of the new standards documents has been to clear up the confusion among the terms "science," "technology," and "engineering." According to the Framework,

> In the K–12 context, "science" is generally taken to mean the traditional natural sciences: physics, chemistry, biology, and (more recently) earth, space, and environmental sciences. . . . We use the term "engineering" in a very broad sense to mean any engagement in a systematic practice of design to achieve solutions to particular human problems. Likewise, we broadly use the term "technology" to include all types of human-made systems and processes—not in the limited sense often used in schools that equates technology with modern computational and communications devices. Technologies result when engineers apply their understanding of the natural world and of human behavior to design ways to satisfy human needs and wants. (NRC, 2012, pp. 11–12)

Definitions alone might not make a big difference, but combining these definitions with an entirely new approach to standards is very likely to be a game changer. Together, the Framework and the NGSS (NGSS Lead States, 2013) have the potential to change the way science is taught in this country.

The Three Dimensions of the NGSS

In order to explain how technology and engineering are integrated in the new standards, it is helpful to understand the three "dimensions" introduced in the Framework and how they appear in the NGSS.

Dimension 1: Science and Engineering Practices

In the National Science Education Standards (NRC, 1996), the set of abilities known collectively as "science inquiry"—what students should be *able to do*—were described separately from the list of what students should *know*. Although the National Science Education Standards (p. 20) advocated combining inquiry and content, it did not specify how to do so. In contrast, the NGSS merge specific practices and core ideas. But before we describe what that looks like, we first describe what has become of inquiry in the NGSS. In its new form, the term "inquiry" has been replaced with eight "practices of science and engineering." Each of the practices is described in some detail, and what is most important for this book is that each practice refers to both science inquiry and engineering design. Following is a description of the eight practices for the elementary school grades, with an emphasis on engineering.

Practice 1: Ask questions and define problems. Just as science inquiry begins with a question, engineering design begins with the definition of a problem. With guidance from a knowledgeable teacher, students' interests in creating things can lead to the formulation of problems to be solved or goals to be met. With prompting, students in Grades K–2 can define a simple problem that can be solved through the development of a new or improved object or tool. During Grades 3–5, students learn to define a problem that requires the development of an object, tool, process, or system that has several criteria for success and constraints on materials, time, and/or cost.

Practice 2: Develop and use models. Whether they are doing science or engineering, students frequently use models. As an engineering practice, students construct models to help them design and test solutions to problems. In Grades K–2, students can develop a simple model based on evidence to represent a proposed object or tool. In Grades 3–5, they can develop a diagram or physical prototype and use it to test their design.

Practice 3: Plan and carry out investigations. There are many different kinds of investigations in science, ranging from controlled laboratory experiments to field biology investigations. In science, investigations are used to answer questions about the natural or designed world. In engineering, students plan and carry out investigations to learn more about the problem they are trying to solve or to test possible solutions. In Grades K–2, students can make observations (firsthand or from media) and/or measurements of a proposed object, tool, or solution to see if it solves a problem or meets a goal. In Grades 3–5, students learn to model and test different designs to see which solves the problem best.

Practice 4: Analyze and interpret data. Science and engineering both involve analyzing and interpreting data. Students in Grades K–2 can analyze data from tests of an object or tool to see if it works as intended. In Grades 3–5, students can represent data in tables and various graphical displays to compare and evaluate the results of different designs and use the data to refine a design solution.

Practice 5: Use mathematics and computational thinking. In addition to analyzing and interpreting data, mathematical thinking includes representing relationships between variables with equations and using computers and other digital tools for automatically collecting, analyzing, and graphing data as well as using simulations. In Grades K–2, students can learn to use quantitative data to compare two alternative solutions to a problem. In Grades 3–5, students can decide if quantitative or qualitative data are best for determining the best solution. They can also create graphs and charts generated from simple algorithms to compare alternative solutions to an engineering problem.

Practice 6: Construct explanations and design solutions. In science, the end result is an explanation for a phenomenon. In engineering, the end result is a solution to a problem. Students in Grades K–2 can use tools and materials to design and build a device that solves a specific problem and compare multiple solutions. In Grades 3–5, students can apply scientific ideas to solving a design problem, generate and compare multiple solutions to a problem based on how well they meet the criteria and constraints of the problem, and identify the evidence that supports one design over another.

Practice 7: Engage in argument from evidence. Although in science students use evidence to argue for or against an explanation for a phenomenon, in engineering students use evidence and reasoning to determine the best possible solution to a problem or to defend their choice of a given solution. In Grades K–2, students can make a claim about the effectiveness of an object, tool, or solution to a problem that is supported by evidence. In Grades 3–5, students can make a claim about the merit of a solution to a problem by citing relevant evidence about how well it meets the criteria and constraints of the problem.

Practice 8: Obtain, evaluate, and communicate information. Both science and engineering involves critical reading and the ability to communicate ideas in writing and speech. In Grades K–2, students can obtain information from a variety of sources that could be helpful in solving a problem and communicate design ideas orally, in written form, or using models. In Grades 3–5, students can obtain and combine information from text that includes tables, diagrams, and charts to inform a solution to a problem. They can also communicate technical information orally and in writing, including various forms of media such as tables, diagrams, and charts.

These eight practices of science and engineering are very important in the NGSS because they are woven into all of the performance expectations, which comprise the heart of the standards.

Dimension 2: Crosscutting Concepts

The second dimension is a set of seven crosscutting concepts. These concepts were also present in earlier standards documents, called "themes" in Benchmarks for Science Literacy, and "unifying concepts and processes" in the National Science Education Standards. The purpose of this dimension is to illustrate that although the different disciplines of science concern different phenomena, they represent a unified way of understanding the world. For example, although "energy" may be treated somewhat differently when studying chemical reactions, ecosystems, and the Earth as a body in space, the concept of "energy" is the same in each case. The seven crosscutting concepts described in the Framework are carried over into the NGSS as follows:

1. *Patterns.* Observed patterns of forms and events guide organization and classification, and they prompt questions about relationships and the factors that influence them.

2. *Cause and effect: Mechanism and explanation.* Events have causes, sometimes simple, sometimes multifaceted. A major activity of science is investigating and explaining causal relationships and the mechanisms by which they are mediated. Such mechanisms can then be tested across given contexts and used to predict and explain events in new contexts.

3. *Scale, proportion, and quantity.* In considering phenomena, it is critical to recognize what is relevant at different measures of size, time, and energy and to recognize how changes in scale, proportion, or quantity affect a system's structure or performance.

4. *Systems and system models.* Defining the system under study—specifying its boundaries and making explicit a model of that system—provides tools for understanding and testing ideas that are applicable throughout science and engineering.

5. *Energy and matter: Flows, cycles, and conservation.* Tracking fluxes of energy and matter into, out of, and within systems helps one understand the systems' possibilities and limitations.

6. *Structure and function.* The way in which an object or living thing is shaped and its substructure determine many of its properties and functions.

7. *Stability and change.* For natural and built systems alike, conditions of stability and determinants of rates of change or evolution of a system are critical elements of study.

In addition to these seven crosscutting concepts, the writing team decided to add two other important ideas that were included in the Framework in a chapter on engineering, technology, and applications of science:

8. *The interdependence of science, engineering, and technology.* Without engineers to design the instruments that scientists use to investigate the world, modern science would be impossible. Conversely, new scientific discoveries enable engineers to invent and modify technologies. Science and engineering drive each other forward.

9. *The influence of science, engineering, and technology, on society and the natural world.* Scientific discoveries and technological decisions profoundly affect human society and the environment.

Feedback from the public (and especially from science teachers) noted that ideas about the nature of science were missing from the Framework and the NGSS. Since concepts relating to the nature of science also cut across all of the science disciplines, these ideas were also included along with the other crosscutting concepts listed earlier.

Dimension 3: A Small Set of Disciplinary Core Ideas

One of the criticisms of today's science curriculum is that it's "a mile wide and an inch deep" (Schmidt, McKnight, & Raizen, 1997). The problem of too much to cover in too little time is not new for those of us who have been in science teaching for decades, but the advent of high-stakes tests has brought the problem to the surface.

The Framework and NGSS are the first set of science standards to substantially reduce the amount that students are expected to learn. Furthermore, the content is more coherent than previous efforts. It is organized in just 12 core ideas that grow in sophistication and complexity across the grades. Eleven of the core ideas are in the traditional fields of life, physical, and Earth and space sciences. The 12th core idea is engineering design. In other words, students are expected to learn the essential process used by engineers to solve problems and achieve goals, just as they are expected to learn about the concepts of

Table 0.3 Twelve Core Ideas in the Next Generation Science Standards

Physical Science	Life Science	Earth and Space Science	Engineering
• Matter and its interactions • Motion and stability: Forces and interactions • Energy • Waves and their applications in technologies for information transfer	• From molecules to organisms: Structures and processes • Ecosystems: Interactions, energy, and dynamics • Heredity: Inheritance and variation of traits • Biological evolution: Unity and diversity	• Earth's place in the universe • Earth's systems • Earth and human activity	• Engineering design

energy and heredity. The 12 core ideas that thread through the standards from kindergarten to Grade 12 are listed in Table 0.3.

Each of the core ideas is further broken down into components, and each of those is integrated into the NGSS in ways that are grade-level appropriate. By organizing the content in this way, teachers can see how their contributions build on the work in prior grades and lay the foundation for further learning.

A Progression of Core Ideas for Engineering

Table 0.3 lists "Engineering Design" as the 12th core idea for all students. Like the core ideas within the traditional science disciplines, these ideas grow in complexity and sophistication over time. Performance expectations for this core idea at all grade levels are shown in Table 0.4. Although this volume is concerned with the elementary school level, it is important for teachers and administrators to be familiar with the entire span of the learning progression.

Combining the Three Dimensions

The NGSS combine disciplinary core ideas practices, and crosscutting concepts in sentences called "performance expectations." These statements illustrate what students are expected to be able to do in order to demonstrate not only their understanding of the important ideas from the Framework but also how they should be able to *use* what they've learned. Each performance expectation begins with one of the practices and explains how students are expected to use that practice in demonstrating their understanding of the disciplinary core idea. Crosscutting concepts are sometimes explicitly integrated into these sentences, and sometimes the crosscutting concept is simply clear from the context.

Table 0.4 Learning Progression for Engineering Design

K–2	3–5	6–8	9–12
Ask questions, make observations, and gather information about a situation people want to change to define a simple problem that can be solved through the development of a new or improved object or tool.	Define a simple design problem reflecting a need or a want that includes specified criteria for success and constraints on materials, time, or cost.	Define the criteria and constraints of a design problem with sufficient precision to ensure a successful solution, taking into account relevant scientific principles and potential impacts on people and the natural environment that may limit possible solutions.	Analyze a major global challenge to specify qualitative and quantitative criteria and constraints for solutions that account for societal needs and wants.
Develop a simple sketch, drawing, or physical model to illustrate how the shape of an object helps it function as needed to solve a given problem.	Generate and compare multiple possible solutions to a problem based on how well each is likely to meet the criteria and constraints of the problem.	Evaluate competing design solutions using a systematic process to determine how well they meet the criteria and constraints of the problem.	Design a solution to a complex real-world problem by breaking it down into smaller, more manageable problems that can be solved through engineering.
Analyze data from tests of two objects designed to solve the same problem to compare the strengths and weaknesses of how each performs.	Plan and carry out fair tests in which variables are controlled and failure points are considered to identify aspects of a model or prototype that can be improved.	Analyze data from tests to determine similarities and differences among several design solutions to identify the best characteristics of each that can be combined into a new solution to better meet the criteria for success.	Evaluate a solution to a complex real-world problem based on prioritized criteria and trade-offs that account for a range of constraints, including cost, safety, reliability, and aesthetics, as well as possible social, cultural, and environmental impacts.
		Develop a model to generate data for iterative testing and modification of a proposed object, tool, or process such that an optimal design can be achieved.	Use a computer simulation to model the impact of proposed solutions to a complex real-world problem with numerous criteria and constraints on interactions within and between systems relevant to the problem.

14

Unlike the vague statements from prior standards that generally began with the phrase "students will know that. . . .," performance expectations specify what students should be able to *do* to demonstrate their understanding. Although performance expectations are not so specific as to designate a given teaching activity or assessment item, they are sufficiently specific to provide the same clear learning goals for curriculum, instruction, and assessment.

Recall that each practice could be used for science or engineering. Keeping in mind that science involves the investigation of natural phenomena in the traditional disciplines, while engineering involves designing solutions to problems, it is possible to figure out which refer to science and which to engineering. Table 0.5 lists several performance expectations from the NGSS. See if you can determine which ones are science and which ones are engineering. The first two statements are classified for you. Fill in the rest of the blanks to test your ability to distinguish science from engineering practices.

Table 0.5 Are These Performance Expectations Science or Engineering?

(The editor's preferred answers are below.[1])

First-grade students who understand energy can:	This is an example of:
Make observations to determine the effect of sunlight on Earth's surface.	Science
Use tools and materials to design and build a structure that will reduce the warming effect of sunlight on an area.	Engineering
Second-grade students who understand matter and its properties can:	**This is an example of:**
1. Plan and conduct an investigation to describe and classify different kinds of materials by their observable properties.	
2. Analyze data obtained from testing different materials to determine which materials have the properties that are best suited for an intended purpose.	
Third-grade students who understand ecosystems can:	**This is an example of:**
3. Make a claim about the merit of a solution to a problem caused when the environment changes and the types of plants and animals that live there may change.	
4. Construct an argument with evidence that in a particular habitat some organisms can survive well, some survive less well, and some cannot survive at all.	
Fourth-grade school students who understand Earth and Human Activity can:	**This is an example of:**
5. Generate and compare multiple solutions to reduce the impacts of natural Earth processes on humans.	
6. Obtain and combine information to describe that energy and fuels are derived from natural resources and their uses affect the environment.	

[1] Answer Key: 1. Science, 2. Engineering, 3. Engineering, 4. Science, 5. Engineering, 6. Science

The layout of the NGSS is shown in the figure below. Each set of performance expectations has a title at the top of the page. Below the title is a box containing the performance expectations. Below that are three foundation boxes, which list (from left to right) the specific science and engineering practices, disciplinary core ideas (DCIs), and crosscutting concepts that were combined to produce the performance expectations above. The bottom section lists connections to performance expectations (PEs) in other science disciplines at the same grade level, to PEs of the same core idea for younger and older students, and to related Common Core State Standards in mathematics and English language arts.

Structure of the NGSS

MS-PS3 Energy

Performance Expectations

Science and Engineering Practices	Disciplinary Core Ideas	Crosscutting Concepts

Connections to:

- Related core ideas at this grade level
- Related core ideas across grade bands
- Common Core State Standards in Mathematics
- Common Core State Standards in English Language Arts

Summary

The new standards are complex, so it's worth pausing for a moment to summarize the most important key ideas.

A Framework for K–12 Science Education (NRC, 2012):

- Was created by a blue-ribbon panel of Nobel Prize–winning scientists, engineers, university professors, and educational researchers
- Provides the blueprint for the NGSS
- Describes three dimensions to be included in the new standards: (1) 12 disciplinary core ideas; (2) practices of science and engineering; and (3) crosscutting concepts
- Calls for engineering to be included at the same level as Newton's laws and the theory of evolution

Next Generation Science Standards: For States, By States (NGSS Lead States, 2013):

- Is organized by 12 core ideas in four disciplines: (1) physical science, (2) life science, (3) Earth and space science, and (4) engineering
- Presents standards in the form of performance expectations, which combine disciplinary core ideas with practices and crosscutting concepts
- Identifies which core ideas are to be taught at which grade, K–5, and by grade band in middle and high school
- Provides clear and common targets for curriculum, instruction, and assessment

Engineering is woven throughout the NGSS, which means that students must be able to demonstrate that they can *use* a given core idea in science to solve a practical engineering problem. Secondly, engineering design is also a core idea that all students are expected to learn at successively higher levels as they mature and move through the grades. In other words, engineering design is both a practice (what students should be able to do) and a disciplinary core idea (what students should know and understand).

While existing instructional materials will need to be modified to meet the new standards—and there are several examples of such modifications in the chapters in this book—thanks to the NGSS, the problem to be solved is far more specific—and therefore more easily solved—than at any time in the past.

Cary Sneider
Portland State University

References

NGSS Lead States. (2013). *Next Generation Science Standards: For states, by states.* Washington, DC: The National Academies Press.

National Research Council. (1996). *National science education standards.* Washington, DC: The National Academies Press.

National Research Council. (2012). *A framework for K–12 science education: Practices, crosscutting concepts, and core ideas.* Washington, DC: The National Academies Press.

Schmidt, W. H., McKnight, C. C., & Raizen, S. A. (1997). *A splintered vision: an investigation of U.S. science and mathematics education.* Boston, MA: Kluwer Academic Press.

1

Engineering Is Elementary

Engineering for Elementary School Students

Christine M. Cunningham, Museum of Science, Boston, Massachusetts

Teamwork is an important part of engineering design at the elementary level.

Image courtesy of the Museum of Science, Boston.

E ngineering is Elementary® (EiE) is a curriculum that fosters engineering and technological literacy among students in Grades 1–5. EiE is intentionally designed to integrate with the science topics students study in elementary school. It's also designed to support 21st-century skills. Students who are learning with EiE work in teams to apply their knowledge of science and mathematics, use inquiry and problem-solving skills to address an engineering design challenge, and tap their creativity as they engage in the engineering design process.

The EiE curriculum is interdisciplinary, using storybooks about children from around the world to introduce students to engineering problems—so in addition to promoting STEM learning, EiE also connects with literacy and social studies. Finally, EiE units align with Next Generation Science Standards (NGSS) (NGSS Lead States, 2013) and other state and national standards. Research shows the curriculum helps children master science and engineering practices and promotes a positive attitude toward engineering as a future career.

To date (July 2013), EiE has been used by more than 55,000 teachers and has reached more than 4 million students. EiE (eie.org) was developed by the EiE team at the Museum of Science, Boston. The curriculum is published by the museum and is available at eiestore.com.

Engineering Adventures, created by the same team that developed EiE, was designed for elementary-age children in out-of-school time settings such as afterschool or summer programs. Engineering Adventures is featured in Chapter 9.

Goals

EiE is the flagship curriculum of a larger project, also called Engineering is Elementary, which is part of the National Center for Technological Literacy at the Museum of Science, Boston. The goals of the EiE project are to

- introduce children in Grades 1–5 to engineering and technology concepts and skills;
- promote engineering and technological literacy in children;
- increase elementary educators' abilities to teach engineering and technology to their students;
- increase the number of schools in the United States that include engineering at the elementary level; and
- conduct research and assessment about engineering teaching and learning at the elementary level.

Central to the EiE project is a commitment to ensure that *all* children, particularly those who are underserved and/or traditionally underrepresented in technical fields, engage in engineering. To meet its goals, the EiE project develops curricular materials, offers PD workshops, and conducts research to evaluate impact.

Units

We designed the EiE curriculum to integrate both engineering and technology concepts and skills with elementary science topics. The project team started by identifying the 20 most commonly taught elementary science topics. We then designed 20 corresponding curriculum units, each one focused on a particular field of engineering (such as mechanical or environmental engineering). Each unit also includes a storybook that introduces a child from a different country and/or culture around the world who uses the engineering design process to solve a real-world problem (see Table 1.1).

Each EiE unit asks children to apply what they know about science as they explore an engineering design challenge and engineer a solution. As we describe later, under EiE Impacts, our research shows this helps reinforce what children have learned about a particular science topic. It's important to note that the EiE curriculum assumes students are currently studying (or have already studied) the science topics addressed in a particular unit; the curriculum does not teach these concepts. We recommend that teachers use EiE lessons in conjunction with, or soon after, they teach a particular science topic; this can be an opportunity to reinforce science concepts.

EiE units follow a consistent format. Each unit includes a preparatory lesson plus four "unit lessons," organized as follows:

Preparatory Lesson: This lesson helps students explore the meaning of *engineering* and *technology* and improve their understanding. The lesson also introduces the Engineering Design Process.

Lesson 1: Engineering Story: To set the context for the unit, children (or the teacher) read an illustrated storybook about a child who uses the Engineering Design Process to solve a real-world problem. This lesson includes a series of questions teachers can use before, during, and after reading the book to encourage students to reflect upon the story and its engineering components. This lesson also reinforces literacy skills.

Lesson 2: A Broader View of an Engineering Field: The second lesson helps students get a broad perspective of a particular engineering field. Through hands-on activities, students learn about the type of work engineers do and the kinds of technologies they produce.

Lesson 3: Scientific Data Inform Engineering Design: The third lesson is designed to help students understand the linkages between science, mathematics, and engineering. Children collect and analyze scientific data that they will use in Lesson 4 to inform their designs.

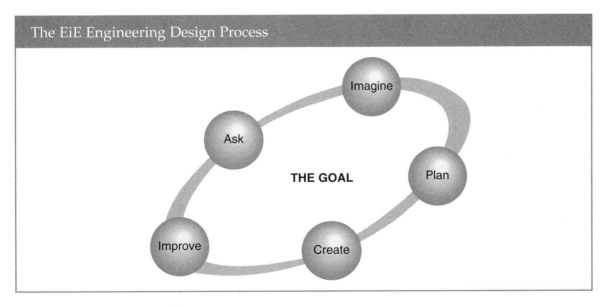

The EiE Engineering Design Process

Image courtesy of the Museum of Science, Boston.

Table 1.1 EiE Curriculum Units and Corresponding Science Topics

	Science Topic	Unit Title	Engineering Field	Story Setting
EARTH SCIENCE	Water	**Water, Water Everywhere:** Designing Water Filters	Environmental	India
	Air & Weather	**Catching the Wind:** Designing Windmills	Mechanical	Denmark
	Earth Materials	**A Sticky Situation:** Designing Walls	Materials	China
	Landforms	**A Stick in the Mud:** Evaluating a Landscape	Geotechnical	Nepal
	Astronomy	**A Long Way Down:** Designing Parachutes	Aerospace	Brazil
	Rocks	**Solid as a Rock:** Replicating an Artifact	Materials	Russia
LIFE SCIENCE	Insects/Plants	**The Best of Bugs:** Designing Hand Pollinators	Agricultural	Dominican Republic
	Organisms/ Basic Needs	**Just Passing Through:** Designing Model Membranes	Bioengineering	El Salvador
	Plants	**Thinking Inside the Box:** Designing Plant Packages	Package	Jordan
	Ecosystems	**A Slick Solution:** Cleaning an Oil Spill	Environmental	USA
	Human Body	**No Bones About It:** Designing Knee Braces	Biomedical	Germany
PHYSICAL SCIENCE	Simple Machines	**Marvelous Machines:** Making Work Easier	Industrial	USA
	Balance & Forces	**To Get to the Other Side:** Designing Bridges	Civil	USA
	Sound	**Sounds Like Fun:** Seeing Animal Sounds	Acoustical	Ghana
	Electricity	**An Alarming Idea:** Designing Alarm Circuits	Electrical	Australia
	Solids & Liquids	**A Work in Process:** Improving a Play-Doh Process	Chemical	Canada
	Magnetism	**The Attraction Is Obvious:** Designing Maglev Systems	Transportation	Japan

	Science Topic	Unit Title	Engineering Field	Story Setting
	Energy	**Now You're Cooking:** Designing Solar Ovens	Green	Botswana
	Floating & Sinking	**Taking the Plunge:** Designing Submersibles	Ocean	Greece
	Light	**Lighten Up:** Designing Lighting Systems	Optical	Egypt

Lesson 4: Engineering Design Challenge: The unit culminates with an engineering design challenge similar to the one described in the storybook. Students follow a simple, five-step Engineering Design Process (EDP)—Ask, Imagine, Plan, Create, Improve to solve the challenge. This simplified EDP was developed by the EiE project expressly for the curriculum.

Knowing that elementary science topics may be taught at different grade levels depending on the district or state, we designed the curriculum to be flexible with respect to grade level. Each unit includes both a "Basic" version suitable for lower elementary grades and an "Advanced" version for upper elementary grades. To use the EiE curriculum effectively, teachers should identify the science units they teach, then choose the EiE unit that corresponds to that content. For example, a teacher who explores air and weather with her class could complement this instruction with the EiE unit Catching the Wind: Designing Windmills.

We also designed the curriculum to be flexible with respect to the order in which the various units are taught. Students may learn science topics in a different order depending on the school, district, or state. Each EiE unit is designed as a stand-alone; the units do not build upon each other and so can be used in any order. Finally, there's no expectation that a student will ultimately complete all 20 units. Typically, a school will select one to four units for each grade level, corresponding to the science topics taught in each grade.

EiE in Action: Aligned With the Next Generation Science Standards

What does EiE look like in the classroom? To answer that question, we'll explore an EiE unit called Best of Bugs: Designing Hand Pollinators. Along the way, we'll point out how this unit addresses the NGSS. We hope this written exploration helps you visualize how EiE helps students engage both with engineering and science content and with the practices in these fields. To see how the Best of Bugs unit works in a real classroom, you're invited to view the short Classroom Videos available at http://eie.org/classroom_video/unit/insectsplants.

Two science topics that elementary school children often study are the life cycles of insects and the life cycles of plants. We designed the curriculum unit Best of Bugs: Designing Hand Pollinators to complement science units about insects, plants, and/or ecosystems. The unit lets students explore the field of agricultural engineering, the role of insects in natural systems, especially as pollinators, interdependencies in ecosystems, and the technologies used in integrated pest management (IPM) and for pollinating plants by hand.

The Best of Bugs: Designing Hand Pollinators Curriculum Unit

The Best of Bugs: Designing Hand Pollinators

Insects, Plants, and Agricultural Engineering for Elementary Students

Engineering is Elementary
National Center for Technological Literacy
Museum of Science, Boston

Image courtesy of the Museum of Science, Boston.

This unit addresses NGSS that focus on interdependent relationships in ecosystems, matter and its interactions, and engineering design. Table 1.2 shows the disciplinary core ideas addressed in the unit.

Table 1.2 NGSS Disciplinary Core Ideas in the Best of Bugs

Number	Disciplinary Core Idea	Subidea
LS1.A	Structure and function	All organisms have external parts that they use to perform daily functions.
LS2.A	Interdependent relationships in ecosystems	Plants depend on water and light to grow, and also depend on animals for pollination or to move their seeds around.
PS1.A	Structure of matter	Matter exists as different substances that have observable different properties. Different properties are suited to different purposes. Objects can be built up from smaller parts.

As they engage with the unit, children have opportunities to demonstrate mastery of the NGSS performance expectations listed in Table 1.3.

In the following description of the lessons, as we reference the Core Ideas and Performance Expectations, we include the number in parentheses (e.g., 2-PS1–1).

Finally, the unit invites students to use engineering practices as they develop solutions for their challenge. These include the following:

- Asking questions and defining problems
- Developing and using models
- Planning and carrying out investigations
- Analyzing and interpreting data
- Using mathematics and computational thinking
- Constructing explanations and designing solutions
- Engaging in argument from evidence
- Obtaining, evaluating, and communicating information

We indicate when these practices occur in the following lesson descriptions by **bolding** them as they arise.

Preparatory Lesson

Like all EiE units, Best of Bugs starts with a preparatory lesson that helps students develop a common understanding of what technologies are and who designs them.

Table 1.3 NGSS Performance Expectations Consistent With Best of Bugs

Number	Disciplinary Core Idea	Performance Expectation
2-PS1-1	Matter and Its Interactions	Plan and conduct an investigation to describe and classify different kinds of materials by their observable properties.
2-PS1-2	Matter and Its Interactions	Analyze data obtained from testing different materials to determine which materials have the properties that are best suited for an intended purpose.
2-LS2-2	Ecosystems: Interactions, Energy, and Dynamics	Develop a simple model that mimics the function of an animal in dispersing seeds or pollinating plants.
K-2-ETS1-1	Engineering Design	Ask questions, make observations, and gather information about a situation people want to change to define a simple problem that can be solved through the development of a new or improved object or tool.
K-2-ETS1-2	Engineering Design	Develop a simple sketch, drawing, or physical model to illustrate how the shape of an object helps it function as needed to solve a given problem.
K-2-ETS1-3	Engineering Design	Analyze data from tests of two objects designed to solve the same problem to compare the strengths and weaknesses of how each performs.

Working in small groups, students open a "mystery bag" to reveal a technology—an everyday item such as a spoon, key, or sticky note. The students are asked to **evaluate** these technologies. Working through a series of **questions**, the students reflect on and **communicate** to the class the need the object serves, how it works, and the materials it's made from and why. Finally, through a whole-class discussion, students develop a definition of technology and learn that all technologies are designed by engineers.

NGSS Connections: The preparatory lesson asks children to question what problems technologies were designed to solve and to reflect upon why the material was designed the way it was (K-2-ETS1–1, K-2-ETS1–2).

Lesson 1. Setting the Context

To set the context for the design challenge in an engaging way, students read the storybook *Mariana Becomes a Butterfly*. The main character, Mariana, a girl from the Dominican Republic, is puzzled by a change in one of her garden plants, which a friend brought to her from Hawaii. At first it produced delicious berries, but now Mariana can't get any berries to grow. With the help of her Tía (Aunt) Leti, an agricultural engineer, Mariana soon discovers the problem: in its new surroundings, the plant lacks a pollinator.

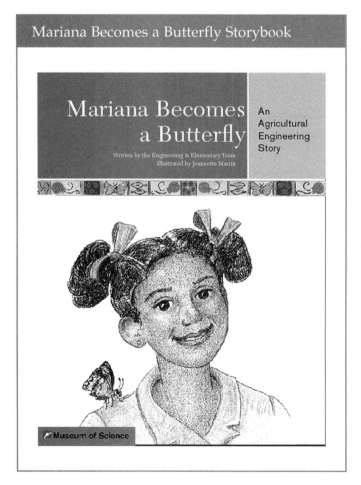

Image courtesy of the Museum of Science, Boston.

Tía Leti introduces Mariana to the challenges of maintaining balance in natural systems, to how pollination works, to the concept of IPM, and to the problems that can result when nonindigenous species are introduced to a new ecosystem. Tía Leti also introduces Mariana to the engineering design process, and Mariana uses her knowledge to engineer a hand pollinator for her new plant.

As the storybook introduces the unit's engineering design challenge **(defining a problem)**, it also introduces scientific vocabulary, reinforces science content, and introduces the EDP—all in an accessible context. After reading the story, students work in pairs to reflect upon what they have learned. In particular, they consider the EDP and describe what Mariana does in each step of the process (ask, imagine, plan, create, improve). Worksheets prompt the students to think more about the vocabulary, geography, and science topics featured in the story.

NGSS Connections: Lesson 1 calls attention to "structure and function" for both plants and insects (LS1.A). It also points out how plants and insects are interdependent in the pollination system (LS2.A). Students ask questions about Mariana's challenge, make observations, and gather information about the situation she wants to change. They define a simple problem that can be solved by developing a new tool—a hand pollinator (K-2-ETS1–1). This tool is a simple model that mimics the function of an animal in pollinating plants (2-LS2–2).

Lesson 2. Introducing Agricultural Engineering

In Lesson 2, students put on a play, *Honeybrook Farm Apple Orchard,* acting out the roles of insects, farmers, and agricultural engineers in an apple orchard. The play introduces agricultural engineering, the engineering discipline that applies science and technology to farm production, the work of agricultural engineers, and in particular to the engineering practice called IPM, an engineered response to a challenge based in the natural world.

The play follows Farmer Bob and Farmer Anne as they encounter various orchard pests that threaten their apple crop, including fruit tree leaf rollers, weevils, and apple moth larvae. With the help of agricultural engineers, the farmers use IPM to solve their pest problem without applying pesticides.

After they present the play, students work together to identify the pest problems in the orchard in each season—and possible solutions. They discuss the natural systems in an orchard, and how agricultural engineers' understanding of the science of the systems helps them to use the technology of IPM to manage the system.

Mariana With Her Pollinator

Image courtesy of the Museum of Science, Boston.

NGSS Connections: Lesson 2 highlights the interdependence of plants and insects in the apple orchard ecosystem—showing ways that insects can both harm and help an apple crop (LS2.A). Together with Farmer Bob and Farmer Anne, students learn about the pest insects that destroy apples and how they can be managed using IPM—a technology that takes advantage of the way natural systems work (K-2-ETS1–1).

Lesson 3. Engaging in the Design Process

In Lesson 3, students start to engage with the engineering design process by **defining the problem** and then **asking questions** related to the design challenge. (They engage in the "Ask" step of the Engineering Design Process.) First, they revisit the challenge: they must design a hand pollinator that will pick up and drop off model pollen from a model flower (**developing and using models**). Next, they figure out the properties of a good hand pollinator—it should both pick up and drop off pollen. Then, students focus on **planning and carrying out** a structured, controlled **investigation** that will help them understand more about scientific and engineering principles. They ask, what materials work best for picking up and dropping off pollen? What are the properties of these materials?

Students are presented with various materials that might be used to engineer a hand pollinator—including marbles, tape, erasers, aluminum foil, pompoms, and pipe cleaners. They discuss criteria of a successful pollinator—it must pick up and deposit pollen. The students' task is to identify materials that can successfully transfer pollen.

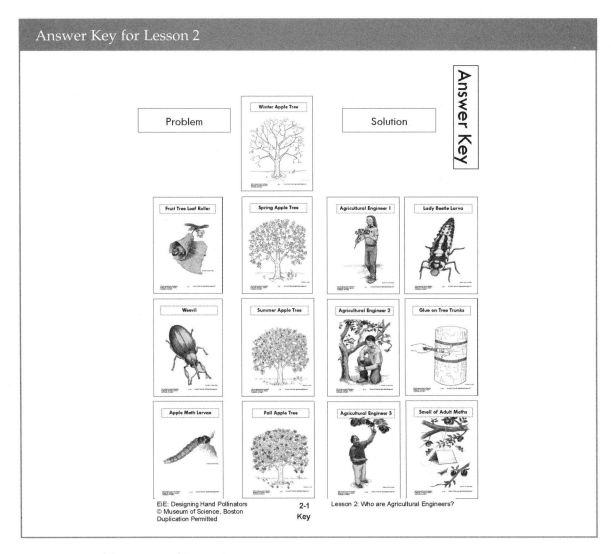

Answer Key for Lesson 2

Image courtesy of the Museum of Science, Boston.

They begin by thinking about the properties of the materials. As a class, they create a chart that lists these materials and their properties (see opposite page). Then they predict which properties of the materials are important in the design of a hand pollinator and which are not.

The students need to test the materials. How should they do this? How do they know their test is "fair"? Working in small groups, children observe a real flower with male (stamen) and female (pistil) parts and find the location of the pollen. They draw parallels between the real flower and a diagram of a flower. They discuss the need to create a **model** flower so they can perform their tests.

As a class, the children also develop a standardized method for testing the various materials. They dip each material in baking soda, which represents pollen, then gently tap the material against a cup three times to dislodge the pollen. The pollen falls onto black paper "flowers" so students can easily observe whether or not pollen is being deposited. Each group then decides which materials work best.

After testing, the students share (**communicate**) their data with the larger class. The class **analyzes and interprets** the results for each material. Through experimentation and observation, the students identify materials that have enough texture to pick up pollen but hold the pollen loosely enough to be tapped off onto the "flower." Students often make connections between the fuzzy materials they are using and bees' legs.

The class also discusses discrepant events. Why did some groups get different testing results? Did they use different testing methods? Students begin to think about which materials they might choose to design a hand pollinator.

NGSS Connections: Students explore materials and their properties as well as the design of experiments. They discuss which properties are important for their hand pollinator and then consider which materials have these properties (PS1.A). Students reflect upon the parts of real plants and flowers (LS1.A) and discuss how their model flower represents the parts of the real flower. They conduct an investigation where they describe different kinds of materials by their observable properties (2-PS1–1). They analyze the data obtained from testing materials to determine which will pick up pollen best (2-PS1–2). The students are actively asking questions, making observations, and gathering information (K-2-ETS1–1) that will inform the designs of their hand pollinators. To

Materials and Their Properties Chart for Lesson 3

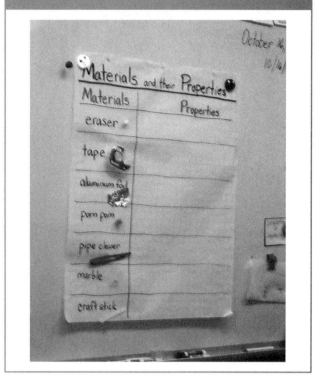

Image courtesy of the Museum of Science, Boston.

Children Testing Pollinator Materials

Image courtesy of the Museum of Science, Boston.

Student Worksheet for Evaluating Materials

Name: _____ Date: _____

Evaluating Pollination Materials

B

Material	Does it pick up pollen? (circle ONE answer)	Does it drop off pollen? (circle ONE answer)	How much pollen does it drop off? (circle ONE answer)
marble	Yes No	Yes No	No pollen Some pollen A lot of pollen
tape	Yes No	Yes No	No pollen Some pollen A lot of pollen
eraser	Yes No	Yes No	No pollen Some pollen A lot of pollen
foil	Yes No	Yes No	No pollen Some pollen A lot of pollen
pompom	Yes No	Yes No	No pollen Some pollen A lot of pollen
pipe cleaner	Yes No	Yes No	No pollen Some pollen A lot of pollen
other:	Yes No	Yes No	No pollen Some pollen A lot of pollen

EiE: Designing Hand Pollinators   3-4   Lesson 3: Exploring Pollination Materials
© Museum of Science, Boston
Duplication Permitted

Image courtesy of the Museum of Science, Boston.

compare materials, children analyze the results from their controlled tests to identify materials that perform best (K-2-ETS1–3).

Lesson 4. Designing, Building, and Testing a Hand Pollinator

In the final lesson, students continue the EDP as they **design** a hand pollinator that will work with a specific kind of flower, represented by a model. Four different model flowers are available; each has a complicated shape (see following figure), such that

Four Flowers and Their Models

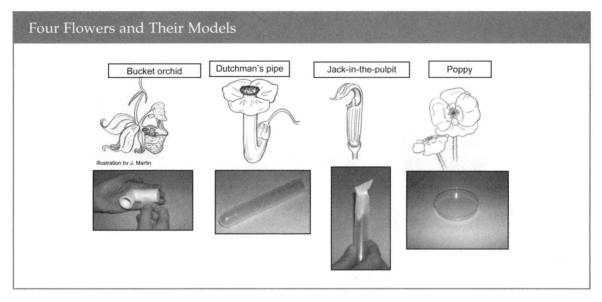

Bucket orchid · Dutchman's pipe · Jack-in-the-pulpit · Poppy

Illustration by J. Martin

Image courtesy of the Museum of Science, Boston.

pollen is less accessible than it was in the model flower students used in Lesson 3. In some cases, the pollen lies deep within the blossom, so students must think carefully about two aspects of design: the tip of the pollinator, which picks up and drops off pollen, and the handle, which must be able to reach the pollen inside the flower The students work in pairs to design, build, and test a hand pollinator that will work with their model flower.

The students begin by reviewing what they learned about materials and their properties in Lesson 3 and reminding themselves which materials worked best for the criteria they are addressing—picking up and dropping off pollen.

Now that they have **defined the problem** and developed their knowledge of flower structures and the properties of various materials, students move to the next phase of the EDP. They begin to brainstorm, or imagine, solutions. Initially each student works independently, sketching two to four possible solutions. Representing ideas in diagrammatic **models** allows children to express their thoughts so they can evaluate them further.

After brainstorming independently, students share their ideas with a partner, and together the two students choose one design idea they want to pursue. This step requires students to **construct explanations or arguments** about why they think a design is particularly strong. The students choose one design and **plan** more details. What materials will it be made from? What will it look like? The partners draw another diagram or **model** of their design and identify the materials it uses.

The next step is to test the design and **carry out an investigation,** gathering data on how their design performs with respect to the criteria. Once they have collected data, students **analyze and interpret the data** they collected—was the hand pollinator able to pick up pollen? To drop off pollen? How do they know? The students also identify which parts of the pollinator (**their designed solution**) worked well, what they would change, and why.

As they think about ways they can improve their design, students **engage in argument from evidence, and evaluate and communicate information.** After they redesign, build, and test their pollinators, they reflect on whether the redesigned pollinator worked better than the initial design and how they know this.

Girls Testing Their Pollinator

Image courtesy of the Museum of Science, Boston.

Each set of partners shares their sketched model and their final product with the class—a step that enables deeper learning. Students must **communicate** what materials they used and why they chose them, explain why their design worked well for their particular model flower, articulate what changes they tried as they improved their design, and report whether the changes worked. They also demonstrate how their hand pollinator functions.

After each group presents their findings, the class reflects on whether the hand pollinator—or some part of the technology—would work to pollinate a *different* model flower. This discussion helps students realize that teams designing pollinators for different flowers had different goals, which produced different designs.

NGSS Connections: As they design a hand pollinator that models how an insect pollinates plants (LS2.A, 2-LS2–2), children are asked again to reflect upon the structures of plants and flowers and understand how they can differ from organism to organism (LS1.A). The students draw upon what they have learned about materials that are effective for pollination (PS1.A) as they engage in the engineering design process to develop and improve solutions (K-2-ETS1-1, K-2-ETS1–2, K-2-ETS1–3).

Who Should Teach EiE?

We believe that engineering is a basic literacy for the 21st century. Every child should have the opportunity to learn more about how the human-made world around him or her is created and hone his or her problem-solving abilities. Thus, we designed EiE for *all* elementary-age students.

Generally, the educator who teaches science teaches EiE. In the majority of schools, the students' primary teacher incorporates EiE into her lessons. In schools that have elementary science specialists, these specialists usually teach EiE lessons.

Sharing Pollinator Designs With the Class

Image courtesy of the Museum of Science, Boston.

EiE Development

We used a rigorous development process for EiE that mirrored the EDP. We worked closely with practicing teachers. Each unit was tested in approximately 75 classrooms nationwide (see figure on next page). Valuable feedback from teachers informed lesson and unit revisions. Overall, we spent about 3,000 hours developing each EiE unit, which is 8–10 hours of classroom instruction.

Instructional Materials

The EiE curriculum includes the following components:

Teacher Guide: The road map for the EiE curriculum. EiE Teacher Guides are presented in a three-ring binder format that includes the following:

- *Introductory materials* that provide background information about the unit and the field of engineering covered, how the curriculum links to standards, and other helpful information.
- *Lesson plans* that include a detailed "materials preparation" section, instructions for each activity, a set of suggested questions to spark classroom discussion and reflection, and helpful hints for teaching the activities.
- *Duplication masters* for the worksheets students use as they complete the activities. Worksheets for both basic and advanced-level students are included.
- *Student assessments* that teachers can use to assess their students' understanding of basic engineering and technology concepts. Rubrics for each lesson are also included. These show how to assess student learning for each individual lesson objective.

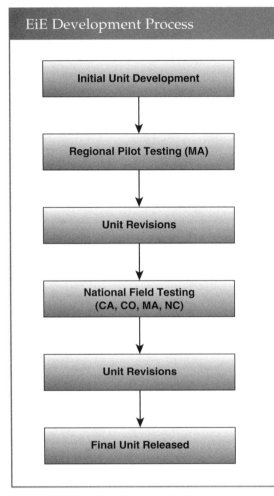

Image courtesy of the Museum of Science, Boston.

Storybook: One copy of the unit storybook is included with each Teacher Guide, or classroom sets can be purchased. Some teachers, particularly those at the younger grades, read the story aloud to their classes. Other teachers prefer that each student have a copy of the storybook.

Materials kits include everything you need to teach a class of 30 students. (Refill kits are also available.) For schools and districts that have a limited budget or prefer to source materials in other ways, a complete list of the supplies needed for the unit activities is included in the Teacher Guide and also available online. We deliberately designed EiE activities to use inexpensive and readily available materials such as craft sticks and pipe cleaners.

Classroom posters feature the EDP as well as the storybook characters. For many elementary teachers, engineering is a new discipline—one they don't feel prepared to teach. To support implementation of the EiE curriculum, we offer PD workshops. (See next section for details.) We have also developed a suite of free resources available on the project website (http://eie.org), including the following:

Video resources (http://eie.org/engineering-elementary/resources) include dozens of short videos that collectively provide free, informal, on-demand PD for teachers who are implementing EiE. Our video library includes the following:

- *How-to videos* that supplement the lesson setup instructions in each Teacher Guide. Each 3- to 5-minute video shows how to prep for one EiE lesson.
- *Classroom videos* that help teachers new to EiE prepare for the classroom experience. Each 10- to 12-minute video shows an experienced teacher using EiE in a real classroom. Each classroom video comes with reflection questions that draw attention to notable pedagogical strategies. EiE's classroom video library is still growing; by 2016, viewers will be able to review all four lessons in each of the 20 units, as taught by two different teachers.

Extension lessons (http://eie.org/engineering-elementary/resources) are free, downloadable extension lessons created by teachers and EiE staff. These lessons extend core EiE lessons by linking them to mathematics, social studies, science, fine arts, and language arts content.

Student assessments (http://eie.org/content/student-assessments): In addition to the assessments provided in EiE Teacher Guides, we offer a larger set of unit-specific assessments available online. We've created both formative and summative assessments to measure children's understandings of general engineering concepts as well as the engineering and science concepts specific to each of the 20 units.

Professional Development

EiE supports teachers who are implementing the curriculum by offering PD workshops (http://eie.org/content/professional-development). These workshops give teachers strategies for fostering student-centered, inquiry-based learning.

The specific goals of each EiE PD workshop include the following:

- Help teachers increase their knowledge of engineering, technology, and the EDP—and how they are related
- Familiarize teachers with the EiE curriculum, including the structure and format of EiE units and EiE's pedagogical approach
- Boost teachers' confidence about teaching engineering
- Boost teachers' ability to implement open-ended engineering design challenges

Our PD workshops are designed to support preservice teachers, inservice teachers, and teacher educators. For example, our "Everyone Engineers" (EE) workshops give teachers an introduction to the EiE project, our philosophy, and our pedagogical strategies. Educators and administrators who want to learn more about EiE often attend EE workshops as well. We also offer "Teacher Educator Institutes" for professional teacher educators who want to become qualified to offer EiE PD to local teachers in their region. With this approach, we have developed a strong network of EiE collaborators across the country who provide EiE PD.

No matter where they are taught, all EiE PD workshops reflect our view that the following set of principles and practices are critical to effective engineering education:

Hands-on, Active Learning. The EiE curriculum emphasizes hands-on activities that let students interact with and manipulate materials as they answer questions and solve engineering design challenges. Hands-on learning is a key part of our PD workshops as well. Workshop facilitators do very little lecture-style teaching, focusing instead on learner-driven experiences.

Participants as Learners. EiE workshop participants engage in the same activities and discussions their students will experience in the classroom. Not only does this approach help educators get familiar with the format, structure, and flow of EiE lessons, but when they experience the lessons from a student's point of view, teachers also get a clear picture of the areas where students may require extra support.

Establishing Foundational Knowledge. We begin every EiE workshop for new teachers with introductory activities in which participants explore the questions "What is technology?" and "What is engineering?" using simple, everyday objects and materials. This exercise helps each participant construct baseline foundational knowledge of technology, engineering as a profession, and the EDP.

Modeling Effective Pedagogical Strategies. Our facilitators model the types of pedagogical approaches and strategies that permeate the EiE units—for example, using open-ended questions or encouraging learners to give evidence and explain the rationale behind their ideas.

Informal Formative Assessments. Many workshop activities begin with the facilitators conducting a brief, informal assessment of participants' prior knowledge of terms or concepts.

Group Work and Discussion. Workshop participants work in pairs, small groups, or large groups throughout the workshop, for both activities and discussion sessions.

Reflecting as Learners (putting on your "student hat"). Participants reflect on the activities they complete from the perspective of a student rather than the teacher. Through reflection, they connect their experience to prior knowledge and previous activities, other subject areas, and to the EiE unit as a whole.

Reflecting as Educators (putting on your "teacher hat"). After each workshop activity, participants discuss what that particular activity will look like in the classroom, focusing on such topics as students' misconceptions, materials management, differentiation, and classroom management.

EiE Impacts

In addition to developing classroom and PD curricula, the EiE project conducts rigorous research, evaluation, and assessment of these products. External evaluators have also reviewed EiE materials. The results of these research and evaluation studies are available on the EiE website at http://www.eie-curriculum/research/articles.

A summary of major findings includes the following results:

- Children who use EiE along with a science curriculum perform significantly better than control group students (who have studied only science) on questions about engineering and technology (Cunningham, Lachapelle, & Lindgren-Streicher, 2005; Jocz & Lachapelle, 2012; Lachapelle & Cunningham, 2007; Lachapelle et al., 2011a; Lachapelle, Phadnis, Hertel, & Cunningham, 2012).
- Children who use EiE along with a science curriculum perform significantly better than control group students on questions about science concepts (Lachapelle et al., 2011a, 2011b).
- Children who use EiE are more likely than control group students to indicate that they are interested in engineering as a career (Cunningham & Lachapelle, 2010; Lachapelle et al., 2012).
- Increased interest in engineering as a career among students who participated in EiE versus control group students was found to be true for all subgroups, including boys and girls, historically underrepresented racial and ethnic minorities, students from low-income families, and English language learners (Lachapelle et al., 2012).
- Assessments show that student interest, engagement, and performance are enhanced when participating in EiE as compared with science curricula alone or school in general (Weis & Banilower, 2010).

The impact of EiE on students is perhaps best captured by some of the students' own words:

I like being able to do the project with my friends and be able to pretend that it's not just a project but the real world like being able to pretend you're a real biomedical engineer.

[I liked] how [EiE] didn't give us limited options. We set a goal and created it the way we thought best.

Now I know how engineers feel when things that they design don't work the first time, but I still want to be one.

I think that learning about technology and engineering process through the [EiE unit] was a fun way of learning. You did an excellent job preparing the kits and the directions were not the least bit confusing! Great job! P.S. Usually I don't really like science, but for that unit I liked it.

I wish we had school tomorrow so we could do [EiE] some more.

Looking Forward

The EiE project continues to support teachers and students by adding to our suite of curriculum and PD offerings. We do this in a variety of ways, including the following initiatives:

- **Mapping all 20 EiE units against the NGSS.** We have already mapped EiE lessons against national inquiry-based science curricula (FOSS, GEMS, STC, Insights, and Science Companion), against the Standards for Technological Literacy, and against the NGSS and science standards for states that have not yet adopted the NGSS.
- **Adding to our library of classroom videos.** We have already collected video footage from two classrooms for 12 of the EiE units. By 2016, classroom videos for all four lessons in each of the 20 units will be complete (160 videos total).
- **Developing new PD workshops** that help educators visualize and implement Next Gen engineering standards and practices with their students.
- **Developing online PD.** The reality of school budgets means that many teachers will not be able to attend an EiE PD workshop. We plan to create Web-based PD—both synchronous and asynchronous—that will support teacher learning and implementation over time and on demand.
- **Creating lessons that reinforce Common Core English language arts and mathematics standards**. We plan to create lessons related to the EiE units and challenges that address math or English standards.
- **Creating PD that reinforces Common Core State Standards.** We are currently pilot-testing PD workshops that link Common Core mathematics and EiE units.
- **Bringing engineering education to preservice teacher programs.** Over the past six years, we have been working with college faculty to help them introduce engineering into education and science courses for preservice teachers.
- **Conducting a gold-standard efficacy study of the EiE curriculum.** We are currently conducting a National Science Foundation–funded research study with more than 300 teachers in three states that examines the efficacy of EiE. One question our study asks is whether the core design principles EiE espouses impact student learning. Additionally, we are exploring how to best scaffold children's engineering learning.

The EiE project is also working to promote students' learning of engineering and technology concepts in settings beyond school classrooms. Our Engineering Adventures program (see Chapter 9) invites children in out-of-school time programs for Grades 3–5 to engineer using our five-step engineering design process. Our new Engineering Everywhere team is developing out-of-school-time programs for middle school students. We are just beginning to explore the terrain of preK–K engineering programming.

Conclusion

The EiE curriculum was developed almost a decade before the NGSS were created. But the EiE curriculum developers were far-sighted. EiE materials closely align with the core ideas and practices included in the new standards. The 20 EiE units and the design challenges they include have been shown to help students develop and demonstrate mastery of NGSS performance expectations.

The EiE team has spent the past decade thinking carefully about how to capitalize on children's natural interest in engineering. Thoroughly tested in the classroom and systematically revised based on evaluations and assessments, our materials are highly engaging—and highly effective in helping children learn engineering concepts and practices. We look forward to continuing to support teachers and children as they apply their creativity and innovation to generate solutions to problems now . . . and in the future.

References

Cunningham, C. M., & Lachapelle, C. P. (2010). *The impact of Engineering is Elementary (EiE) on students' attitudes toward engineering and science.* Paper presented at the ASEE Annual Conference and Exposition, Louisville, KY.

Cunningham, C. M., Lachapelle, C. P., & Lindgren-Streicher, A. (2005). *Assessing elementary school students' conceptions of engineering and technology.* Presented at the ASEE Annual Conference & Exposition, Portland, OR.

Jocz, J., & Lachapelle, C. (2012). *The Impact of Engineering is Elementary (EiE) on students' conceptions of technology.* Boston, MA: Museum of Science.

Lachapelle, C. P., & Cunningham, C. M. (2007). *Engineering is Elementary: Children's changing understandings of science and engineering.* Presented at the ASEE Annual Conference and Exposition, Honolulu, HI.

Lachapelle, C. P., Cunningham, C. M., Jocz, J., Kay, A. E., Phadnis, P., Wertheimer, J., & Arteaga, R. (2011a). *Engineering is Elementary: An evaluation of years 4 through 6 field testing.* Boston, MA: Museum of Science.

Lachapelle, C. P., Cunningham, C. M., Jocz, J., Kay, A. E., Phadnis, P., Wertheimer, J., & Arteaga, R. (2011b). *Engineering is Elementary: An evaluation of years 7 and 8 field testing.* Boston, MA: Museum of Science.

Lachapelle, C. P., Phadnis, P., Hertel, J., & Cunningham, C. M. (2012). *What is engineering? A survey of elementary students.* Presented at the 2nd P-12 Engineering and Design Education Research Summit, Washington, DC.

Lachapelle, C. P., Phadnis, P., Jocz, J., & Cunningham, C. M. (2012). *The impact of engineering curriculum units on students' interest in engineering and science.* Presented at the NARST Annual International Conference, Indianapolis, IN.

NGSS Lead States. (2013). *Next Generation Science Standards: For states, by states.* Washington, DC: The National Academies Press.

Weis, A. M., & Banilower, E. R. (2010). *Engineering is Elementary: Impact on historically underrepresented students survey results.* Chapel Hill, NC: Horizon Research.

2

Physical Science Comes Alive!

Integrating Engineering and Science Through Design and Troubleshooting of Cars and Gadgets[1]

Gary Benenson, City College of New York, and the following teachers from New York City Public Schools:
Emmy Matias-Leonard, The Earth School
Barbara Martucci, PS 92
Travis Sloane, PS 267
Jody Hilton, Christopher Ave. Community School
Donna M. Johnson, PS 21
Cherubim Cannon, Angula Bumbury Camacho, and Janice Porter, PS 5; Brooklyn, NY

Q: What happens when you give a group of teachers access to cups, lids, paper plates, rubber bands, paper clips, sticks, and masking tape?

A: They become transformed into children, creating simple to futuristic wind-up toys! From the minute I was introduced to **Fantastic Elastic**, all I could think about was how my students were going to love being immersed in this unit.

Barbara Martucci, PS 92, Central Harlem

1 This material is based upon work supported by the National Science Foundation under Award # 0733209. Any opinions, findings and conclusions or recommendations expressed in this material are those of the authors and do not necessarily reflect the views of the National Science Foundation.

Closed and open views of a mystery box made by fourth- and fifth-grade students using the ElectroCity unit. The hidden switch at the top rear of the box uses the foil and battery to turn the motor on and spin the propeller when the box is closed.

a   b

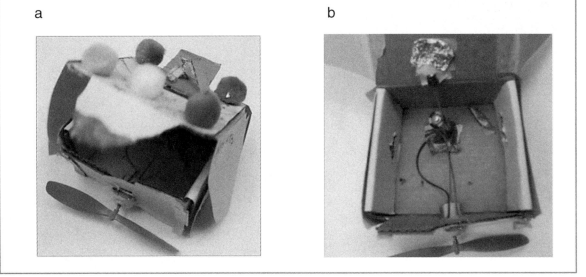

Images courtesy of Evi Abeler.

Overview

Physical Science Comes Alive! consists of curriculum and professional development materials to support integration of engineering, science, literacy, and art in the elementary grades. Students design their own vehicles and gadgets, which don't typically work at first, and learn science and engineering principles in the course of troubleshooting and redesigning these devices. There are rich opportunities for writing, customizing, and modeling. Students document their work by writing and illustrating material lists, troubleshooting guides, "how-to" manuals, descriptions of "how it works," and reflections.

Table 2.1 summarizes all eight units, which are available online at no charge, along with video support (CityTechnology.org). Classroom sets of materials cost between $100 and $300 per unit and are available from SEMPCO, Inc. in Nashua, New Hampshire. Following are descriptions of four of the units by a group of teachers in New York City who played major roles in the development, pilot-testing, and redesign of the materials.

Invent-a-Wheel

In this unit, my kindergarten students learned about friction and gravity as they investigated ways to get a toy sled to slide down a ramp. Initially, both the ramp and the sled were made of ordinary cardboard but incurred too much friction for the sled to slide easily. My students redesigned their sleds and ramps by investigating the properties of materials such as plastic spoons, paper fasteners, paper clips, straws, stirrers, tape, craft sticks,

Table 2.1 Physical Science Comes Alive! Curriculum Units		
Grades	**Force and Motion**	**Energy Systems**
PreK–1	*Mech-a-Blocks:* Students use brightly colored pegboard shapes and pegs to create, model, and explore structures and mechanisms.	*Invent-a-Wheel:* Students explore slides and sliding, finding ways to reduce friction, and design and test gravity-powered cars.
2–3	*MechAnimations:* Students develop spatial thinking as they use pegboard and cardboard to make levers and linkages and design mechanisms that animate stories.	*Fantastic Elastic:* Students design, make, and test rubber-band-and-balloon-powered cars, then write instruction manuals and troubleshooting guides.
4–5	*ArithMachines:* Students increase their proportional reasoning skills as they use MechAnimations to develop quantitative relationships between inputs and outputs.	*EnerJeeps:* Students invent switches to control motors, attach the motors to model cars in various ways, and add lights and horns.
	Pop-ups: Students create 3-D paper mechanisms, make measurements, track motion, and explore geometric and algebraic relationships between distances.	*ElectroCity:* Students invent visible, remote, and hidden switches to control LEDs, buzzers, and motors and to electrify puppets, pop-ups, and mystery boxes.

felt, sandpaper, cardstock, wax paper, and aluminum foil. Toward the end of the unit, they tried rollers, and eventually incorporated the rollers on the sleds, creating wheels and cars.

In the first lesson, the students came up with a way to make the small cardboard pieces move. While apparently just playing, the students spent 25 minutes pushing, flipping, walking, wiggling, dropping, pulling, and occasionally throwing their materials. In fact, they were doing much more: by exploring new ways to make the cardboard move, they were not only collaborating and learning from one another's ideas but also learning about force, motion, and energy. As a class, we then created a list of all the ways we had come up with to make the cardboard move. This list then became the basis for a discussion on movement and forces. By focusing on opposing pushes and pulls, students learned to think critically about how to classify the movements, which also provided an opportunity for me to assess their understanding.

After creating the groundwork for a shared common language, the students now had more ability to converse about their ideas and questions. Furthermore, their understanding of science concepts supported a shift toward the application and synthesis of these concepts through engineering design. This shift was evident when students redesigned their sleds so they could slide down a ramp covered by a sandpaper or felt surface that increased friction. The following figures show top and bottom views of how two students modified their sleds: both added weight to the light piece of cardboard. In addition, the sled in the first figure used paper fasteners to reduce friction, while the one in the second figure used plastic spoons instead. In both cases, students applied the new knowledge they had gained from experimenting with the materials.

Redesigned Sled With Paper Fasteners

a. top view   b. bottom view

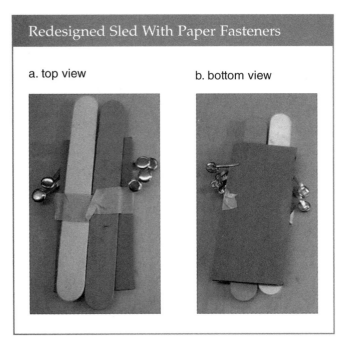

Images courtesy of Travis Sloane.

Redesigned With Spoons

a. top view   b. bottom view

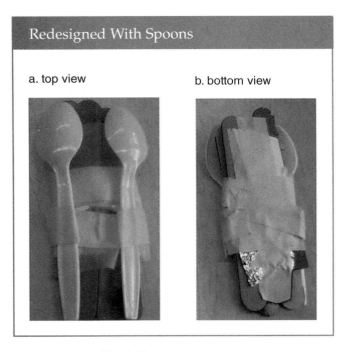

Images courtesy of Travis Sloane.

To document their ideas, students wrote in journals to record their successes and failures. The figure on the next page shows the redesign process a student took to create the final and successful design pictured on the left. The student used a drawing to show each sled she designed and an "X" to indicate that it did not slide down the ramp. In addition to writing in the journals, we held numerous class discussions for students to share their ideas. After each discussion, we created a class chart showing outcomes that could be used along with the journals for deciding on next steps. This process of design and redesign shows that students are taking an idea, creating a model to test it, and then analyzing the outcomes to identify what does not work. Then they come up with new ideas that might work better.

Subsequently, I provided the students with new materials to find even better solutions. The new materials consist of round objects that roll, such as straws, crayons, pencils and wooden skewers. Students realized quickly that taping the round objects to their sleds would not work and began to look for other solutions. Through trial and error and natural curiosity, students eventually learned that the round objects can be used to roll the sled down the ramp. In fact, with the use of rollers, the ramp can start at an even lower height than it did before. However, they also realized that when the sled reached the bottom of the ramp, the rollers kept rolling, leaving the sled behind.

Through guided discussion students looked at the strengths and weaknesses of both the sliding sled and the rolling sled. Ultimately, they designed sleds with rollers that rolled freely and did not fall off their rollers at the bottom of the ramp. The students learned that a roller that is attached firmly to a vehicle is called a "wheel," and the sled has become a "car." Throughout the curriculum, students created and tested prototypes, analyzed the data, and determined which modifications would produce the best results. By looking at the form and function of materials, students studied the strengths and weaknesses of materials that permit a sled to slide or roll.

The final challenge for the students was to compare their sleds with wheels to see how they could redesign them to meet their own design goals. Examples of these challenges were cars that

- could go faster.
- were slower.

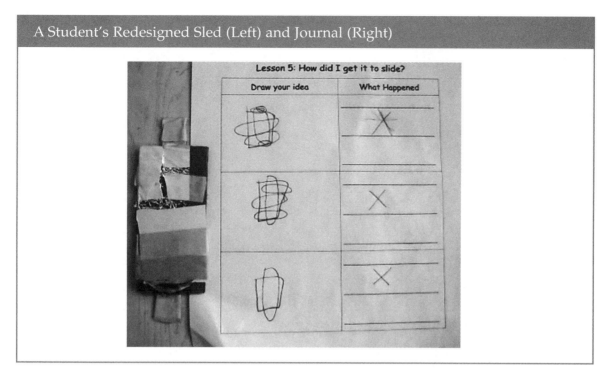

A Student's Redesigned Sled (Left) and Journal (Right)

Images courtesy of Travis Sloane.

- go straight.
- turn or go in circles.
- jump off the top of a ramp.
- have fewer than four wheels.

These activities enable kindergarten students to meet all three early childhood Next Generation Science Standards (NGSS) performance expectations in engineering design. As specified in K-2-ETS1–1, students begin by making observations and gathering information. They identify "a situation people want to change"—the sled won't go down the ramp—and look for a solution "through the development of a new or improved object or tool" by adding weight and/or reducing friction, as illustrated on page 42, (see opposite). Next, they add rollers and eventually wheels. In comparing the results, they are addressing K-2 ETS-1–3: "Analyze data from tests of two objects designed to solve the same problem, to compare the strengths and weaknesses of how each performs." At every step, they record their results, as illustrated in the figure above and outlined in K-2 ETS-1–2: "Develop a simple sketch, drawing or physical model to illustrate how the shape of an object helps it function as needed to solve a given problem" (NGSS Lead States, 2013).

Fantastic Elastic

The Fantastic Elastic curriculum helped my students develop concepts of energy through design, construction, and testing of elastic powered vehicles. I first introduced the unit by showing my second graders a few of the wind-ups I had created. I was immediately bombarded with questions:

- *How did you know what to do?*
- *Is it hard to do?*

- *When can we make some?*
- *Does it always work?*
- *What makes it move?*
- *How fast can it go?*
- *What if I make one and it doesn't do anything?*
- *What if the rubber band breaks when you wind it?*
- *How will I know what rubber band to use?*
- *What happens if it only moves a little bit and then stops?*
- *Can we take them home?*

Then I set out the materials and gave the students time to explore. Students quickly began noticing that just looking at an object doesn't necessarily tell you how to construct it. This is when the next set of questions came up:

- *How do I get it to work?*
- *Why doesn't the rubber band stay on?*
- *How do I get the rubber band to go through the bead?*
- *How did you get yours to work?*

This was the first opportunity when students got to become the leaders of the lesson. Students become aware of their own growth. Nathaniel was the first to succeed. He tested his out and it moved. He excitedly asked if he could make another one, which he completed in no time. He said,

I found that once you do the first one, you can do the second one much faster.

Sayyid said something similar:

When you showed us the wind up, I thought it was going to be easy to make but I had a hard time with the rubber band. After I made the first one it got easier to make the next one because I knew what to do with the rubber band.

Collaboratively, students performed troubleshooting to identify and solve the problems with their wind-ups. Students learned that troubleshooting requires identification of the malfunctions within a system. Then they generated a list of possible causes for each problem. After that they tried to fix the problem. All of this information is recorded on a chart, which has three columns: Issue, Cause, and Fix.

Students were then able to create their own troubleshooting guides by taking the information from the classroom chart and using it to fix their own individual problems. Many students were able to come up with causes and fixes for their wind-ups after completing the troubleshooting lesson. However, there were still students who could not. This is when students became facilitators, helping other students troubleshoot:

- *Why do you think it doesn't work?*
- *Show me what you have done so far.*
- *What do you think you need to do next?*
- *Did you try _____?*
- *See what would happen, if you _____.*

Making a Wind-Up (Left) and Then Racing Them (Right)

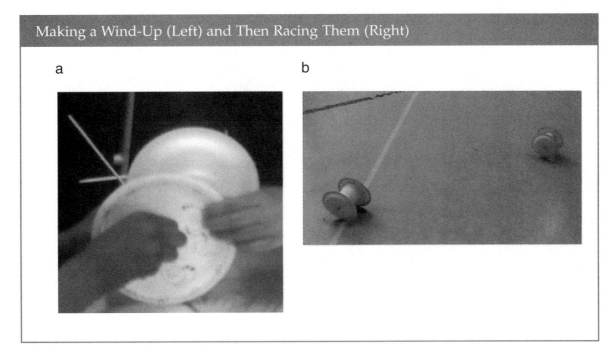

a   b

Images courtesy of Barbara Martucci.

The most powerful thing a teacher can experience is when students not only solve their own problems but also help one another. The figure above shows two students collaborating on making a wind-up and a race between two students' wind-ups.

After students had designed, troubleshot, and redesigned their wind-ups, they were often so proud of the outcomes that they wanted everyone to be able to duplicate it. For this purpose, they learned to create step-by-step instruction manuals that show how to construct a wind-up. This is another example of a design problem. Like the wind-up itself, an instruction manual is designed, tested, and redesigned to fix any issues that have come up. After creating an instruction manual, each student exchanged it with a classmate to see if it was possible for them to construct the wind-up just by following the steps in the manual. Students almost always left out details, which they didn't discover until they had watched someone else try to follow the steps. They conferred with one another about the missing details and then made revisions based on the issues that had come up in the conference. They realized quickly that the first manual was only a draft, which had to go through testing, troubleshooting, and redesign, just like a wind-up. Once this was done, they were ready to publish and celebrate complete instructional manuals. The next figure (see p. 46) shows students working on their manuals.

Focusing on engineering practices really enhanced my lessons. They motivated and stirred up new interest in my science classroom. Students viewed themselves as engineers: designing, sketching, constructing, reconstructing, manipulating, testing, observing, modifying, or adding to the intricacies of their devices.

As they designed, built, troubleshot, redesigned, and observed their wind-ups in motion, my students were introduced to energy concepts that they would learn more formally later, including potential, kinetic, mechanical, heat and elastic energy, friction, and energy storage and transfer. These concepts were challenging for both the teacher

Writing Instruction Manuals

a   b

Images courtesy of Thinkstock.

and the students but were strongly supported by having real experiences and examples to illustrate the abstractions.

While they observed their wind-ups in motion, the students questioned where the energy came from. By slowly winding up their toys, they realized that the energy was being transferred from their muscles to twisting the rubber band, where it was stored as elastic potential energy, and was later released as kinetic energy when their wind-ups began to move. My students had never before had the opportunity to make scientific discoveries in this manner. They were so enthralled that before the unit was completed, they were already collecting materials to build new kinds of wind-ups at home.

This unit promotes investigations of how one variable can affect another. There was a group that was obsessed with making models that went *faster* than others, so they concentrated on the rubber bands. Another group wanted their models to go *farther* than other models and were also focused on the rubber bands, while a third group was looking at changing wheel size as a way to increase the distance traveled. At the end of every session, I asked them to do a brief write-up in their journals in which they addressed three questions:

1. *What did you notice?*

2. *What problem were you trying to solve or fix?*

3. *What will you plan to do next time?*

Then they shared their answers with the whole group. Often these sharing sessions led to a flurry of rethinking and redesigning the wind-ups, illustrating the power of cross-fertilization.

Students' daily reflection journals were an integral part of their science and engineering growth. They recorded plans for their next steps, scientific discoveries, their appreciation of help from team members, and their zeal to share and help others. Their journals revealed how ecstatic they were when they made discoveries or solved engineering problems. Introverts became extroverts as they had "voice" in the classroom, and some students became expert teachers. Writing and sharing their journals boosted the students' writing skills and self-confidence. Students who were normally quiet were eager to share their journal entries as it gave them an opportunity to boast about their accomplishments. One third grader wrote,

> What I learned today was how energy works and how wind-ups are not so easy to make. I learned that energy can make it stop and go. When I did the wind-up, I had a few problems like my rubber band didn't go through the clear plastic lid. My rubber band would not stay in my hand. So I got a paperclip and stuck it through the hole and it grabbed the rubber band and put it through the hole. Ever since I started making wind-ups, I have been crazy and stupid. I love school and I love wind-ups so much! When I learned about the energy, I was so surprised.

Fantastic Elastic is closely aligned with the NGSS Performance Standard, 3–5 ETS-1 (NGSS Lead States, 2013). Students identify a simple design problem (3–5-ETS1–1), generate and compare multiple solutions (3–5-ETS1–2), plan and carry out fair tests, and use the results to improve their prototypes (3–5-ETS1–3).

More broadly, the unit develops nearly all of the Science and Engineering Practices identified in *A Framework for K–12 Science Education* (NRC, 2012, pp. 41–77). Students begin by asking questions and defining problems that they want to solve (Practice 1). They select their materials, design and build their elastic-powered prototypes, and later use them in energy investigations (Practice 2: Developing and using models). They use their prototypes to find answers to puzzling questions. They investigate the effects wheel size, cup length, and rubber band type on the operation of their wind-ups (Practice 3: Planning and carrying out investigations). Using the engineering strategy of troubleshooting and redesigning, they diagnose problems and propose possible causes for the malfunctioning of their wind-ups, which informs their efforts at redesign through multiple approaches (Practice 6: Constructing explanations and designing solutions). They make a variety of devices with different design features and explain why they work the way they do. In the process, they interpret data and draw conclusions from it (Practices 4: Analyzing and interpreting data and Practice 7: Engaging in argument from evidence). Their reflection journals and instructional manuals provide opportunities to communicate their ideas to their classmates and create step-by-step directions someone else could follow later (Practice 8: Obtaining, evaluating, and communicating information).

EnerJeeps and ElectroCity

My fourth-grade students were not enthusiastic about learning about electricity from the textbook. Although there are process skills to practice and questions to answer, the students did not have an exciting project to look forward to. I needed to motivate them.

The EnerJeeps unit solved this problem. Students were very excited to know that they would be able to make and keep a toy electric car by the end of the unit. They looked forward to completing each task because they realized that they would learn science content that could help them to improve the design of a car. Near the end of every lesson, there were students who would not want to stop working and actually begged to continue through their lunch break. Some even asked to come back to the classroom during recess to work on their projects.

As a teacher, I found the unit very easy to use. Everything you need is available online (CityTechnology.org). The website includes learning goals, background content, detailed lesson plans, and duplication masters for all student planning, data collection, reflection, and assessment. There are also many valuable tips related to lesson preparation.

The idea of being the engineers gave the students a sense of ownership that they never would have had if I had given step-by-step instructions on what to do. They found it amazing that they were able to plan each step independently and then actually implement their ideas. The first activity consisted of just getting the motor to run. I provided motors and batteries, but no guidance at all. This task elicited high excitement and many cries of "I did it, I did it!" as students figured out how to make it work.

The idea of creating an on/off switch elicited a lot of discussion among the students when they realized that nearly every electrical appliance is controlled by some type of switch. The hardest part of the curriculum was actually making a switch and inserting it in a circuit. Materials for making a switch consisted of paper clips, paper fasteners, and binder clips. They understood why a switch was needed, but it took them time to realize that just connecting the motor to the battery directly, or touching and removing a wire, does not involve a switch. A student who kept working during his lunch period was the first to create a working switch. The figure below shows a rotary switch made using a paper clip, and a toggle switch made from a binder clip.

The next problem was making a car that could actually be driven by the motor. Students learned that this involved a lot more than just connecting a wheel to a motor. Possible drive mechanisms included direct-drive, friction-drive, belt-drive, and propeller-drive alternatives. One student wanted to know why her car only went in circles. When she examined the car closely, she could see that the only wheel touching the ground was the one attached to the motor. She was then able to redesign the car so that all the wheels touched the ground.

Rotary Switch Using a Paper Clip (Left); Toggle Switch Made From a Binder Clip (Right)

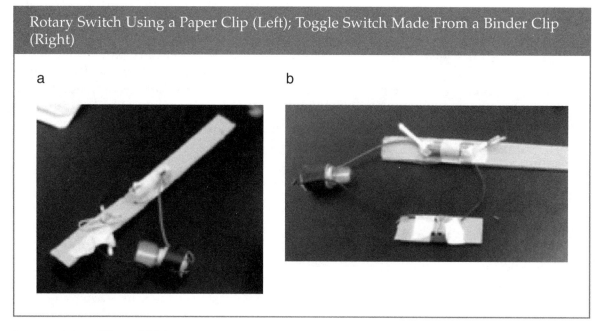

a

b

Images courtesy of Donna M. Johnson.

Another obstacle that the students faced was how they would attach the wheels. They tried to put the wheels on without making them fit tightly onto the axles and were baffled as to why the car wouldn't move when placed on the floor. The figure below shows and example of a loose wheel. These problems and many others like them were solved by the group through brainstorming.

The EnerJeeps curriculum generated a lot of issues that the students had to solve on their own. They were constantly being challenged to look closely at their cars and think carefully about how to correct the problems. They also learned to keep detailed sketches and diagrams to help them replicate and explain their designs to others. This acceptance of drawing as well as writing encouraged students with disabilities and English language learner students to start expressing their designs on paper and orally. They were able to compare cars with one another to discover whose design was most effective. Some students made multiple cars using alternative design ideas because they wanted to see how different designs would behave. An example of a belt-drive vehicle is shown on the next page (p. 50). Sometimes a student would feel at a loss but a classmate would quickly come to his or her aid with helpful advice. It was thrilling to see students take ownership over their own learning and help each other!

Like EnerJeeps, ElectroCity is an upper-elementary-grade unit that focuses on electric circuits and energy transformations. In ElectroCity, students design their own mystery boxes, pop-up cards, masks, dioramas, and puppets that use visible or hidden switches to control light, sound, and motion. The first few lessons of EnerJeeps and ElectroCity are similar, but they diverge once students begin creating their projects. The students who did ElectroCity were successful in creating all sorts of designs. Their creations included the following:

Loosely Fitting Wheel

Images courtesy of Donna M. Johnson.

Belt-drive car; the motor at center bottom turns a rubber band, which is attached to the drive wheel at bottom right. Note also the horn at top left and two tail lights near top right.

Image courtesy of Janice Porter.

- A "money alarm" that makes a noise when someone snatches a dollar bill
- Pop-ups that light up or sound off when opened
- Boxes that shake when the lid is closed
- Color mixers, with multicolored wheels that spin inside a box when the lid is opened
- A "microwave" that makes noise when the door is closed
- A " Laundromat," with washers and dryers that spin when the doors are closed
- A "popcorn maker" that spins and makes beads jump when activated
- Electric puppets, whose eyes light up when the mouth is closed

Two sample projects are shown below. The figure on the opening page of this chapter (p. 39) shows a mystery box that is designed to look like an airplane, whose propeller spins when the box is closed. The figure on the next page (p. 51) illustrates a pop-up card that lights up when opened.

To accomplish their goals, students developed new kinds of hidden switches and showed how a switch can control a circuit. The students were excited about learning engineering, including testing designs, troubleshooting existing problems, and redesigning what didn't work. Meanwhile, they also learned that being an engineer also requires writing and drawing for communication, using standard circuit symbols, and reflecting on one's work. The students took ownership of their learning and demonstrated the knowledge they had acquired by designing their own devices. As engineers, they brainstormed about materials they would like to incorporate in their designs and anticipated possible problems that might occur. Before starting the curriculum, almost none of my low-income minority students would have thought they were capable of doing engineering, let alone of pursuing careers as engineers. By engaging in basic engineering practices, the students realized that by nature they are thinkers, problem solvers, and designers. The most important lesson the students took away from the curriculum is that they already have the capacity to do engineering.

Much like Fantastic Elastic, EnerJeeps and ElectroCity develop students' abilities to use scientific and engineering practices, and address the NGSS Performance Standard 3–5

Closed and open views of a pop-up card with a light that turns on when the card is opened. The text in the yellow balloon reads: "What a great lunch for a hawk in its nest."

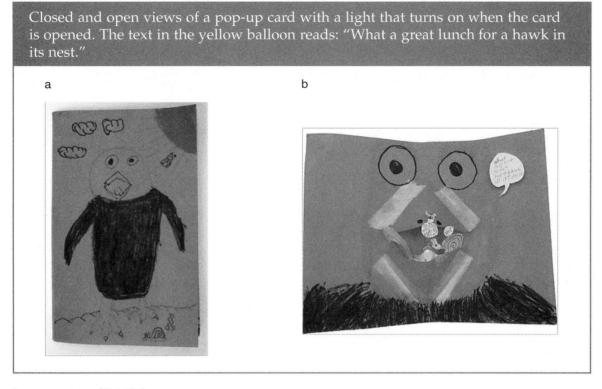

a

b

Images courtesy of Evi Abeler.

ETS-1. In addition, they are closely aligned with most of the crosscutting concepts that comprise Dimension 2 of *A Framework for K–12 Science Education:*

- **Patterns.** Just as scientists look for patterns to better understand the world around them, "engineers often look for and analyze patterns, too. For example, they may diagnose patterns of failure of a designed system under test in order to improve the design" (NRC, 2012, p. 86). That is just what students are doing when they troubleshoot their electric cars and other electrical devices.
- **Cause and Effect: Mechanism and Prediction.** "In engineering, the goal is to design a system to cause a desired effect, so cause-and-effect relationships are as much a part of engineering as of science. Indeed, the process of design is a good place to help students begin to think in terms of cause and effect, because they must understand the underlying causal relationships in order to devise and explain a design that can achieve a specified objective" (NRC, 2012, p. 88). Most devices do not work initially. In order to troubleshoot, students learn to identify the cause of a problem so they can fix it.
- **Systems and System Models.** "Models can be valuable in predicting a system's behaviors or in diagnosing problems or failures in its functioning, regardless of what type of system is being examined. A good system model for use in developing scientific explanations or engineering designs must specify not only the parts, or subsystems, of the system but also how they interact with one another" (NRC, 2012, p. 93). Every circuit or vehicle is a system that students learn to model by creating a diagram, which serves as a resource for both design and troubleshooting.
- **Matter and Energy.** "The ability to examine, characterize, and model the transfers and cycles of matter and energy is a tool that students can use across virtually all areas of science and engineering" (NRC, 2012, p. 95). In understanding how to

construct a circuit, the students develop an appreciation for how energy flows and is transformed from electrical energy to sound, light, or mechanical energy.

- **Structure and Function.** By constructing switches and including them in circuits, students are required to think about how the functioning of a built system "depends on the shapes and relationships of certain key parts" (NRC, 2012, p. 93).

Conclusion

Unlike most industrial nations, the United States has virtually no experience in teaching and learning engineering in K–12, particularly in the elementary grades (NAE & NRC, 2009, p. 20). Inaugurating this endeavor will be at best highly challenging, in light of an already overburdened curriculum, lack of resources, and inertia. As with physical science, there is a strong likelihood that the engineering aspects of the NGSS will simply be ignored, particularly in settings that are predominantly low-income, ethnic minority, early childhood or elementary, English language learner and/or special education (NRC, 2007, pp. 7–5, 8–15, 10–15). What strategies are available to surmount these barriers?

This is a classic design problem, which we pose for ourselves much the same way as our students tackle the design of wind-ups, electric cars, or mystery boxes. Like any other design task, the design of engineering curriculum begins with a goal, draws upon resources, is limited by constraints, and is tested to acquire data, and then typically redesigned based on that data in light of the design criteria. None of these factors is static. In the course of an actual design project, the designers' understanding of the goals, resources, constraints, test methods, data, and criteria will almost certainly change over time. Following are the main lessons we've learned as we've engaged in this work over the last six years:

1. **Consult, listen, and collaborate.** Too often curriculum design takes place in rarefied environments that are culturally distant from classrooms, schools, and communities, resulting in curriculum products that remain on the shelf. Like any other design process, curriculum design should attend to users' voices and concerns, which should be the most basic source of data to inform redesign. Curriculum ideas and products are far more likely to gain traction if teachers and children have been part of the design team. We once scrapped a curriculum almost completely after teachers reported that their students did not find it very engaging. A key principle of our project is that teachers and students have veto power over any idea, no matter how intriguing it was at first.

2. **Integrate across subject areas.** The problem of "not enough time" is a key constraint in every classroom. Integrating engineering with science, math, literacy, and art in a single project is an obvious strategy for introducing curriculum that can serve more than one purpose and thereby fit into a school day in a variety of ways.

3. **Use inexpensive or recycled materials.** A complementary obstacle to "not enough time" is "no money for materials." In an era of downsizing and cutbacks, few schools and districts will buy expensive materials for a subject they neither understand nor appreciate. We have avoided the use of handheld computers or laptops, which we think are not appropriate, let alone necessary, for teaching engineering design at an elementary level. All of the materials for our units are inexpensive, and some are virtually free. The materials needed to make a wind-up cost about 5 cents in bulk, and nearly everything can be

found in the cafeteria or office supply cabinet. For specialized materials, such as electrical components, we have worked hard with SEMPCO to find inexpensive sources. We don't buy battery holders, bulb holders, or switches because it's both cheaper and far more instructive when students make their own.

4. **Consider curriculum, professional development, materials, and assessment in a unified way**. All four of these components are necessary to any successful educational initiative, but too often they are developed in isolation from one another. Our experience has taught us that these four design challenges should be taken on in parallel rather than in sequence. For example, assessment studies often reveal weaknesses in a lesson, leading to ideas for curriculum improvement; and teachers in our professional development sessions have given us ideas for simplifying materials.

We hope these lessons will be valuable to others, as guidelines for meeting the new engineering demands of the NGSS.

Acknowledgments

The coauthors of this chapter include an engineering professor and eight teachers who played major roles in the development, pilot-testing, and redesign of the materials. Gary Benenson, the project director of Physical Science Comes Alive! is the overall editor of the chapter and primary author of the Overview and Conclusion. Travis Sloane contributed the section on Invent-a-Wheel, which describes his experiences with kindergarten students. The next section, Fantastic Elastic, combines the classroom observations of four teachers who taught the unit in Grades 1–3: Emmy Matias-Leonard, Angula Bumbury-Camacho, Barbara Martucci, and Jody Hilton. ElectroCity and EnerJeeps are related units that both involve electric circuits. The section on these units was written by three teachers who taught the materials in Grades 3–5: Cherubim Cannon, Janice Porter, and Donna Johnson. Most of the work reported here took place in low-income schools in Harlem, Bedford-Stuyvesant, and Brownsville. Recommendations and suggestions for this chapter were additionally provided by Jim Neujahr, co-project director, and Anja Hernandez, project coordinator, Physical Science Comes Alive! and Joachin Rodriguez and Tchnavia Merrick, science teachers at PS 41 and Harbor Arts and Sciences, both in Manhattan.

References

NGSS Lead States. (2013). *Next Generation Science Standards: For states, by states.* Washington, DC: The National Academies Press.

National Research Council. (2012). *A framework for K–12 science education: Practices, crosscutting concepts, and core ideas.* Washington, DC: The National Academies Press.

National Academy of Engineering & National Research Council. (2009). *Engineering in K–12 Education: Understanding the status and improving the prospects.* Washington DC: The National Academies Press.

National Research Council. (2007). *Taking science to school: Learning and teaching science in grades K–8.* Washington DC: The National Academies Press.

3

Engineering by Design TEEMS™

Kindergarten Through Second Grade

Diana Cantu, Teacher Effectiveness Coach for K–5
EbD TEEMS™ STEM, Center for Teaching and Learning™,
International Technology and Engineering Educators Association

Kindergarten Student Designing and Building a Birdhouse

Images courtesy of Engineering byDesign™.

Engineering byDesign™ is a comprehensive K–12 curriculum that was developed by the International Technology and Engineering Educators Association's **STEM** Center for Teaching and Learning™. This chapter will focus on the K–2 elementary-level component of the curriculum, EbD TEEMS™, where TEEMS stands for Technology, Engineering, Environment, Mathematics, and Science. We've added the extra "E" to create a stronger link among the four science, technology, engineering, and mathematics (STEM) fields and to engage the students in a fun, real-world context.

There are three fun and engaging modules, called Building Blocks, that make up the K–2 curriculum: A Home for All Seasons (kindergarten); Agriculture Around Us (first grade); and Our Environment, Our Health (second grade). Each Building Block is organized around an environmental context and real-world design challenge that require students to learn and apply targeted technology, engineering, mathematics, and science concepts (ITEEA, 2013). Many of these design challenges were inspired by the National Academy of Engineering's (NAE) Grand Challenges for Engineering.

All Building Blocks are designed for flexible use to meet the varying needs of today's elementary classrooms. Instruction for each Building Block takes approximately 6–8 weeks, based on an average of 3–4 hours of implementation per week. However, the length can vary depending on the frequency and duration of time allotted for STEM learning experiences. Some lessons can take as little as 20–30 minutes, while others may take several hours to complete.

Birdhouse Created by Kindergarten Students

Image courtesy of Engineering byDesign™

By addressing standards in several different subjects in the same lesson, Building Blocks allow you to cover more material in less time, while helping you illustrate cross-curricular connections. Seeing such connections is imperative for students if they are to understand the world around them. The world functions together in an integrative fashion, not in silos.

The goals of EbD-TEEMS™ are to

- provide culturally and cognitively diverse students with STEM learning experiences that are meaningful, engaging, and appropriate to their stage of development;
- foster development of a global perspective for personal and social responsibility; and
- initiate comprehensive reform in elementary schools by serving as a model for integration and providing a foundation for advanced STEM learning in future grades.

Engineering byDesign™ is accessible at http://www.iteea.org/EbD/ebd.htm or through the ITEEA's Consortium of States as described later in this chapter.

Following is an overview of the three Building Blocks for Grades K–3.

A Home for All Seasons (Kindergarten)

In the kindergarten Building Block, students use integrative STEM strategies to learn about and create various animal homes covered throughout the Building Block. A Home for All Seasons challenges young learners to explore various animal homes ranging from hives, to caves, to underground dens, and various other types of homes.

Students apply what they learn in the "Home Sweet Home" design challenge, where they must create a birdhouse using certain materials and constraints in order to show mastery of the core concepts covered within the Building Block. Students will surprise you as they construct complex homes with features only a kindergarten imagination could envision.

Agriculture All Around Us

In the first-grade Building Block, Agriculture Around Us, students use integrative STEM strategies to engage in activities related to managing Earth's land resources, with a focus on soil management and conservation. Science concepts include plants, nutrients, soil, and food and fiber systems; mathematics concepts include place value, length, 3-D shapes, tallying data, and using data tables. Through an experiential and problem-based approach, students work together to investigate global agricultural issues and begin to develop an understanding of stewardship and innovation.

A design challenge provides an opportunity for students to apply their new knowledge and skills in a meaningful way as they design a sustainable garden to grow the raw materials necessary for a specific product (ITEEA, 2013). The design challenge for this Building Block was inspired by the NAE's Grand Challenges for Engineering: Management of the Nitrogen Cycle.

Our Environment, Our Health

In this Building Block, —Our Environment, Our Health—second-grade students explore a hot topic in 21st century global news: dependence on fossil fuels and the reduction of carbon emissions. Through the environmental context of reducing, reusing, and recycling,

Students Learning About a Garden

Image courtesy of Home Gardening Association, U.S. Department of Agriculture, retrieved from http://healthymeals. nal.usda.gov/resource-library/bulletin-board-resources/school-gardens-bulletin-board-resources.

Changing the Oil Can Be a Messy Job

Image courtesy of Thinkstock.

and problems associated with fossil fuels, students engage in design and inquiry-based instruction while also using integrative STEM concepts. Science and mathematics concepts reinforced in the Building Block include pollution, matter, fossil fuels, natural resources, place value, length, recording data, and graphing data (ITEEA, 2013).

The design challenge in this Building Block provides an opportunity for students to apply knowledge and skills in a meaningful way as they create absorbent mats to capture an oil spill. Inspired by the NAE's Grand Challenges for Engineering: Reduce Carbon Emissions, students connect their learning with both the present and the future. Students are further challenged to not only create an original design but also to consider containment *and* mobility of their mats.

The Engineering Design Process

In each Building Block, students engage in the engineering design process—a core idea and essential practice in the Next Generation Science Standards (NGSS) (NGSS Lead States, 2013). At this level, the process is simplified to four phases, as shown on the opposite page. Students begin by stating the problem they are going to engage. They are instructed to then look for ideas to solve the problem. This can be done through observation or research or

Students Developing a Mat to Absorb Excess Oil

Image courtesy of Engineering byDesign™.

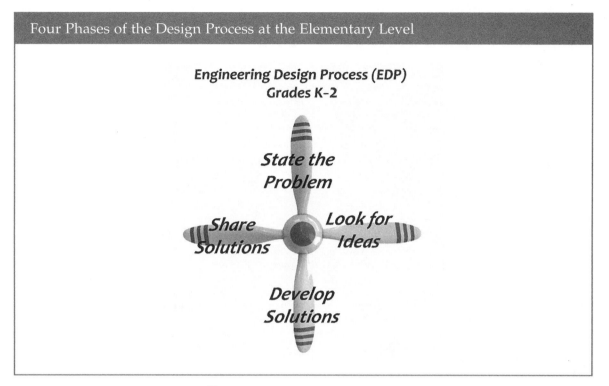

Four Phases of the Design Process at the Elementary Level

Engineering Design Process (EDP)
Grades K-2

State the Problem

Share Solutions

Look for Ideas

Develop Solutions

Image courtesy of Engineering byDesign™.

both. Next, students turn those ideas into possible solutions. At this stage, students should be encouraged to look at multiple ideas for solutions before choosing the solution they wish to pursue. Finally, students share their solutions, much like an engineer or scientist does, in order to compare and contrast various ides for solving the same problem. This phase is particularly important to illustrate that a given problem can have many solutions.

STEM Integration

Table 3.1 illustrates how each of the EbD-TEEMS™ Building Blocks integrates all four of the STEM fields in an environmental context. Notice how each of the units includes science concepts, a major technological system, an engineering design challenge, and important mathematical ideas and skills.

Key Elements of the Instructional Model

Each Building Block in EbD-TEEMS™ follows a 6E Learning Cycle that includes: *(pre) Evaluate, Engage, Explore, Explain, Elaborate, and (post) Evaluate*. Together, the six phases of a Building Block, illustrated in Figure 3.6, form a progression of learning that takes students from the basics to the application of newly learned concepts in order to invent or innovate solutions to a design challenge. This 6E model is used throughout the K–5 curriculum. The 6E Learning Cycle, revised by J. Bertrand (2013), is an adaptation of the 5E learning model proposed by Rodger Bybee (Bybee, 1997; Bybee & Landes, 1990), adapted to a technology and engineering context in which students must start by evaluating the problem to be solved and conclude by evaluating the solution to see if they solved the problem.

Table 3.1 Integrated STEM in the EbD-TEEMS™ Building Blocks*					
		Science	**Technology**	**Engineering**	**Mathematics**
Building Block	**Environmental Context**	**Core Concepts**	**The Designed World**	**Design Challenges**	**Math Focal Points**
Kindergarten *A Home for All Seasons*	Animal Shelters & Habitats	Animal Properties, Seasons, Nature, Habitats	Construction Technologies	Design a bird house	Counting, Size, Attributes, 2-D and 3-D Shapes
First Grade *Agriculture Around Us*	Food & Fiber Systems/ Agriculture	Plants, Nutrients, Food & Fiber, Soil	Agriculture and Related Biotechnologies	Manage the nitrogen cycle*	Place Value, Length, 3-D Shapes, Data Tables
Second Grade *Our Environment, Our Health*	Environmental Health	Pollution, Matter, Fossil Fuels, Resources	Manufacturing Technologies	Design an absorbent mat to contain an oil spill*	Place Value, Length, Record Data, Graph Data

*Inspired by NAE Grand Challenges.

In addition, the EbD-TEEMS™ instructional model has a number of important additional features. Each Building Block

- encourages and supports student engagement in inquiry and design-based learning experiences;
- recommends award-winning literature at the appropriate grade level in order to create a context and for student learning (You can substitute different readings if you wish);
- supports literacy development through explicit and intentional use of proven vocabulary and reading comprehension strategies;
- encourages expository and technical writing through the use of STEM notebooks;
- emphasizes the T and E of STEM education (now an integral part of the NGSS);
- helps students develop environmental stewardship and an unbiased awareness of global issues;
- provides opportunities for students to develop collaboration and communication skills;
- introduces students to Grand Challenges for Engineering as identified by the NAE;
- highlights the career of a real-life person who conducted research, developed potential solutions, or played some other important role in the featured environmental issue;
- can be used to complement elementary science and math programs;
- is currently undergoing alignment with the NGSS; and
- supports mathematics development by providing opportunities for students to reinforce challenging concepts through application.

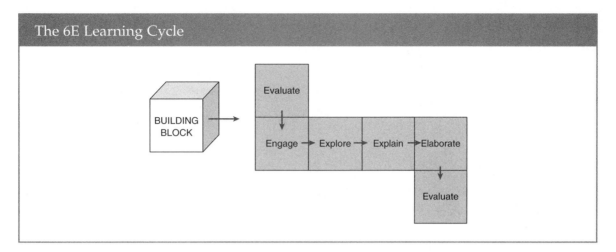

The 6E Learning Cycle

Image courtesy of Engineering byDesign™.

Working in Tandem With the Next Generation Science Standards

Engineering byDesign™ was created to support the Common Core State Standards (NGA & CCSSO, 2010), Standards for Technological Literacy (ITEEA, 2000, 2005, 2007), Principles and Standards for School Mathematics (NCTM, 2000), and Benchmarks for Science Literacy (AAAS, 1993/2008). The curriculum is currently being modified to better align with the NGSS (NGSS Lead States, 2013). However, as shown in Table 3.2, it is already well aligned with performance expectations from the NGSS for Grades K–2.

The kindergarten Building Block, a Home for All Seasons, is especially well aligned with the following learning expectation in the NGSS life science standards: *K-LS1–1,* Use observations to describe patterns of what plants and animals (including humans) need to survive.

STEM Notebooks

TEEMS™ uses a STEM notebook as a means to process and reflect on learning through each Building Block. Learners are encouraged to write, draw, make tables and diagrams, and conference about items contained in their STEM notebooks. STEM notebooks could also serve as source of formative assessment as they provide evidence of student learning, aid in the identification of misconceptions, and serve as a demonstration of student progress. For teachers, STEM notebooks can serve as a source of information for planning in order to adjust lessons to meet the needs of students.

STEM notebooks are used throughout the Engineering byDesign™ curriculum. STEM notebooks are structured similar to professional scientific or engineering laboratory notebooks. They can be a hardbound, softbound, or a spiral-bound notebook. Lined pages are suggested, although gridlines on either the top half of the page or every other page for sketching and making graphs can also be used. Students are encouraged to number every page while keeping the first five pages as a table of contents. The last several pages should be used as a glossary for new vocabulary terms. The following are suggested components and guidelines that should be included in the STEM notebook:

- **Question or Problem**—What do you want to find out or solve?
- **Prediction**—What do you think will happen? If . . . then, or I think . . . because . . .

- **Materials**—List all of the materials, including amounts and safety equipment.
- **Procedures**—Write a numbered list of the steps that you will follow or have followed.
- **Observations**—Record what you see, hear, smell, or feel during an investigation.
- **Ideas**—List all of your thoughts, reflections, and brainstorms.
- **Data**—Record measurements, amounts, and other numerical information.
- **Drawings**—Sketch what you observe or ideas that you have.
- **Conclusions**—What have you learned? What evidence do you have to support your ideas?

Table 3.2 K–2 Engineering Design Standard From the NGSS

	Performance Expectations From the NGSS (NGSS Lead States, 2013)	K–2 EbD-TEEMS™ Activities (ITEEA, 2013)
K-2-ETS1-1	Ask questions, make observations, and gather information about a situation people want to change to define a simple problem that can be solved through the development of a new or improved object or tool.	Students use STEM notebooks in which they record questions, make observations, and gather information about a given situation. In addition, students begin to develop ideas about the development of a new or improved object or tool in order to solve their grade-level design challenge.
K-2-ETS1-2	Develop a simple sketch, drawing, or physical model to illustrate how the shape of an object helps it function as needed to solve a given problem.	In their STEM notebooks, students sketch their ideas for solving a grade-appropriate design challenge.
K-2-ETS1-3	Analyze data from tests of two objects designed to solve the same problem to compare the strengths and weaknesses of how each performs.	Once students have created a solution for the grade-level design challenge, they share their ideas while comparing and contrasting various solutions. Students can then engage in a redesign if they believe an improvement can be made to their design.

Maintaining a STEM notebook is an important process in the curriculum. Students will find themselves referring back to their STEM notebooks when confronted with their grade-level design challenge or activity. In addition, these notebooks serve as a great resource not only for students and teachers but also as a communication tool for parents to understand what their children are learning. Parents will also enjoy perusing through the various pages to see how their child has grown in concepts and learning progression throughout the year.

Instructional Materials

We understand budgets are tight, and teachers have limited resources. So we designed the Building Blocks to use materials and supplies that can easily be found in the classroom,

Student Using a STEM Notebook

Image courtesy of Engineering byDesign™.

purchased locally, or donated by parents or community members. Materials lists are provided in the following categories:

Typical classroom supplies are materials already available in a classroom such as pencils, chart paper, glue, scissors, etc.

Equipment includes reusable items needed for mixing, molding, gluing, carving, or holding. Examples of equipment can include bowls, spoons, forks, glue guns, paintbrushes, safety goggles, etc.

Recyclable items can be easily collected at home by either students and/or teachers. These can include items such as cardboard boxes, cereal boxes, Styrofoam trays, newspaper, clear plastic containers, etc.

Consumables are items that will be used up and cannot be salvaged. Examples include plastic bags, balloons, clay, gravel, pebbles, etc.

Additional materials include anything that does not fit in the other categories, such as hammers, screws, nails, saws, etc.

Students are taught from the beginning how to safely use equipment in order to construct their projects. This includes use of safety glasses, gloves when handling glue guns, and adult supervision when handling new tools. The students continue to build their knowledge and skills in using tools throughout the K–12 curriculum.

One important issue to keep in mind is food allergies. Teachers should send a note home to determine if the children have any food or substance allergy(s) prior to instruction so there is time to find substitutes.

The Future of EbD-TEEMS™

"The Engineering byDesign™ Program is built on the belief that the ingenuity of children is untapped, unrealized potential that, when properly motivated, will lead to the next generation of technologists, innovators, designers, and engineers." (ITEEA, 2013, para. 1)

We have been pleased to see that the mission of EbD-TEEMS™ is entirely consistent with the important role of engineering design in the NGSS. Nonetheless, some further improvements will be needed to fully align our curriculum with the NGSS. Many talented curriculum writers and subject-matter experts are already hard at work to properly align each Building Block with the NGSS standards.

EbD-TEEMS™ can be your go-to curriculum in order to create a STEM-enriched classroom that considers the environment we live in as a context for learning. In addition to meeting the required STEM content, you can create a fun, rigorous, and challenging environment for your students that will help them become active and responsible 21st century learners!

To learn more about any of the Engineering byDesign™ programs, visit http://www .iteea.org/EbD/ebd.htm.

Access to Engineering byDesign™

The Engineering byDesign™ course curricula can be purchased by any individual, school, district, or state, for a low price at www.iteea.org. However, schools can become a part of the Engineering byDesign™ school network to access the full benefits of the entire Engineering byDesign™ program and learning community. These benefits include the following:

- Online access to the curriculum and the latest updates
- Exclusive access to EbDonline™ to converse with online facilitators and teachers around the country who are also implementing the same courses
- Online assessments for the students in their classes—access to real-time student performance data

To become an Engineering byDesign™ network school, you can download and complete a network agreement at www.iteea.org. Additionally, Engineering byDesign™ has created a consortium of states to serve as leaders in collaborating for higher quality education. Any schools within a consortium state are provided with free access to the Engineering byDesign™ program. The leaders in these states work together to create consistency in the advancement of STEM education. The state leaders implement the Engineering byDesign™ curriculum in their school systems and together evaluate student achievement to make informed decisions in enhancing technological and engineering literacy for all through an integrative STEM study. These state members develop the necessary professional growth opportunities for teachers and propose any needed changes to the curricula. With the increase of states in the consortium, state decisions can become a powerful tool in shaping the future of education, and furthering students' technological and engineering literacy. The figure on the next page illustrates the current consortium of states for Engineering byDesign™.

Access to the Engineering byDesign™ Portal

The Engineering byDesign™ network of schools and consortium states have access to the curriculum through the EbDportal™. The EbD portal™ is a cloud-based solution for providing curriculum, assessment, and professional development. Through the portal, teachers can access the dynamic course curriculum and EbDonline™ for ongoing professional

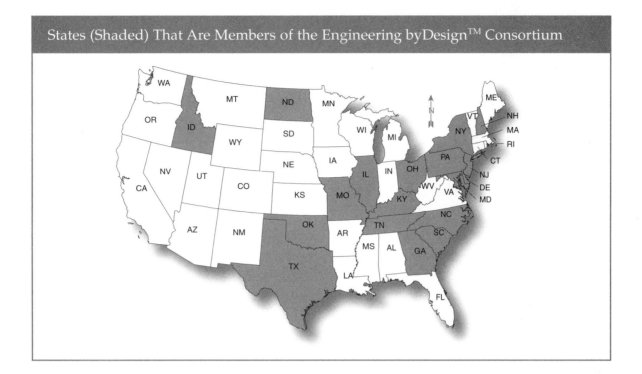

States (Shaded) That Are Members of the Engineering byDesign™ Consortium

development. Additionally, teachers can assign and mange student assessments through the portal to make data-driven decisions about their instruction.

References

American Association for the Advancement of Science. (1993/2008). *Benchmarks for science literacy.* New York, NY: Oxford University Press.

Bertand, J. (2013). *6E learning cycle* [PowerPoint slides]. Retrieved from http://www.iteea.org/EbD/ebd.htm.

Bybee, R. W. (1997). *Achieving scientific literacy: From purposes to practices.* Portsmouth, NH: Heinemann.

Bybee, R. W., & Landes, N. M. (1990, February). Science for life & living: An elementary school science program from Biological Sciences Curriculum Study. *The American Biology Teacher, 52*(2), 92–98.

International Technology and Engineering Educators Association. (2000, 2005, 2007). *Standards for technological literacy: Content for the study of technology.* Reston, VA: Author.

International Technology and Engineering Educators Association. (2013). *Engineering byDesign: A standards based model program.* Reston, VA: Author. Retrieved from http://www.iteea.org/EdB/ebd.htm.

National Council of Teachers of Mathematics. (2000). *Principles and standards for school mathematics.* Reston, VA: Author. Retrieved from http://www.nctm.org/standards/default.aspx?id=58.

National Governors Association Center for Best Practices & Council of Chief State School Officers. (2010). *Common Core State Standards.* Washington, DC: Authors.

NGSS Lead States. (2013). *Next Generation Science Standards: For states, by states.* Washington, DC: The National Academies Press.

4

BSCS Science Tracks

Connecting Science and Literacy

Nancy M. Landes, BSCS: Colorado Springs, Colorado
Janet Carlson, Center to Support
Excellence in Teaching, Stanford Graduate School
of Education, Stanford, California

BSCS Science Tracks engages students in thinking deeply about technology and engineering.

Image courtesy of BSCS.

T he intent of standards in science and engineering education is to define in a concise way what all students should know and be able to do to become scientifically literate citizens. BSCS Science Tracks provides a model of what standards-based science and engineering education looks like in elementary school classrooms, Grades K–5.

In BSCS Science Tracks, students learn and apply basic science concepts through engaging experiences that involve them both physically and mentally in the processes of scientific inquiry and engineering design. Each module clearly defines the standards that students are to meet and provides a sequence of developmentally appropriate experiences that allow students to develop a true understanding of the concepts presented, not just a superficial overview of related vocabulary and facts.

The Go-To Guide for Engineering Curricula is a perfect descriptor for the Science and Technology modules (units of instruction) of BSCS Science Tracks. BSCS Science Tracks and its predecessor, Science for Life and Living: Integrating Science, Technology, and Health, were among the first curricula in elementary science to incorporate engineering design into the curriculum framework as endorsed by the National Science Education Standards (NSES) (NRC, 1996) and Benchmarks for Science Literacy (AAAS, 1993/2008). Both the Standards and the Benchmarks considered scientific inquiry and engineering design to be essential components of the content of a comprehensive science education as do the current Next Generation Science Standards (NGSS) (NGSS Lead States, 2013).

BSCS Science Tracks includes everything the busy teacher needs to help students meet high standards, including

- complete lesson plans in physical science, life science, earth and space science, and science and technology (engineering design);
- well-defined assessment strategies;
- a structure for collaborative learning;
- the BSCS 5E Instructional Model that connects learning experiences;
- background information about the science content and engineering design; and
- BSCS Science Tracks *Handbook: A Resource for Educators.* The Handbook is full of practical suggestions for everything from establishing a safe and manageable learning environment, to using notebooks as effective tools to promote learning, to helping students construct their understanding of science concepts and engaging them in problem solving through engineering design. The curriculum does not require teachers to have special laboratory facilities or equipment and supports teachers with content background information in science and engineering.

Following is a brief overview of the K–5 BSCS Science Tracks Science and Technology (engineering design) modules, which are published by Kendall/Hunt Publishing Company, Dubuque, Iowa (http://www.kendallhunt.com).

Kindergarten: Using Tools to Solve Problems

Because children are natural inventors and like to make things, they should be encouraged to explore and use the technology that exists in the world around them. The first lesson focuses on the technology we use to fasten things together. Lesson 2 emphasizes the use of simple tools that extend the senses of sight and hearing. In lesson 3, students design their own "plumbing system" to solve the problem of moving water from one place to another. Each lesson includes independent learning centers along with a whole-class introduction to the concepts.

Grade 1: Testing Materials

This module provides sequential, connected experiences to help students understand that people select a material for a specific purpose according to the properties of the material. As students engage in the processes of technological design and problem solving, they learn to view testing as a way to find out about materials. Students realize they can learn as much from tests that fail as from tests that succeed. They learn to risk their ideas without losing their confidence.

Grade 2: Designing Sound Systems

Sound is an important part of a child's world, one that children are eager to investigate. In the first half of this module, students engage in scientific inquiry as they investigate how vibrating objects produce sound. To conclude the module, students participate in the process of technological design; they use what they have learned about sound to design simple systems (musical instruments) that produce sound and explain how their design works to produce sound.

Extending the Senses

Image courtesy of BSCS.

Testing a "Puffing Machine"

Image courtesy of BSCS.

Designing Cymbals

Image courtesy of BSCS.

Grade 3: Designing Structures

The lessons in this module place students in the role of imaginative architects and engineers who design, construct, test, and evaluate solutions to problems. Students are challenged to design and build strong towers and bridges. They learn about shapes and patterns that add strength to structures; design, build, and test the structures; and communicate their findings. Testing requires students to gather and analyze data and recognize patterns in the data.

Grade 4: Solving Air Pollution Problems

This module challenges students to design solutions to problems that require the application of ideas and procedures rather than construction with actual materials. The technological problems presented in this module center around air pollution. Students examine the effects of air pollution on the respiratory system, collect and analyze data of visible and invisible air pollution, and design solutions to air pollution problems in their local environment.

Grade 5: Designing Environmental Solutions

In this module, students assess their own and society's impacts on the environment and evaluate those impacts. They consider environmental issues, such as the depletion of rain forest resources, oil spills, and using disposable versus cloth diapers. All these issues

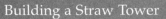

Building a Straw Tower

Image courtesy of BSCS.

Analyzing Data About Air Pollution

Image courtesy of BSCS.

present trade-offs and constraints and relate to human use of resources and the related environmental impacts. By wrestling with environmental dilemmas, students come to understand that designing solutions to environmental problems is a complex process.

Image courtesy of BSCS.

BSCS Science Tracks Curriculum Framework

Table 4.1 is an overview of the entire BSCS Science Tracks Curriculum Framework. The six modules briefly summarized earlier are listed in the right-hand column under "Science and Technology." In the remainder of the chapter, we focus on this column since these modules best illustrate *The Go-To Guide for Engineering Curricula.* The entire Framework is listed here to illustrate that these modules are part of a comprehensive elementary curriculum that includes all of the major science fields.

Technology and Engineering in the Curriculum

Each module in the K–5 Science and Technology sequence begins with a lesson titled "Doing Technology," in which students learn about the nature of technology and engineering design as illustrated on the next page. "Doing technology" in BSCS Science Tracks has the same meaning as "engineering design" in *A Framework for K–12 Science Education* (NRC, 2012) and the NGSS (NGSS Lead States, 2013).

BSCS Science Tracks and A *Framework for K–12 Science Education*

We recognize that the purpose of the NGSS is to provide a common set of learning expectations for curriculum, instruction, and assessment. The NGSS is based on *A Framework for K–12 Science Education: Practices, Crosscutting Concepts, and Core Ideas*, which projects a broad vision for the future of science education. In many cases, the Framework provides more expansive descriptions of what students are expected to know and be able to do

Table 4.1 BSCS Science Tracks Curriculum Framework

Reading Level	Physical Science	Earth & Space Science	Life Science	Science & Technology
PreK/K	Investigating My Senses	Investigating Myself and My Family	Investigating Here, There, and Everywhere	Using Tools to Solve Problems
1	Investigating Properties	Investigating Weather	Investigating Animals & Their Needs	Testing Materials
2	Investigating Position & Motion	Investigating Earth Materials	Investigating Plants	Designing Sound Systems
3	Investigating Electrical Systems	Investigating Objects in the Sky	Investigating Life Cycles	Designing Structures
4	Investigating Physical & Chemical Properties	Investigating the Changing Earth	Investigating Ecosystems	Solving Air Pollution Problems
5	Investigating Heat & Changes in Materials	Investigating Weather Systems	Investigating Human Systems	Designing Environmental Solutions

Doing Technology Model in BSCS Science Tracks

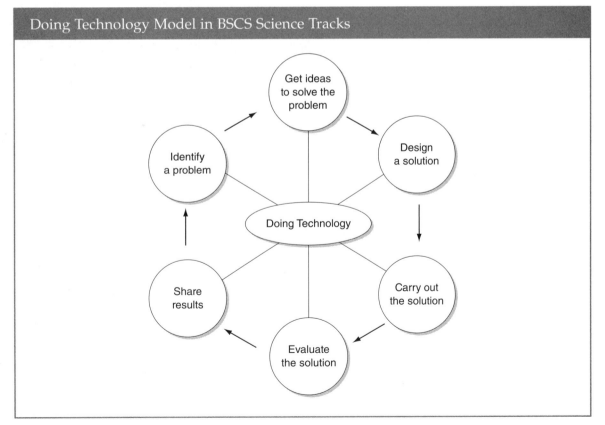

Image courtesy of BSCS.

than does the NGSS. That is the case with the practices of science and engineering, which weave throughout the new standards, and which all students are expected to master. As shown in Table 4.2, "doing technology" in BSCS Science Tracks is very similar to the way that "engineering design" is described in the Framework.

To help you envision what engineering design might look like in your classroom, following are detailed descriptions of the first-grade and fifth-grade lessons in BSCS Science Tracks.

Through these lessons, students acquire both the understanding of engineering design and the abilities to do it. We hope you become as excited as we are at BSCS with the rich and engaging, yet practical, engineering experiences we have designed for your students.

Grade 1: Testing Materials

The Testing Materials module, Grade 1, introduces students to the processes of technological design by placing them in the role of imaginative engineers who solve problems

Table 4.2 Correlation of Doing Technology and Engineering Practices in the Framework

Doing Technology in BSCS Science Tracks	Practices in the Framework
Identify a problem: "People who do technology try to fix problems or prevent problems from happening. Engineers, architects, and scientists work together to solve problems. The first step in solving a problem is to identify clearly what the problem is" (BSCS, 2006a, p. 4).	*Asking questions and defining problems:* "Engineering begins with a problem, need, or desire that suggests an engineering problem that needs to be solved. Engineers ask questions to define the engineering problem, determine criteria for a successful solution, and identify constraints" (NRC, 2012, p. 50).
Get ideas to solve the problem: "Engineers and designers talk about many ideas to solve a problem. They think about whether a product or structure is safe and how it might affect the environment and people. They draw or write about all the parts of their designs" (BSCS, 2006b, pp. 6–7).	*Constructing explanations and designing solutions:* "Each proposed solution results from a process of balancing competing criteria of desired functions, technological feasibility, cost, safety, esthetics, and compliance with legal requirements. There is usually no single best solution but rather a range of solutions" (NRC, 2012, p. 52).
Design a solution: As students develop proposals to build something or get something to work better, they describe and communicate many ideas. Students recognize that designing a solution might have constraints, such as cost, materials, time, or safety.	*Planning and carrying out investigations:* Engineers use investigation both to gain data essential for specifying design criteria or parameters and to test their designs. Like scientists, engineers must identify relevant variables, decide how they will be measured, and collect data for analysis. Their investigations help them to identify how effective, efficient, and durable their designs may be under a range of conditions (NRC, 2012, p. 50).

Doing Technology in BSCS Science Tracks	Practices in the Framework
Carry out the solution: In implementing their proposed solutions, students build and test models before constructing a final solution. Students use appropriate tools, measurements, and techniques to build their models, collect data, and implement their solutions. They show the ability to balance simple constraints when they implement their solutions. "As engineers carry out their solutions, they gather data (evidence) about how well their solutions work" (BSCS, 2006b, p. 9).	*Developing and using models:* Engineering makes use of models and simulations to analyze existing systems so as to see where flaws might occur or to test possible solutions to a new problem. Engineers also call on models of various sorts to test proposed systems and to recognize the strengths and limitations of their designs (NRC, 2012, p. 50). *Analyzing and interpreting data:* Engineers analyze data collected in the tests of their designs and investigations; this allows them to compare different solutions and determine how well each one meets specific design criteria—that is, which design best solves the problem within the given constraints (NRC, 2012, p. 51).
Evaluate the solution: Engineers evaluate their solutions by looking at their evidence and asking themselves questions such as, Based on our data, did our solution work to solve the problem we identified? How well did it work? How might we change it to make it better? Did our solution cause any new problems? They talk about how their product, structure, or machine works. They tell how they changed the design to make it work better.	*Engaging in argument from evidence:* Engineers use systematic methods to compare alternatives, formulate evidence based on test data, make arguments from evidence to defend their conclusions, evaluate critically the ideas of others, and revise their designs in order to achieve the best solution to the problem at hand.
Share results: Students communicate both the process and product of technological design—both what they did and how they did it. Students learn to share and critique their own and others' work and compare results based on which solution best solved the given problem. "Engineers share what they do with others. They communicate by telling and writing. They communicate with pictures and diagrams. They tell about the design and the steps or process that they used to carry out the design. They tell people about the problem and how they solved it. They tell how their product or structure works. They tell how they changed the design to make it work better" (BSCS, 2006a, pp. 10–11).	*Obtaining, evaluating, and communicating information:* Engineers cannot produce new or improved technologies if the advantages of their designs are not communicated clearly and persuasively. Engineers need to be able to express their ideas, orally and in writing, with the use of tables, graphs, drawings, or models and by engaging in extended discussions with peers. Moreover, as with scientists, they need to be able to derive meaning from colleagues' texts, evaluate the information, and apply it usefully (NRC, 2012, p. 53).

and test their solutions. The problems students encounter involve the selection of materials based on properties. Just like professional engineers, students consider the purpose of an object, explore materials (as shown below), conduct "fair tests" to find out about their properties, and then select the appropriate materials for making the object. Students collect data and record their results.

The module consists of six lessons that follow the BSCS 5E Instructional Model (Bybee 1997; Bybee & Landes, 1990): Engage, Explore, Explain, Elaborate, Evaluate. This module addresses the crosscutting concept (from the NGSS) of Structure and Function and reinforces three performance expectations from the NGSS for the K–2 grade band:

K-2-ETS1–1. Ask questions, make observations, and gather information about a situation people want to change to define a simple problem that can be solved through the development of a new or improved object or tool.

K-2-ETS1–2. Develop a simple sketch, drawing, or physical model to illustrate how the shape of an object helps it function as needed to solve a given problem.

K-2-ETS1–3. Analyze data from tests of two objects designed to solve the same problem to compare the strengths and weaknesses of how each performs.

Introduction: Doing Technology provides an introduction to the practices of engineering design. Students also learn about collaborative learning and set up their engineering notebooks.

Lesson 1: I'll Huff and I'll Puff begins as students listen to the story of "The Three Little Pigs" and discuss the problems the first two pigs had with their houses. Teams make a "puffing machine" and test objects to find out which ones will or will not move with a puff of air. They write letters to the three pigs telling them the results of their tests. The intent of the lesson is to *engage* students by presenting them with an interesting

Examining the Properties of a Material

Image courtesy of BSCS.

engineering problem and to find out what children know about the properties of materials and engineering design. They also have practice sorting objects by their properties, using tools, collecting data, and evaluating a design.

Lesson 2: Let It Soak In starts with poem "Wet Pet," which helps to introduce the property of absorbency. Teams *explore* different materials by conducting "fair tests" of a variety of objects to find out which ones absorb water. Students then list materials that are useful to people because of their absorbent or nonabsorbent properties. The purpose of the lesson is for students to recognize that the property of absorbency makes some materials useful for specific purposes and to provide practice in collecting data, evaluating a product, and communicating their findings to the rest of the class using a chart.

Lesson 3: Jeepers Creepers—Find the Keepers involves students in *exploring* a variety of "keepers," such as cardboard boxes, file cabinets, aquaria, refrigerators, and pencil boxes. They connect the purpose of each "keeper" to the material of which it is made and decide why the properties of the material make it a good choice for the particular kind of keeper. The class records its data in a big book of keepers. The intent of the lesson is for students to have practice in identifying a problem and proposing a solution, to recognize that objects are made of materials that suit a particular purpose, and to develop their abilities to communicate detailed descriptions of objects.

Lesson 4: Materials Matter involves a game in which students make and play a card game to *explain* why specific objects should and should not be made of certain materials. They also have to justify their explanations. The lesson is supported by a vignette of Stephanie Kwolek, the scientist/engineer who invented the material KEVLAR®. The purpose of the lesson is for students to learn that some materials, because of their properties, are better than others for making particular objects. During the lesson they have opportunities to evaluate a solution and share results, draw and describe objects based on their properties, and learn about a real engineer who developed a material with special properties.

Lesson 5: Beds for Bears begins with the story of "Goldilocks and the Three Bears," and then students form teams. Each team selects appropriate materials for each of the three bears' beds. They then exchange the beds and test them to find out which is the hardest, the softest, and in between. Teams critique their solutions and display their results. The purpose of this activity is for students to *elaborate* their understanding of how to choose materials for a specific purpose based on their properties. During this lesson the students engage in the practices of engineering design, test possible solutions to a problem, and communicate data and results.

Lesson 6: Puffy Pig needs a house for protection from wind and rain. Teams identify the problem, plan, and build a house to protect Puffy Pig. They test their houses with the "puffing machine" (Lesson 1) and dropper bottle (Lesson 2), revise their design, retest, and share their results. They also share their design process with another team, noting how their choices of specific materials are justified in light of the materials' properties and suitability for solving the problem. This lesson emphasizes the practice of arguing from evidence, as the students listen to their classmates and critique one another's designs. During this lesson, teachers (and the students themselves) can *evaluate* students' understanding of materials and their properties and skills in engineering design.

Literacy Connections in Grade 1

Time is a precious commodity in the elementary classroom. Did you know that science/engineering and reading share many process skills, such as activating prior knowledge, predicting, making observations and inferences, and drawing conclusions? The lessons in the Testing Materials module incorporate literacy strategies, such as developing scientific vocabulary, creating an interactive word wall and reinforcing the use of the science/engineering words in sentences, sorting words into categories, creating a glossary as students learn new words through their experiences, using read-aloud/think-aloud strategies, creating and using a technology notebook, learning about text structures and supports for reading, and focusing on comprehension and conceptual outcomes.

Grade 5: Designing Environmental Solutions

In *Designing Environmental Solutions,* students assess their own and society's impacts on the environment and evaluate those impacts. Are they good, bad, or neutral? Who defines what is "good," "bad," or "neutral"? Prompted by illustrations (as below), students consider environmental issues, such as the depletion of rain forest resources, oil spills, and using disposable versus cloth diapers. Students then apply what they learn about constraints and trade-offs to local environmental problems.

This module consists of seven lessons that also follow the BSCS 5E Instructional Model (Bybee 1997; Bybee & Landes, 1990): Engage, Explore, Explain, Elaborate, Evaluate. This module addresses the crosscutting concept (from the NGSS) of Influence of Science, Engineering, and Technology on Society and the Natural World and reinforces three performance expectations from the NGSS for the 3–5 grade band:

Considering the Consequences of an Oil Spill

Image courtesy of BSCS.

3–5-ETS1–1. Define a simple design problem reflecting a need or a want that includes specified criteria for success and constraints on materials, time, or cost.

3–5-ETS1–2. Generate and compare multiple possible solutions to a problem based on how well each is likely to meet the criteria and constraints of the problem.

3–5-ETS1–3. Plan and carry out fair tests in which variables are controlled and failure points are considered to identify aspects of a model or prototype that can be improved.

Introduction: Doing Technology provides an introduction to the practices of engineering design. Students also learn about collaborative learning and set up their engineering notebooks.

Lesson 1: How Do Your Choices Affect the Environment? begins with a story that *engages* students in the module concepts. The students list the characters' choices of products and activities. Teams highlight their personal choices of products and activities in a collage and then evaluate the effects of those choices on the environment. The students express their ideas about what makes a product or activity "good" or "bad" for the environment, and they recognize that the technologies humans produce have both risks and benefits, and can affect the environment in both positive and negative ways.

Lesson 2: Rain Forest Detectives is organized around a fictitious mystery related to the production of aluminum cans and the destruction of rain forest habitat. The students play the game "Timber!" and *explore* the ways that a renewable resource can be depleted if the rate of destruction exceeds the rate of replenishment. They choose a resource and analyze how the use of that resource helps and harms living and nonliving things. They recognize that people's use of resources has intended benefits and unintended consequences and that the supply of some resources is limited. Through this experience, students learn that it is important to research and analyze a problem situation before beginning to design a solution. Testing a solution involves investigating how well a design performs under a range of likely conditions. Students use graphic organizers to help structure their data and ideas.

Lesson 3: Oil Spills concerns the constraints and trade-offs of using petroleum and petroleum products. Students *explore* the pros and cons of this technology by reading about actual oil spills and discussing causes and consequences. Then, teams design a procedure for cleaning up an oil spill based on cost, time, and thoroughness and put their plans into action cleaning up a simulated spill. They then assume various roles and debate the constraints of cost, time, and thoroughness of alternative methods of cleaning up oil spills. Finally, they use a rubric to critique one another's presentations. The purpose of the lesson is for students to recognize that designing solutions to environmental problems involves trade-offs and no solution is ideal. It is also to provide practice reading, writing, listening, and speaking skills, and practicing arguing from evidence.

Lesson 4: The Diaper Debate is an *exploration* of the constraints and trade-offs involved in deciding between cloth versus disposable diapers. Students assume roles of different families and decide which of the options would be best when faced with constraints of cost, convenience, or environmental impact. They create a "discussion web" and use scoring rubrics to examine and critique solutions, and examine their personal contributions to solid waste disposal and suggest alternatives. The intent of the lesson is for the students to recognize that personal choices have environmental consequences, that resources can be extended by reusing or recycling them, and that people can use a systematic approach to analyze the risks and benefits of the ways they use resources. They also learn that it is important to examine two sides of an issue before reaching a conclusion.

Lesson 5: Designing Environmental Solutions engages students in making a considered decision about an environmental problem by helping them *explain* their understanding of the module concepts. Students read a scenario about petroleum scarcity in the future and then apply the model to the problem, using an evaluation chart and a rating scale. Students determine the *best* solution for the class by rating each team's best solutions. The purpose of the lesson is to help the students develop a systematic approach to solving environmental problems and to communicate their understanding of the benefits and drawbacks of technological solutions. It is also to help students recognize that it is helpful to try to determine in advance how proposed solutions might affect people and the environment.

Lesson 6: Debating the Issues involves students in debating possible solutions to three environmental dilemmas: paper versus plastic bags, landfills versus incinerators, and plastic versus glass drink bottles. Each team selects one problem and develops an argument for one possible solution. In a debate format, teams present opposing arguments to compare the alternative solutions. As a class, students determine preferred solutions to the three problems and evaluate "debate" as a way to solve environmental problems. This lesson provides practice in arguing from evidence, one of the eight practices in the NGSS, as well as improving their reading, writing, listening, and speaking skills. It also reinforces and *elaborates* students' skills in engineering design to propose solutions to an environmental problem.

Lesson 7: Taking Action is the last lesson in the module. Students read about others who have implemented solutions to environmental problems in their communities. Teams choose a local environmental issue to "take action." They frame an action plan and, if possible, carry it out and share their results. The purpose of this lesson is for students to *evaluate* various solutions that have actually been implemented to solve environmental problems and to *evaluate* their own understanding of the essential ideas in the module: that people can use a systematic approach to thinking critically about the risks and benefits of technological solutions to problems, designing solutions to environmental problems involves constraints and trade-offs, that no solution will be perfect, and that it is important to try to predict all the different possible effects of a solution before implementing it.

Literacy Connections in Grade 5

By Grade 5, the literacy strategies in BSCS Science Tracks become more sophisticated. Students engage in the following strategies to help them read and interpret informational text and ideas effectively: reading descriptive text and determining the most important ideas and details; collecting and comparing evidence and taking effective notes from the text; using a graphic organizer to organize ideas; increasing comprehension by considering a cause-effect organizational pattern in informational text; applying a discussion web to look at two sides of an issue; and incorporating reading, writing, listening, and speaking in a debate format.

Features of the Instructional Materials

First and foremost, BSCS Science Tracks is designed to improve student learning in science and technology/engineering. As you can see from the previous examples, the program enables students to develop an understanding of important concepts in science and engineering and to experience and develop the abilities and understandings inherent in the processes of scientific inquiry and engineering design. This is exactly what the NGSS propose. By including engineering design as a core idea *and* as a practice, students are expected to understand the processes of engineering design and be able to carry out those processes with a good measure of skill. As illustrated on the next page, the work of students in the classroom is similar to the work of professional engineers, though at a lower level of sophistication.

Conceptual Outcomes and Assessment Indicators

Each lesson specifies outcomes and assessment indicators that relate directly to the NSES and *Benchmarks* that provide the foundation for each module. The hands-on nature of science makes it motivating and fun; however, it is important to make certain that science and engineering are minds-on, too. The outcomes and assessment indicators help keep the teacher's and students' focus on developing conceptual understanding.

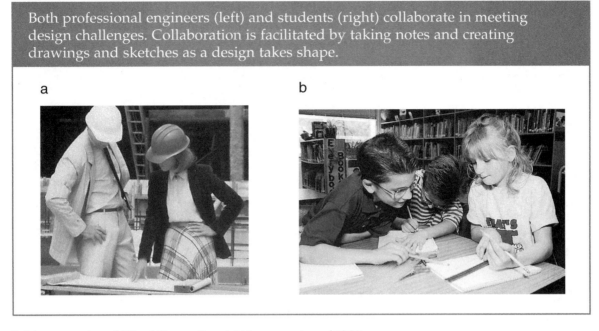

Both professional engineers (left) and students (right) collaborate in meeting design challenges. Collaboration is facilitated by taking notes and creating drawings and sketches as a design takes shape.

Left image courtesy of ©Corel Corporation; right image courtesy of BSCS.

The lesson outcomes are divided into the following categories: conceptual, scientific inquiry or technological design (both abilities and understandings), literacy (reading, writing, speaking, listening), and collaborative learning (teamwork).

The outcomes are sequenced for developmental understanding. Each conceptual outcome leads to or is connected in some way to the next. It is the conceptual flow that leads students to the overarching conceptual understanding.

The assessment indicators provide a way for the teacher to assess whether students have achieved the identified outcomes. Students will achieve module and lesson outcomes at different times. The more the teacher knows about students' current conceptions and understanding of the lesson concepts, the better able she or he will be to assess and facilitate students' conceptual development. The introduction in each "Module Overview" provides information about typical conceptions and misconceptions that students hold about the module concepts.

Scientific and Engineering Practices

Science as inquiry and technological (engineering) design are defined as *abilities to do* scientific inquiry and engineering design and as *understandings about* scientific inquiry and engineering design. Scientific inquiry outcomes are identified for each lesson in the science modules. Technological (engineering) design outcomes are identified for each lesson in the science and technology modules.

Literacy Outcomes

Science for all adds an additional challenge to the teaching of science. Your students might range from nonreaders to proficient readers. The goal of this program is not to teach students how to read; however, literacy strategies are included in each module to help build conceptual understanding, support reading comprehension, and develop scientific vocabulary. Literacy strategies are embedded in the lessons and are intended to help students understand, discuss, and apply scientific concepts and processes. Teachers are encouraged to explicitly teach the literacy strategies, model those strategies for students, provide guided practice, and provide independent practice, such as writing and reading from their own notebooks as illustrated below.

Collaborative Outcomes

According to research, students learn more effectively when they learn collaboratively. However, simply placing students in teams does not ensure that they will work collaboratively. The collaborative nature of this program is deliberate. Team size, team jobs, and team skills are based on the developmental level of the students. The introductory lesson of each module introduces students to the team jobs and skills. Teaching, reinforcing, monitoring, and processing the skills are essential if students are to work and learn effectively together.

BSCS 5E Instructional Model

The BSCS 5E Instructional Model guides the conceptual flow of each module. The BSCS 5Es are based on constructivist learning theory—the principle that children (and adults!) construct their understanding of concepts over time and that their views of the world are constantly evolving as they "try on" new ideas. As you may already know, the BSCS 5Es sequence learning experiences through five stages, ensuring that students have opportunities to construct their understanding of module outcomes over time.

Literacy strategies are important in all of the BSCS Science Tracks modules.

Image courtesy of BSCS.

The 5E stage of each lesson is identified in both the Teacher Edition and the Student Guide. Research about teaching and learning informs us of the importance of the integration of metacognitive instruction. Reviewing and discussing how each stage supports learning will help students become more aware of how they learn so that they are better equipped to take control of their own learning. We highly recommend that you review the following "E" words with the students so that the learning process becomes explicit for them, too.

Engage. Research into children's learning suggests that students come to learning situations with prior knowledge, which may or may not be congruent with the concepts presented. The *engage* lessons provide the opportunity for you to find out what students already know or what they think they know about the topic and the concepts to be developed.

Explore. At this stage, students should have many experiences with objects, events, and organisms in their environment that relate directly to the concept to be developed. The *explore* lessons provide a common set of experiences and a broad range of experiences within which students can compare what they think about what they are observing and experiencing.

Explain. *Explain* lessons provide opportunities for students to connect their previous experiences and to begin to make conceptual sense of the main ideas of the module. This stage also allows for the introduction of formal language, scientific terms, and content information that might make students' previous experiences easier to describe and explain.

Elaborate. In *elaborate* lessons, students apply or extend the concepts in new situations and relate their previous experiences to new ones.

Evaluate. Although this is the final stage of the instructional model, it does not connote finality in the learning process nor does it imply that this is the only stage in which student learning is assessed. In reality, the evaluation of students' conceptual understanding and ability to use skills begins with the *engage* lesson and continues throughout each stage of the model. Combined with the students' written work and performance of tasks throughout the module, the *evaluate* lesson can serve as a summative assessment of what students know and can do.

Continuous Assessment

Typically, we in American education think of assessment as synonymous with a test or some way of determining a summative "grade"—a final outcome. We have been taught to believe that such assessments tell students, parents, other teachers, and the administration of a student's "achievement" or "progress" when compared with the achievement or progress of other students. While this type of evaluation or assessment certainly has its place, it often does not promote learning or students' conceptual development. Therefore, BSCS Science Tracks uses methods of ongoing, or formative, assessment of students' learning, such as the group activity shown on the next page, rather than tests of student progress.

"Observe a skilled teacher as she assesses students' work: looking for more than just information possessed, she depends not on discrete instances but entire performances, sampled frequently over time in the classroom. . . . In this teacher's classroom, you are likely to see tables filled with lab equipment, pieces of student work in various stages of completion, or desks pushed aside to make room for group activities and discussion. Students are likely to be moving around the room questioning, experimenting, talking,

Image courtesy of Comstock.

debating, and looking. They may work on a project for hours, days, or weeks—designing experiments, conducting interviews, crafting oral history projects, deriving equations, and testing theories, or writing and revising multiple drafts of a short story. In each of these cases, students are engaged in a variety of activities, constructing strategies for demonstrating their understanding. Through these activities, students show that they know how to develop ideas; pose questions; experiment with new possibilities; and revise, refine, and present their work" (Zessoules & Gardner, 1991, p. 48).

In this context, assessment looks like instruction. If assessment is continuous, it flows easily back and forth with instruction as students encounter new phenomena or information, reflect on their experiences, and demonstrate what they know and can do as a result of those experiences.

Program Components

BSCS Science Tracks Handbook: A Resource for Educators. This resource offers teachers a more complete understanding of the program, including an overview of research on teaching and learning, and an in-depth description of the BSCS 5E instructional model. It also offers more detail on program features and components and many hints to ensure a successful experience for you and your students.

Teacher Edition for Each Module (Levels 1–5). This resource provides a detailed overview of the module, a list of necessary supplies, teaching and assessment strategies for each lesson, facsimiles of the student pages (with the exception of prekindergarten/kindergarten), copymasters of student handouts, and a list of additional resources. In it, you will find background information, questions, and answers that will help you facilitate student conceptual understanding.

Student Guide. Each module (with the exception of prekindergarten/kindergarten) features a student guide. This book is not a typical "read- about-science" book. It actively engages students in their own learning and helps them become more responsible for their own conceptual development. It includes an effective structure for collaborative learning and encourages students to rely on themselves, their teammates, and their classmates, as well as their teacher. For each module's Student Guide, there is a corresponding Student Guide Spanish Edition.

Materials Kit. A kit of materials is available for each module. The kit contains hands-on materials that might not be readily available to teachers. It also contains materials (with the exception of prekindergarten/kindergarten) specifically for collaborative learning (team jobs posters, team skills posters, and colored wristbands). The kits do not require elaborate storage or classroom space. Forms for taking an inventory are included in each kit. A consumables replacement kit is available for each module, which contains the nonpermanent or "consumable" materials found in the materials kit.

Conclusion

In the United States, unlike in most developed countries in the world, technology as a subject has largely been ignored in the schools. . . . The task ahead is to build technology education into the curriculum, as well as use technology to promote learning, so that all students become well informed about the nature, powers, and limitations of technology. . . . In modern times, technology has become increasingly characterized by the interdependent relationships it has with science and mathematics. (AAAS, 1993/2008, pp. 41–42)

Since the early 1990s, BSCS has incorporated engineering design and technology in its curricular programs from kindergarten through high school, and we applaud the inclusion of engineering design and engineering practices in *A Framework for K–12 Science Education* and the NGSS. However, we know that teaching about engineering and technology might feel like a foreign subject for many elementary teachers. We hope you see from the informative chapters in *The Go-To Guide for Engineering Curricula* that you don't have to create your own engineering curriculum to meet the requirements of the NGSS. BSCS Science Tracks can help you build engineering design into your curriculum seamlessly and with complete confidence that students will be motivated to learn. The modules use readily available materials and provide everything you need to take the plunge into engineering education. We invite you to join us in embracing this opportunity to broaden children's experiences in science and engineering.

References

American Association for the Advancement of Science. (1989). *Science for All Americans.* New York, NY: Oxford University Press.
American Association for the Advancement of Science. (1993/2008). *Benchmarks for Science Literacy.* New York, NY: Oxford University Press.

BSCS. (2006a). *Designing environmental solutions.* Dubuque, IA: Kendall/Hunt.

BSCS. (2006b). *Solving air pollution problems.* Dubuque, IA: Kendall/Hunt.

Bybee, R. W. (1997). *Achieving scientific literacy: From purposes to practices.* Portsmouth, NH: Heinemann.

Bybee, R. W., & Landes, N. M. (1990, February). Science for life and living: An elementary school science program from Biological Sciences Curriculum Study. *The American Biology Teacher, 52*(2), 92–98.

National Research Council. (1996). *National Science Education Standards.* Washington, DC: National Academies Press.

National Research Council. (2012). *A framework for K–12 science education: Practices, crosscutting concepts, and core ideas.* Washington, DC: The National Academies Press.

NGSS Lead States. (2013). *Next Generation Science Standards: For states, by states.* Washington, DC: The National Academies Press.

Zessoules, R., & Gardner, H. (1991). Authentic assessment: Beyond the buzzword and into the classroom. In V. Perrone (Ed.), *Expanding student assessment.* Alexandria, VA: Association for Supervision and Curriculum Development.

5

A World in Motion

From SAE International

Christopher Ciuca, Director of Pre-Professional
Programs, SAE International

Students learn about gear ratios and the trade-offs between speed and torque in designing a motorized toy car.

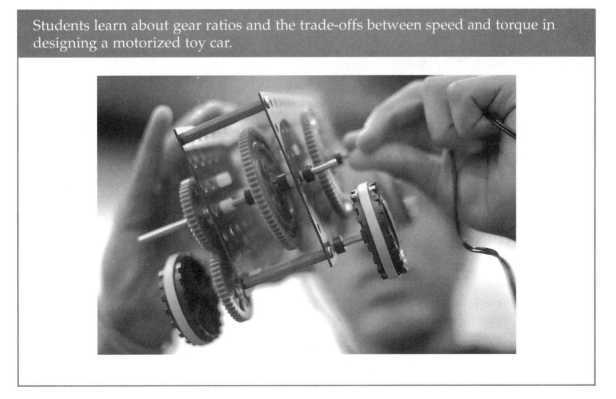

Image by Christopher Ciuca.

A World in Motion (AWIM) brings science, technology, engineering, and mathematics (STEM) education to life in the classroom for students in kindergarten through eighth grade. Benchmarked to the Next Generation Science Standards (NGSS) and Common Core mathematics and English language arts standards, AWIM incorporates STEM disciplines in an integrated setting designed to engage students in hands-on, age-appropriate curricular experiences. AWIM is part of the life-long learning experiences available for students, teachers, and professionals at SAE International (formerly the Society of Automotive Engineers).

Goals

In order to succeed in the society of tomorrow, all children need to understand and apply concepts in STEM in a real-world integrated setting. In addition to becoming literate in these disciplines, students must learn to solve complex problems, communicate clearly, raise questions and resolve problems, assimilate information, and work cooperatively toward common goals. AWIM is built with the intent of accomplishing these goals while engaging students in age-appropriate engineering design challenges to learn about STEM fields as potential areas for future engagement in the STEM workforce.

Engineering Design Experience

AWIM integrates STEM subjects through an approach identified as the Engineering Design Experience (EDE). The EDE places students in the roles of scientists and engineers as they explore a "design challenge." The EDE provides a problem-solving context in which students design a product or devise a solution to a problem throughout a teacher-facilitated challenge. Teams of students examine who the product is for and what must be accomplished; gather and synthesize information; design, develop, and test a prototype design; and prepare a presentation of their design ideas. The engineering design process is outlined here.

Set Goals. Students are introduced to a challenge scenario. They investigate and discuss what is asked of them and share ideas on how to go about solving the problem. Then the students set goals and begin to work in teams, recording their work in design logs.

Build Knowledge. Students work through a variety of structured and age-appropriate activities to build knowledge and skills they will need to design their own solutions or products. First, students build and test a physical model. Then teams change variables on the model, record observations, and discuss results as a team and as a class. They move from simple explorations and opinions to controlled experiments and performance predictions based on the graphs or tables of results they create.

Design. Student teams design their own toy to meet the requirements stated in the toy company's letter. They determine the values of variables, plan construction, and predict performance based on knowledge from previous activities and data collected.

Build and Test. Student teams build and test their design to see how well it meets the performance criteria. Design teams optimize performance based on previous knowledge. Students make certain their solution meets the design criteria and build a case for why they made their design decisions in preparation for the team presentation of their solution.

Present. Student teams present their work to an audience (i.e., their class, whole school, parents, and/or community) and provide arguments for why their solution/design meets the design criteria.

Students complete the EDE for each design challenge. The challenges are aligned to the NGSS (NGSS Lead States, 2013) and Common Core State Standards for mathematics and English language arts (NGA & CCSSO, 2010). The integration of all of the STEM subjects as well as subjects outside of STEM allows the curriculum to easily "fit" in a teacher's already full teaching schedule. This structure is important because it facilitates teachers bringing a real-life inquiry-based approach into the classroom setting.

Although historically AWIM activities have taken place primarily during science or math time in the daily schedule, teachers working in school systems where the curriculum does not exist in silos enjoy the benefits of bringing in teachers from other disciplines as part of the AWIM experience.

The STEM/Industry Volunteer

SAE International is distinctive in that its membership base supports education by providing volunteers who can illustrate the practical application of STEM concepts and serve as content experts for the teachers. This unique feature goes beyond "career day" type activities that introduce students to careers with little connection to the context within the students' everyday interaction with the world. Volunteers provide a face for STEM careers and communicate the needs of the workforce so the students can see themselves as future scientists or engineers. Empirical research supports this approach of connecting real-life

Student Recording His Work in Design Logs

Image by Christopher Ciuca.

STEM volunteers to the schools through the AWIM model. More information is available in a research article and the full evaluation posted at www.awim.org/about/reportcard.

Challenge Design

All AWIM Challenges are designed to take students through a procedure where they actively engage (independently and within groups) through the process skills associated with Critical Thinking, Project Management, Communication, Inquiry & Analysis, and Teamwork & Collaboration. The design of AWIM addresses many process standards as students delve into learning experiences aligned to age-appropriate content standards.

AWIM provides engineering challenges for primary (K–3), elementary (4–6), and middle school (7–8) students. The challenges are not tied directly to any one independent grade level to allow teachers to address specific core concepts appropriate for their particular district or state standards. In this chapter, we describe the primary and elementary challenges. An overview of the middle school curriculum is available at www.awim.org/curriculum/middleschool/.

Challenges for the Primary Grades (K–3)

The set of AWIM Primary Challenges provide an integrated STEM experience for students in kindergarten through third grade. All Primary Challenges are designed around a customized piece of children's literature from varying genres that sets the stage for student learning.

Table 5.1 AWIM Challenge Components

Components Common in All AWIM Challenges (K–8)				
Critical Thinking	**Project Management**	**Communication**	**Inquiry and Analysis**	**Teamwork and Collaboration**
✓ assess a new situation ✓ formulate questions for scientific analysis; generate and evaluate ideas ✓ gather and interpret data ✓ synthesize information and make predictions ✓ integrate and apply learning	✓ define goals and establish objectives ✓ maintain portfolios/ design logs of work ✓ identify and set priorities ✓ organize and present data ✓ propose and test solutions	✓ design a team name, logo, and slogan ✓ develop and produce drawings and diagrams ✓ prepare written and oral reports ✓ prepare presentation aids and materials ✓ deliver oral presentations	✓ conduct formal testing ✓ measure and record outcomes ✓ make qualitative and quantitative observations ✓ establish relationships among variables and make predictions ✓ use the scientific method of experimentation, questioning, trial/variable testing	✓ participate as a member of a team ✓ practice cooperation and compromise to reach group consensus ✓ assign team member roles and responsibilities ✓ understand group dynamics ✓ evaluate team and individual performance

Rolling Things

Students explore the story *The Three Little Pigs' Sledding Adventure*. Based on the scientific concepts presented in the story, students explore toy cars and car performance. Students launch the cars from ramps and investigate the effects that different ramp heights and car weights have on distance traveled. Students make adjustments for performance through variable testing and data collection.

Pinball Designers. Students explore the concept of optimizing a design by developing and building a pinball game. The story of *Malarkey & the Big Trap* introduces students to the concept of improving a design through experimentation and data analysis. Students test the launch ramp to explore how launch position affects the behavior of the pinball. Students make their games more challenging by adding targets, walls, and bumpers to the game board.

Engineering Inspired by Nature. Students investigate methods by which seeds are dispersed in nature through the story *Once Upon a Time in the Woods*. The story leads the students to further explore seeds dispersed by the wind. Students use the designs of nature to develop paper helicopters and parachutes and perform variable testing to improve performance.

Straw Rockets. Students explore the early life of Dr. Robert Goddard through the age-appropriate biography *The Rocket Age Takes Off*. Investigating Goddard's early trials and tribulations to create the first liquid-fueled rocket engine, students begin to uncover the work necessary to optimize a design. Students use the design process to build and perform variable testing on straw rockets. Design goals include farthest and highest flight.

Students Launching Cars From Ramps

Image by Christopher Ciuca.

The Primary Challenges provide teachers with a structure to introduce students to STEM concepts through the following skills and instructional techniques using the EDE:

- Guided Opportunities to Question Ideas and Define Problems
- Literature to Facilitate Questioning of Concepts and Ideas
- Play and Guided Experimentation for Investigation
- Building Physical Models
- Manipulating Variables
- Collecting, Recording, and Analyzing Data
- Building Tables and Graphs
- Making Predictions
- Designing Solutions
- Pair-Share and Group Discussions
- Communicating Ideas
- Turn and Talk Strategies (Partner Interaction)
- Sharing and Interpreting (Whole Group)
- Presenting a Solution

Challenges for the Elementary Grades (4–6)

At the fourth- through sixth-grade levels, the AWIM Elementary Challenges shift student learning experience away from the children's literature to incorporate a more structured research focus. Students explore the EDE while engaged in formal variable testing, data gathering, and decision making based on analysis.

Students Testing Their Balloon-Powered Toy Cars

Image by Christopher Ciuca.

Skimmer Challenge. Students construct paper sailboats and test the effects of different sail shapes, sizes, and construction methods to meet specific performance criteria. Friction, forces, the effect of surface area, and design are some of the physical phenomena students encounter in this challenge.

JetToy Challenge. Students make balloon-powered toy cars that meet specific performance criteria: distance traveled, weight carried, accurate performance, and speed. Jet propulsion, friction, air resistance, and design are the core scientific concepts students explore in this challenge.

Gravity Cruiser Challenge. Students focus on understanding the relationships between the "sweep" of the lever arm, the number of winds the string makes around the axle, and the distance the gravity cruiser travels. They also investigate how the diameter of the wheels, the diameter of the axles, and the amount of weight placed on the lever affect the gravity cruiser's speed and distance.

Below are the skills and instructional practices common to the Elementary Challenges:

- Guided Opportunities to Question Ideas and Define Problems
- Integration of STEM Subjects (and Beyond) to Solve Design Questions
- Play and Guided Experimentation for Investigation
- Building Physical Models
- Manipulating Variables
- Collecting, Recording, and Analyzing Data
- Building Tables and Graphs
- Making Predictions
- Designing Solutions
- Engineering Design Team—Teamwork
- Communicating Ideas
- Presenting a Solution

Linkages to the Practices of Science and Engineering

Both the NGSS and *A Framework for K–12 Science Education: Practices, Crosscutting Concepts, and Core Ideas* (NRC, 2012) emphasize the importance of engaging students in eight practices of science and engineering. These are essential skills that all students are expected to develop through 13 years of schooling. Table 5.2 lists examples showing how the AWIM challenges engage students in each of these practices from both a scientific point of view and an engineering point of view.

Students Engage in All Eight Practices During These Activities

Image by Christopher Ciuca.

Table 5.2 Correspondence Between K–12 Practices and AWIM Program Elements

Practices for K–12 Classrooms	AWIM & Science	AWIM & Engineering
Asking Questions (Science) and Defining Problems (Engineering)	Students develop scientific questions about the phenomena involved in a real-life scenario. For example, student questions might include: • Why does the large nozzle size make my balloon-powered car go faster? • Why do plants not all grow at the base of a parent plant where the seeds fall? • What causes my fuel cell to run an electric motor?	Students look at an engineering problem that needs to be solved. For example, students might determine: • My motorized toy car does not currently climb a 15-degree slope. How can I change the gear ratio to improve the design so that my car climbs the hill? • My skimmer currently turns to the right. How can I change the surface area distribution of the sail to make the skimmer travel straight?

(Continued)

Table 5.2 (Continued)

Practices for K–12 Classrooms	AWIM & Science	AWIM & Engineering
Developing and Using Models	Students construct models and simulations to enable predictions from data. For example, students might construct models and use simulations by: • Building a gravity cruiser to test the effects of weight position/amount on a lever arm to propel a vehicle forward. • Entering different variables (e.g., weights, balloon size, nozzle size) into a computer-based representation of a JetToy car to determine performance differences, then building a physical model based on knowledge gained through virtual testing.	Students use standard models and simulations to investigate flaws and test possible solutions. For example, students might construct and test standard models by: • Building a pinball game field to test the effects of different target and bumper placement. • Building a standard model glider to compare wing surface area and shape for longest flight or accuracy. • Constructing scale drawings of skimmer sail designs, indicating optimum surface area and placement of the sail above the skimmer hull.
Planning and Carrying Out Investigations	Students conduct controlled experiments and record data to develop explanations, test theories, and revise thinking. For example, students might control variables to: • Determine the optimum amount of hydrogen required for a fuel cell to run an electric motor for three minutes. • Test the best straw diameter to design a straw rocket to travel five meters when launched. • Test three different wheel diameters on a gravity cruiser to determine which diameter travels the furthest.	Students perform investigations to gather data needed to design a solution to a problem and test designs. For example, students might perform investigations to: • Determine the optimum mass of a vehicle and height of a ramp required to move a crash box at the bottom of the ramp 20 centimeters. • Examine gear ratios and the trade-offs between speed and torque in designing a motorized toy car.
Analyzing and Interpreting Data	Students conduct investigations and organize data in ways that facilitate analyzing the meaning of the data. For example, students might analyze data by:	Students analyze data to compare different solutions to a problem and determine how well a design will meet performance criteria. For example, students might use the following tools to analyze their data and make informed decisions:

Practices for K–12 Classrooms	AWIM & Science	AWIM & Engineering
	• Building a Glider design log to record data in tables, charts, or spreadsheets, observe patterns in the data, answer questions, and make predictions of future performance. • Investigating inconsistent data for JetToy distance performance and determining if outliers in the data make sense for performance.	• Building a spreadsheet of different wheel sizes and distance performance on a gravity cruiser and determining the appropriate wheel size to win a distance competition. • Displaying controlled variable test data on a graph to design and build a JetToy car that travels 5 meters and stops.
Using Mathematics and Computational Thinking	Students use mathematics and computational thinking to represent physical variables. For example, students might use mathematical calculations and computational thinking to: • Determine the statistical probability of repeating test data for weight carried versus speed of a balloon-powered JetToy car. • Recognize data patterns in performance and probability when testing the repeatability of test results on a pinball game field.	Students use mathematics and computation representations that are integral to design. For example, students might use mathematics and computational thinking to: • Determine the appropriate gear ratio to design and build a motorized toy car with the appropriate amount of torque to haul a 5-pound load 1 meter in less than 10 seconds. • Use mathematical calculations to build a wing assembly for a glider that has the appropriate surface area to keep the glider aloft for a prescribed 15-meter flight.
Constructing Explanations (Science) and Designing Solutions (Engineering)	Students construct performance theories in an effort to explain their experiences. For example, students might construct a theory that: • Reveals their account of how a fuel cell converts energy to power a fuel cell vehicle. • Explains how to build a skimmer that turns to the left when released.	Students design a solution they believe is the best one based on their controlled testing and analysis. For example, students might design a solution that: • Enables them to meet specific design criteria outlined in a request (using data from variable testing) while simultaneously meeting the needs of a customer (based on market research). • Uses the EDE as a guide to a design solution without the limitations of a single process of solving a problem.

(Continued)

Table 5.2 (Continued)

Practices for K–12 Classrooms	AWIM & Science	AWIM & Engineering
Engaging in Argument From Evidence	Students reason and build arguments for the best explanation of a scientific finding. For example, students might build arguments to support their reasoning by: • Referencing scientific data during a class discussion when asked to defend an explanation of why seeds do not always germinate directly under the parent plant. • Identifying flaws in other students' ideas when classmates argue an opposing point.	Students reason and build arguments in an effort to find the best possible solution to a problem. For example, students might build arguments to support their designs by: • Citing scientific research data that defends their design decisions as the best solution to a problem. • Making arguments from evidence both to identify flaws in their decisions and to defend conclusions.
Obtaining, Evaluating, and Communicating Information	Students communicate scientific findings clearly and persuasively in AWIM design logs and presentations. For example, students might obtain, evaluate, and communicate their findings by: • Presenting results of their inquiry and fielding questions during verbal presentations of their scientific findings. • Building design logs that clearly communicate findings and research decisions throughout the AWIM experience.	Students express their ideas orally and in writing persuasively in AWIM design logs and presentations. For example, students communicate the advantages of their designs by: • Using tables and graphs as graphical representations for design decisions during verbal design presentations. • Producing a manuscript of classroom glider designs for publication.

Conclusion

For more than 25 years, SAE International has been dedicated to improving science and technology education. Initially the goal was simply to involve SAE members in providing support to teachers. In recent years, the organization's goals have evolved to include developing and delivering high-quality STEM programing like the AWIM program.

SAE's mission to increase the number of students exploring STEM careers and to meet the ever-changing needs of teachers by providing high-quality STEM educational experiences for students is moving forward, and more than 4 million students have been reached through AWIM to date.

Empirical research examining the program's effectiveness supports short-term and longer term benefits to both students and teachers participating in one or more AWIM challenges. The NRC's work to create *A Framework for K–12 Science Education: Practices, Crosscutting Concepts, and Core Ideas* is further proof that AWIM remains relevant and provides a strong resource for K–12 educators. From the structure AWIM provides through the EDE at all levels, to the standards-based concepts AWIM addresses at grade-appropriate levels, SAE's AWIM program is making a difference in STEM education. Looking toward the future, AWIM is a good representation of the type of programing and instruction outlined in the NRC's Framework as a research-proven educational model that serves as a best practice for implementation of the NGSS.

References

National Governors Association Center for Best Practices & Council of Chief State School Officers. (2010). *Common Core State Standards: English language arts.* Washington, DC: Authors.

National Research Council. (2012). *A framework for K–12 science education: practices, crosscutting concepts, and core ideas.* Washington, DC: The National Academies Press.

NGSS Lead States. (2013). *Next Generation Science Standards: For states, by states.* Washington, DC: The National Academies Press.

6

Engineering Opportunities in FOSS (The Full Option Science System)

Third Edition for Upper Elementary Science Students

Linda De Lucchi and Larry Malone, FOSS Codirectors:
Lawrence Hall of Science, University of California, Berkeley

Introduction

Science is a creative and analytic enterprise, made active by our human capacity to think. Scientific knowledge advances when scientists observe objects and events, think about how their observations relate to what is known, test their ideas in logical ways, and generate explanations that integrate the new information into understanding of the natural world. Thus, the scientific enterprise is both what we know (content knowledge) and how we come to know it (practices). Science is a discovery activity, a process for producing new knowledge.

Engineers apply that understanding of the natural world to solve real-world problems. Engineering is the systematic approach to finding solutions to problems human societies have identified. The fields of science and engineering are mutually supportive, and scientists and engineers collaborate in their work. Often, acquiring scientific data requires designing and producing new technologies—tools, instruments, machines, and

Students Engaged in the FOSS Energy and Electromagnets Module

processes—to perform specific functions. The enterprise of science has progressed to the degree where advancing the frontier of science requires sophisticated observations of kinds that have never been made before.

The best way for students in elementary school to appreciate the scientific enterprise, learn important scientific and engineering concepts, and develop the ability to think well is to actively participate in scientific and engineering practices through their own investigations and analyses. The Full Option Science System (FOSS) was created to engage students and teachers with meaningful experiences in the natural and designed worlds.

FOSS began in 1988 as a small project at the Lawrence Hall of Science, University of California, Berkeley. The purpose of our grant from the National Science Foundation (NSF) was to develop an elementary science curriculum to usher students into the 21st century and prepare them for higher level studies in science and engineering. The goal was for students to become sufficiently scientifically literate to participate in the discourse regarding contemporary science-related issues. The grant was written to focus attention on the upper elementary years, Grades 3–6. The FOSS staff of four curriculum developers eagerly accepted the challenge.

FOSS is now a comprehensive science curriculum for Grades K–8 that has been designed to teach *science* concepts and principles, not *engineering* concepts and principles. However, in the course of pursuing understanding of natural phenomena, students do have many engineering experiences as a kind of serendipitous unintended consequence of their science studies and in extending their science understandings to solve problems.

This chapter will describe the development and evolution of the FOSS elementary program and how the Third Edition, released in 2013, provides engineering experiences for all students. Our discussion will focus on the modules designed for students in upper elementary Grades 4–6.

Goals

FOSS was conceived with three goals that framed the initial development and have continued to inform and guide the revisions of the program during the ensuing 20 years.

I. Scientific literacy for all elementary students

II. Instructional efficiency for all elementary teachers

III. Systemic reform; FOSS at the core of an institutional revolution in elementary school science education

These are lofty goals—engaged students; effective, efficient teachers; and a revised conception of the role of science in elementary education. Looking back, it is surprising how relatively easy it is to achieve goal I, how challenging and rewarding it is to achieve goal II, and how difficult and exhausting it is to make progress with goal III because of inherent political, historical, and churning policy barriers that must perpetually be negotiated.

Instructional Design

The vision of the codirectors of the project was to develop a modular "hands-on" curriculum that would provide a comprehensive general science experience for students, a complete program that would provide students with a coherent preparation for seamless continuation of their academic science careers into middle and high school. One condition of the NSF program funding stipulated that the institution of higher education submitting the proposal (University of California, Berkeley campus) had to have a commitment of participation in the project by an education publisher. The early publishing partner in the FOSS proposal was Encyclopaedia Britannica Educational Corporation (EBEC). The selection of EBEC was a fortuitous choice for the FOSS project, as EBEC was not a traditional textbook-oriented publisher, so the intentions of the FOSS developers to design a curriculum that was not delivered between two sturdy book covers did not cause alarm. With the rapt interest of the publisher, we proceeded to design a science curriculum that centered on student experiences with objects, organisms, and systems engaging students in firsthand experiences that exposed them to the real world of science while wrapping themselves in all of the scientific connective tissue (scientific practices) that transformed the personal experiences into coherent conceptual scientific knowledge.

The pedagogies were simple and based on historically sound curriculum design elements pioneered and employed at the Lawrence Hall of Science. Those pedagogies were the elements of the first iteration of the learning cycle originated by Dr. Robert Karplus, director of the Science Curriculum Improvement Study Project during the 1960s. Each of the original 12 FOSS modules comprised a sequence of activities in which students interacted with carefully selected and organized materials, followed by a process of sense making during which students made their best attempt to process their experiences into explanations (cause and effect), describe relationships, make predictions, and communicate their thinking. Following a verbal debriefing, the teacher would provide a summation of the experience, introducing precise, appropriate vocabulary to impose an appropriate level of conventional interpretation on the experience. The activity often continued with additional related experiences, in which students are challenged to apply their new knowledge to an appropriately novel situation.

This simple, straightforward instructional design was used to develop the initial modules for Grades 3–6. The three senior curriculum designer/developers all had traditional academic preparation in the sciences, with some teaching experience. The scope and sequence of the curriculum was based in part on the experience and intuition of the developers, guided by the advisory board and national trials directors. Expert guidance in terms of a national framework for science education was still some years in the future. We developed and published what we thought typical elementary teachers could teach efficiently and typical elementary students could learn effectively. Testing in participating classrooms confirmed the effectiveness of the FOSS modules with teachers and students to the satisfaction of the developers.

With an additional grant from NSF in 1992, the FOSS staff focused its attention on issues of science education for the primary Grades K–2. By 1995, we had completed the first edition of our comprehensive K–6 science program.

A significant number of schools around the country were ready to accept a fresh alternative science curriculum program; FOSS enjoyed a significant and spirited early implementation through the middle and late 1990s. The questions that interfered with FOSS acceptance most often were "Where is the book? What do the students read? What evidence suggests that students are achieving the goals of the lessons?" As the 20th century was drawing to a close, it was time to review the effectiveness of the FOSS teaching/learning design. We determined that it would probably be advantageous to add a reading component to each module—not a traditional textbook that might be misinterpreted as an alternative to the hands-on active investigations, but a collection of stories and articles (technical articles, expository texts, narrative stories, and biographies) that complement, augment, enrich, and enhance the active-learning experience.

Assessment materials (formative assessments and summative assessments) would be developed for each module. Formative assessments were developed to be used during instruction to monitor student progress with content knowledge, their ability to conduct investigations, and their ability to generate scientific explanations for observed phenomena. The summative assessments were designed to be administered after students completed all of the investigations in a module. The summative assessment looks primarily at student acquisition of science content knowledge, the learning outcome most valued by administrators in school districts. The revision (second edition) also included a forward-looking (for the time) feature—digital resources available through the Internet. A multimedia development team was added to the FOSS staff. Each revised FOSS module also included specific multimedia interactives that were available on the newly implemented FOSS website (FOSSweb.com).

FOSS Second Edition—Legacy Modules

The release of the second edition in 2000 (and updated in 2005) produced a renewed surge of adoptions of FOSS across the country. Several of the FOSS modules were particularly well suited for exercising innate engineering skills. These included **Ideas and Inventions**, **Physics of Sound**, **Levers and Pulleys**, **Solar Energy**, **Variables**, **Models and Designs**, and **Human Body**.

In the **Human Body Module**, students are challenged to discover how many bones comprise the human skeleton. After feeling for bones through their skin and referring to technical illustrations of human body skeleton subsystems, they arrive at a satisfactorily accurate count of about 206 bones. After the bone inventory activity, students are introduced to the human skeletal muscle system. Students are introduced to the idea that muscles are positioned across joints—the locations where separate bones meet, and that movement is accomplished when muscles spanning joints contract.

Students are supplied with sections of wooden sticks (simulated bones) and sections of rubber hose to connect the "bones." Students are challenged to use paper clips (tendons) to attach muscles (rubber bands) to the bone systems so that when the muscle contracts, the joint flexes. When students successfully design a model leg and foot, and fit it appropriately with muscles, they can demonstrate how contracting muscles can perform familiar foot and leg movements. This is challenging (but accessible) engineering for third or fourth graders.

Model Leg and Foot Made From Wooden Sticks and Rubber Bands

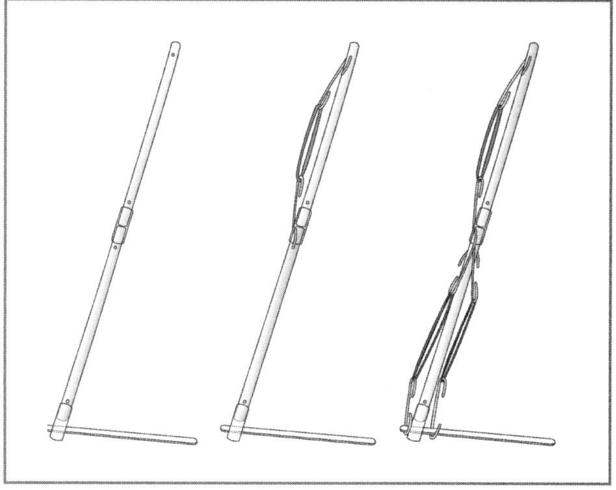

In the **Models and Designs Module**, fifth- and sixth-grade students have several opportunities to exercise engineering skills. In the first investigation, called *Black Boxes,* students are challenged to produce models (drawings) of the interior design of several different black boxes. Black boxes are small opaque plastic boxes containing a marble and one or more simple geometric shapes glued inside. By shaking and tipping the box, students attempt to determine the shape and location of the geometric shapes glued in the boxes. At the conclusion of the exercise, students often express dissatisfaction with their results, desiring to open the boxes to confirm the interior design. When it becomes clear that opening the boxes is not possible, they are challenged to think of alternative means for acquiring additional information to develop more precise solutions to the problem.

Students are given access to a set of empty black boxes, a selection of geometric shapes, and some marbles. Invariably, someone hatches the idea of trying to design and build black boxes that behave exactly like the closed boxes. This is the point in the activity when the natural engineers take over the investigation to solve the problem of the internal design of the black boxes.

Testing a Hypothesis of What Is in the Black Box

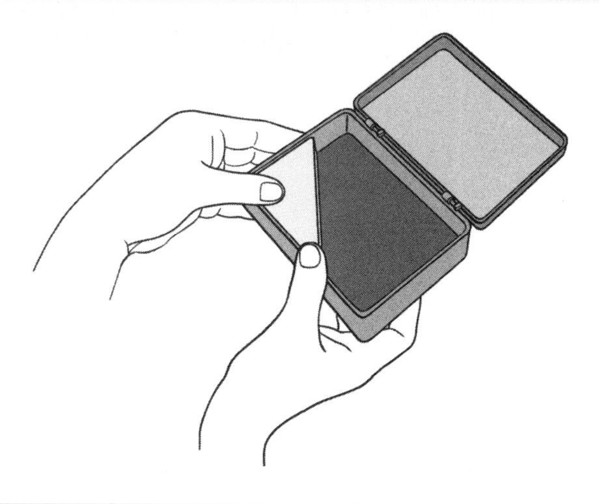

The next investigation is called *Hum Dingers.* The activity starts when the teacher brings forward a mysterious paper bag from which a string dangles. The teacher introduces it as a hum dinger that was given to her by an "inventor." She demonstrates why it is so named by pulling on the string. The pull produces a substantial hum, which terminates in a resounding ding when the string is released. Thus the name *hum dinger*.

Students are challenged to design and construct a model hum dinger, one that hums when its string is pulled and dings when the string is released. The challenge is not to replicate the exact design of the obscured hum dinger apparatus but to create a model hum dinger that emulates the function of the "inventor's" hum dinger, an apparatus that hums when its string is pulled and dings when the string is released.

Working in groups, students inventory the materials they have at their disposal—a diverse collection of wires, paper clips, rubber bands, and other items, including a D-cell, small electric motor, miniature cow bell, sticks, and clothespins, and a section of peg board on which to assemble their model hum dinger apparatus. The task is not trivial. It requires the application of standard engineering practice, including design, construction, testing, evaluation, revision, and further testing and evaluation until eventually the design evolves into a functional hum dinger.

Success may take two or more days and may involve episodes of casual espionage to obtain information about design approaches that are leading to success by other groups. If the additional constraint of cost of materials is added to the challenge, the students will need to consider the efficiency of the design to limit the resources required.

FOSS Third Edition 2013

At the end of the first decade of the 21st century, we once again reinvented the FOSS program. At this time, industry was initiating a conversation about STEM education—the fusion of science, technology, engineering, and mathematics. Simultaneously, some of the most accomplished science and engineering educators in the country were starting the process of creating a new framework for K–12 American science education. And our work through the first decade had given us fresh insights into effective science teaching practices: a clear idea of the critically important role of a student science notebook, deep understanding of the benefits and effective methods of embedded (formative) assessment, the role that the outdoors can play in enhancing the gravitas of the science learning experience, and the critically important advantage of integrating English language arts practices into the FOSS instructional model. We mapped out the conceptual terrain we thought we needed to cover with the third edition of FOSS and began the process of revising existing modules and designing investigations for new modules.

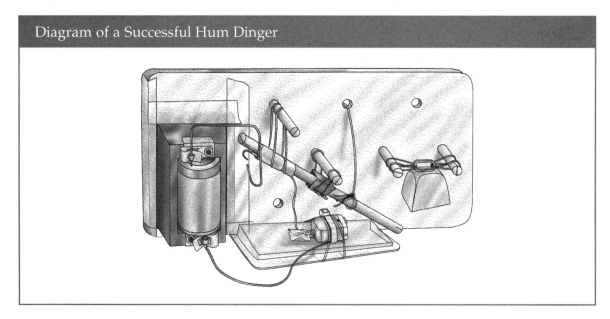

Diagram of a Successful Hum Dinger

We were well into the revision process when the first draft of *A Framework for K–12 Science Education* (NRC, 2012) was released for public review. We were gratified to discover that the FOSS active-learning approach was validated by the language and vision of the Framework. The focus on "inquiry" has been replaced in the Framework with a detailed and clarifying discussion of the scientific and engineering practices. As curriculum developers, we had incorporated the scientific practices comprehensively into the investigations in the revised FOSS modules. We would need to expand those practices to also incorporate the closely related engineering practices.

The revised FOSS program also covered most of the disciplinary core ideas described in the framework. But one of the core ideas that we had not focused a lot of attention on was engineering design. So we had to develop a strategy for how we would address the engineering objectives. We determined that there were four ways to inject engineering experiences into the program.

1. Amplify and make more explicit the opportunities in existing science learning activities that have a design/construct element in the instructional experience.

2. Develop extension activities that guide/encourage students to design and execute projects that use the new science concepts and/or practices introduced.

3. Develop reading and/or multimedia materials that bridge from the science experience to an engineering application.

4. Develop new modules that are explicitly about engineering and design.

The next section will provide examples of these four strategies in the FOSS program.

Engineering Opportunities in FOSS Third Edition

Strategy 1. The first strategy (amplify and make more explicit the opportunities in existing science learning activities) was easily implemented in the Third Edition. We call these opportunities to teachers' attention with an engineering icon in the activity write-up. As shown in Table 6.1, we were successful in addressing each of the engineering design performance expectations for Grades K–5 through this strategy alone.

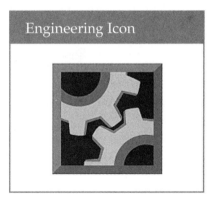

In addition to addressing these performance expectations, nearly all of the modules address the influence of engineering, technology, and science on society, a crosscutting concept. In the next section, we use one of the modules from Table 6.1, **Energy and Electromagnetism** for Grades 4–6, as an example of how engineering design has been incorporated into the FOSS modules.

The **Energy and Electromagnetism Module** has five investigations and requires 10 weeks to complete. In the first two investigations (Investigation 1, *Energy and Circuits*; Investigation 2, *Series and Parallel*), students discover two fundamentally different ways to connect two light bulbs to a D-cell; a series circuit with two bulbs "holding hands" and the D-cell connected to the two free ends of the two bulbs, and a parallel circuit,

Table 6.1   NGSS Engineering Performance Expectations Met by FOSS Modules, Third Edition

PERFORMANCE EXPECTATIONS (NGSS Lead States, 2013)	FOSS MODULES → Air and Weather	Balance and Motion	Materials in Our World	Plants and Animals	Solids and Liquids	Energy and Electromagnetism	Environments	Living Systems	Measuring Matter	Motion, Force, and Models	Water	Weather on Earth
K-2-ETS1-1. Ask questions, make observations, and gather information about a situation people want to change to define a simple problem that can be solved through the development of a new or improved object or tool.		X	X									
K-2-ETS1-2. Develop a simple sketch, drawing, or physical model to illustrate how the shape of an object helps it function as needed to solve a given problem.	X	X	X	X	X							
K-2-ETS1-3. Analyze data from tests of two objects designed to solve the same problem to compare the strengths and weaknesses of how each performs.	X	X	X		X							
3-5-ETS1-1. Define a simple design problem reflecting a need or a want that includes specified criteria for success and constraints on materials, time, or cost.						X			X	X	X	
3-5-ETS1-2. Generate and compare multiple possible solutions to a problem based on how well each is likely to meet the criteria and constraints of the problem.								X	X	X		
3-5-ETS1-3. Plan and carry out fair tests in which variables are controlled and failure points are considered to identify aspects of a model or prototype that can be improved.							X	X		X		X

in which each bulb reaches out to make contact with the D-cell. Students then discover that when bulbs are connected in series, both bulbs go out if one bulb is removed from the circuit. But when bulbs are connected in parallel, removing one bulb does not prevent the second bulb from continuing to burn brightly.

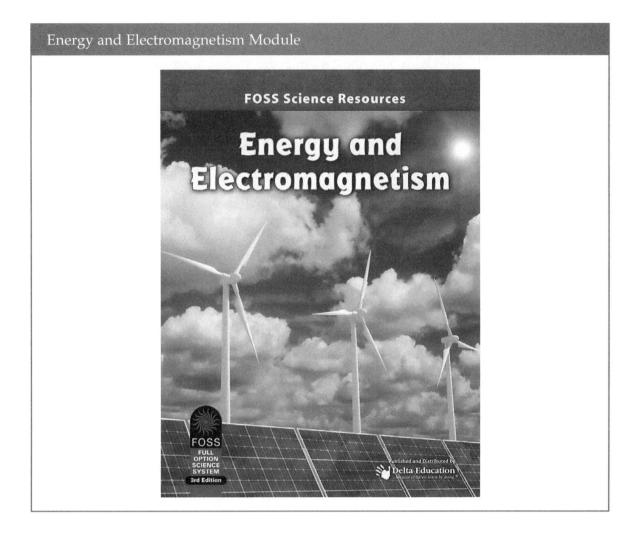

At this point in Investigation 2, students are challenged to solve an engineering problem. A fictitious lighting company has been making strings of holiday lights. Their customers are miffed because when one bulb burns out, the whole string goes dark. Student are challenged to help the engineers at the lighting company discover why their strings of lights all go dark when one bulb burns out and to propose a design that will alleviate the problem of complete darkness when one bulb burns out.

The class reorganizes into two large teams. One team engineers a string of lights with eight light bulbs wired in series, the other team engineers a string of lights with eight bulbs in parallel. Students discover that the series system not only goes dark when a single bulb burns out, but the system also requires two or three D-cells in series to deliver enough energy to get all eight bulbs to burn. The bulbs in parallel are less frustrating and all eight can burn brightly using only the energy provided by one D-cell.

Strings of Lights in Series and Parallel

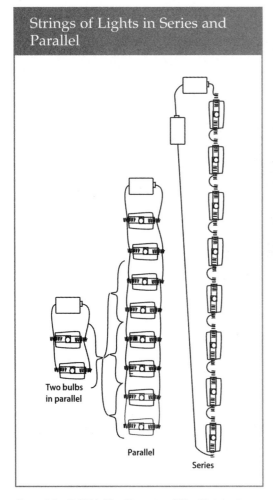

Two bulbs in parallel

Parallel

Series

Students go on in this investigation to apply their understanding of electric circuits using solar cells to run a motor or light a bulb. They design the circuits and then test them, observing the effect on the speed of the motor. They observe that cells in series make the motor run faster but that cells in parallel do not deliver additional power to the motor.

In Investigation 3, *The Force of Magnetism*, students investigate the force of attraction between two magnets. The teacher can describe a standardized experimental setup for students to use to determine the strength of the force of attraction between two magnets. Or if the teacher is inclined to start the learning episode with an engineering problem, she can simply show the available materials and challenge the students to use the materials to invent a way to measure the force of attraction between two magnets. After students have identified elements of a functional system, she might lead a discussion to get everyone's best ideas shared and then guide the process to collectively develop an effective "standardized" design for a system for acquiring data to solve the problem and answer the question. After students collect and graph their data, they should be able to make a general statement about magnetic interaction. "The greater the distance (number of plastic spacers) between two magnets, the weaker the force of attraction."

After students use a standardized experimental design to determine the strength of the force of attraction between two magnets, the experience can be extended or enriched with additional related projects. The teacher might say, "We know what happens to the force of attraction between two magnets when the distance between them is increased by putting plastic spacers between the two attracting magnets, but I have

Connecting Solar Cells to Batteries in Series and Parallel

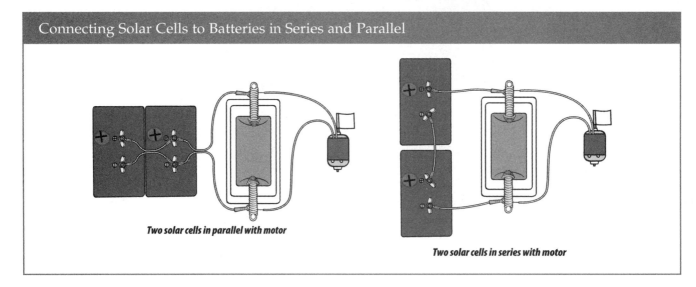

Two solar cells in parallel with motor

Two solar cells in series with motor

Student Team Involved in "Breaking the Force"

Equipment Needed for "Breaking the Force" Activity

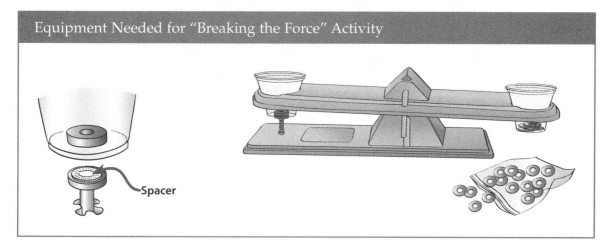

more questions for you to answer. What happens to the force of attraction between two magnets when the distance between them is increased by putting steel washers or copper pennies between them? Or when the distance is increased by putting additional magnets between the two attracting magnets?" And another question: "Is the force of repulsion equal to but opposite to the force of attraction?" These questions are related to the original question, but each new question requires reengineering of the experimental system.

In the final investigation, *Electromagnets,* students observe that a compass needle is deflected when electric current flows through a wire. Any wire through which electric current is flowing has a magnetic field surrounding it. When students wind an insulated wire around an iron core and close a switch to send electric current through the wire, the magnetic field created around the wire induces magnetism in the iron core, making an electromagnet. The magnetism persists as long as the current flows. Opening the switch opens the circuit, causing the magnetism to disappear. Students conduct experiments to discover how the number of winds in the electromagnet coil affects the strength of the magnetism. They discover that the greater the number of winds in the coil, the stronger the magnetism.

Students Experiment With Electromagnets

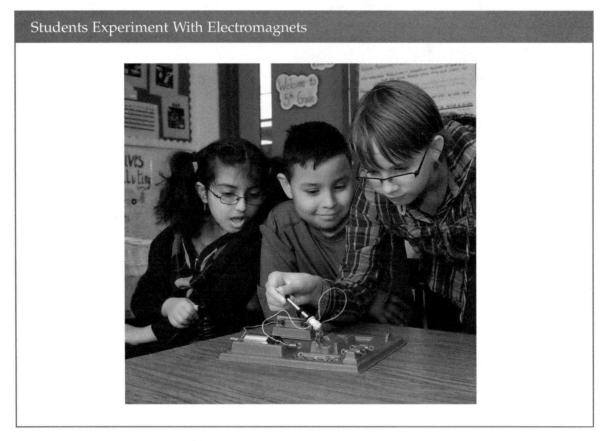

Students are ready to engage in an engineering project. They learn about a historical device, the telegraph, a system that uses an electromagnet to attract a piece of steel with an audible click. After engineering a replica of a telegraph, students use the system to send encoded messages to their teammates. Finally, students wire two telegraph units together to accomplish long-distance telegraphic communication.

Designing and constructing a telegraph accomplishes two goals. First, it provides an authentic opportunity to exercise investigation and engineering skills. Second, the telegraph is perhaps the most straightforward of the electromagnetic devices. Designing and constructing one clearly demonstrates electromagnetic application. Students could go on to engineer a doorbell, burglar alarm, or build an electric motor. Some of these activities are suggested as investigation extensions and some are described in readings.

Strategy 2. The second strategy (develop extension activities that guide/encourage students to design and execute projects that utilize the new science concepts) is also developed in the **Energy and Electromagnetism Module.** At the end of the module, students are presented with Science and Engineering Extensions that include making a rheostat (light dimmer) out of a graphite pencil. Graphite imposes resistance to the movement of the electric current.

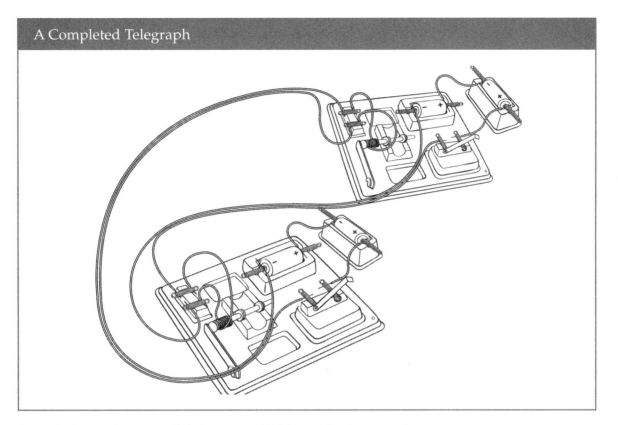

A Completed Telegraph

The greater the distance the current flows through the graphite, the lower the current and the dimmer the bulb in the circuit will glow.

Another extension challenges them to use permanent and temporary magnets to make a model motor. An additional engineering design challenge has students make a functional telegraph device out of common materials such as cardboard, paper clips, nails, wire, paper fasteners, and rubber bands. There are teacher masters (pattern and assembly procedure) that can be used to provide direction. Or the teacher could show students a few of the techniques to get them started and let them design their own device.

Another engineering design opportunity is in the **Motion, Force, and Models Module,** where students systematically explore the variables that affect the amount of energy a spring can transfer to an object.

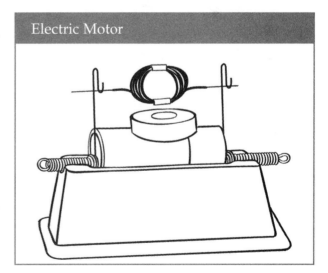

Electric Motor

At the end of this investigation, an additional experience with variables is suggested as a home/family extension. The home activity challenges the whole family to design and compare the performance of paper airplanes. Some designs produce planes that fly long distances in a straight line, others produce planes that fly in a big loop, others result in planes that fly in an arc, returning to the launcher. Some glide smoothly and land softly, and others fly more like rockets. Engineering with paper is

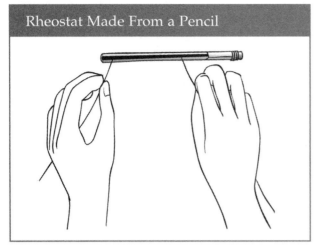

Rheostat Made From a Pencil

fascinating. There is a whole paper folding/engineering art form (origami) with thousands of followers.

Strategy 3. Each FOSS module includes a book of readings (articles) that complement, enrich, and extend the science learning experience introduced in the active investigation. The *Science Resources* book is an opportunity for students to think about the bridge between the science concepts and principles and the applications of those science ideas in the service of human enterprise. For example, in the *FOSS Science Resources: Energy and Electromagnetism* book, the article "Morse Gets Clicking" describes in words and diagrams how the telegraph device was designed and developed, and changed the way people communicated starting in 1844.

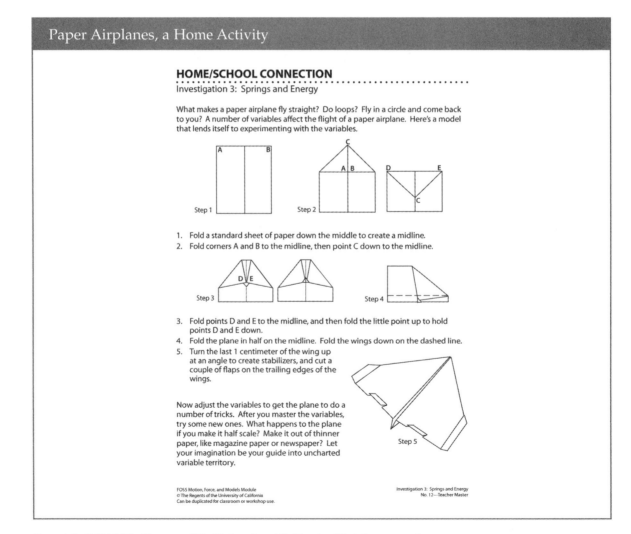

Paper Airplanes, a Home Activity

Another article "Electromagnets Everywhere" provides students with diagrams and descriptions of how motors use magnets to turn a shaft and how a direct-current generator is a direct-current motor in reverse. If you can turn the shaft of the generator using a renewable source of energy, such as wind to turn a windmill, you can generate electricity without relying on fossil fuels. This leads to the design of alternative sources of energy.

In another module, **Motion, Force, and Models,** students learn that objects in motion have energy and that the faster a given object is moving, the more kinetic energy it has. They also learn that when objects collide, energy can transfer from one object to another. An object in motion has a property called momentum, which keeps the object moving. The more momentum an object has, the harder it is to stop. Momentum can be calculated (product of its mass and speed). So, a large object moving at high speed has a lot of momentum, requiring a lot of force to stop it. Conversely, a small object moving at low speed has very little momentum. These concepts of force and motion can lead to a discussion about a safety issue for young, active people, playing sports, or using bikes or skateboards. The *FOSS Science Resources: Motion, Force, and Models* provides a mechanism to introduce the engineering products.

One reading, "Coming to a Stop," reviews the concepts dealing with transfer of energy and momentum. In the next reading, "Concussion Discussion," students learn that a concussion is a brain bruise caused by a traumatic head impact. A concussion does not necessarily compromise the integrity of the skull, the protective vault that surrounds the brain. The brain incurs a bruise primarily because of the property of momentum.

When a skateboarder goes out of control and crashes into a wall or tree, a concussion can happen. The brain, nestled comfortably in the skull, is traveling along at high speed. If the head comes up short against a large unmovable object, the kinetic energy of the moving head applies a force to the large object. The large object pushes back against the head with a force equal to the force exerted by the head. The push-back force stops the motion of the head by reducing its momentum to zero in a matter of a thousandth of a second or so. The problem is that the brain inside the skull also has momentum. When the skull stops, the brain's momentum keeps it moving, and it runs smack into the

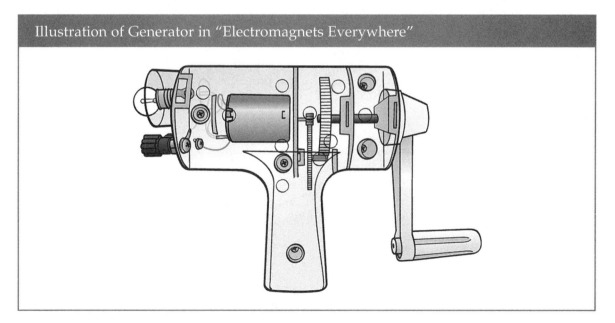

Illustration of Generator in "Electromagnets Everywhere"

inside of the skull. The inside of the skull pushes back on the brain with enough force to bring it to a stop in a fraction of a second. The magnitude of the force is often enough to bruise the nervous tissue and blood vessels in the brain near the area where the brain hit the interior of the skull.

A moving object comes to rest when its momentum is reduced to zero. The way to reduce an object's momentum to zero safely is to extend the length of time it takes to slow down. If the momentum takes longer to get to zero, much less force can be used to accomplish the task. To avert disaster when a skateboarder runs into an object, the skater's head should be covered in a padded helmet. What does padding accomplish? The force applied to the padding causes the padding to compress. The compression force slows the moving object over an extended period of time by applying a lighter, less damaging force. Padding increases the time it takes to reduce a moving object's momentum to zero and decreases the stopping force.

This is essentially the engineering design incorporated into crash helmets, air bags, and chassis-crumple zones in automobiles. Students can read about these products of engineers and understand how they work based on the science involved. Then when presented with the design challenge in the module, they will apply the concepts to the challenge: "Drop a plastic egg filled with beans from a high place. Design a contraption to protect the plastic egg from cracking after it is dropped. You may not seal the egg shut with anything."

The engineering design process to develop these safety products involves materials selection, design, testing, evaluation, redesign, more evaluation, manufacturing, field implementation, ongoing evaluation to make judgments about the design and production, with an eye to effectiveness and efficiencies concerning materials and investments of time and other resources during implementation of the innovation.

Also in the **Motion, Force, and Models Module,** students read a short biographical article about Arthur Fry, the person who developed the omnipresent sticky label. This helps students understand that engineering is not limited to objects and complex systems, but extends to areas like materials engineering. After learning of the invention of a "failed" adhesive, Fry worked and worked on a formula for the adhesive that solved the problem he was experiencing. He needed an adhesive that would hold pieces of paper together, but which would allow the pieces of paper to be separated without damaging or leaving residue on the paper when they were separated. After many attempts, he achieved the solution he was seeking. As a result, we now see little colorful paper flags sticking to papers and books distributed all through our work environments.

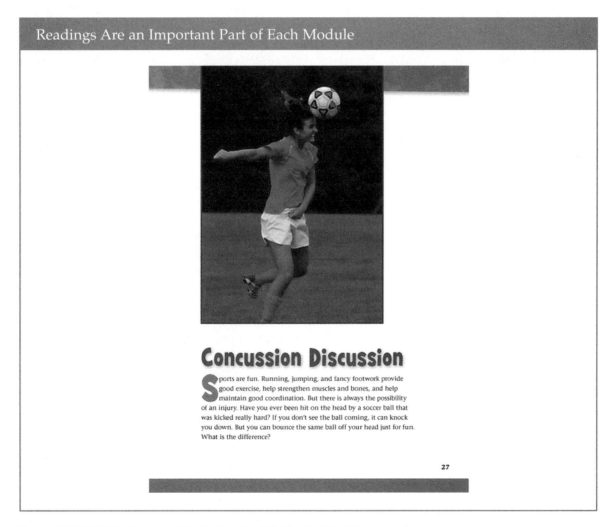

Readings Are an Important Part of Each Module

Concussion Discussion

Sports are fun. Running, jumping, and fancy footwork provide good exercise, help strengthen muscles and bones, and help maintain good coordination. But there is always the possibility of an injury. Have you ever been hit on the head by a soccer ball that was kicked really hard? If you don't see the ball coming, it can knock you down. But you can bounce the same ball off your head just for fun. What is the difference?

27

Strategy 4. The final strategy (develop new FOSS engineering modules) was not possible due to resource limitations but remains a possibility for future collaborations. The legacy module **Models and Designs** described earlier is an example of a module that employs engineering design strategies throughout all four investigations. Even though this module will not be going through the extensive Third Edition revision process, **Models and Designs** will be promoted to the status of legacy module and a STEM module and will always be available to educators, even though it will not officially be part of the FOSS Third Edition program. Other Second Edition modules that have particularly rich engineering opportunities will continue to be available for engineering educators as legacy modules: **Ideas and Inventions, Human Body, Levers and Pulleys, Solar Energy,** and **Variables.**

FOSS and the Next Generation Science Standards: The Happy Marriage Between Science Education and Engineering Education

The Framework asserts that in the context of learning science, students should have ample opportunity to understand how scientific knowledge is acquired and how science knowledge is applied in the service of human needs and desires. Acquisition and application engage engineering practices. The instructional methods used in an active learning science program (e.g., FOSS) are replete with opportunities for engineering. Students continually coordinate and assemble (engineer) systems in order to achieve science-learning goals. The coordination and assembly phase can be relatively passive if instructions simply call for students to follow a predetermined number of steps so the activity becomes an exercise in technical reading, or the design can be implied by a statement of the function (problem) to be achieved by the coordination and assembly phase of the activity. Admittedly this approach will often require more time, so giving students this creative engineering space will require teachers to assume a different stance in the classroom. This presents a significant challenge to meeting the NGSS.

Rising to the level of performance described in the NGSS will require a monumental commitment to professional development in virtually every school district across the country. Teachers will have to learn how to project a sense of trust and expectation that students will be able to rise to the challenge of taking more responsibility for designing their own learning environments. It will require teachers to engineer a problem-solving culture in the classroom. Teachers will have to become comfortable with protests from students claiming they don't know what to do or how to solve the problem. Teachers will have to learn to reply earnestly that they (the students) should talk it up and share ideas as a community of learners to start a process of figuring it out collaboratively. Sometimes the teacher might join with students as a colleague to engage in the engineering/design process as just another member of the learning community.

Conclusion

Although initially intended for teaching only science, FOSS will prove to be an excellent curriculum for teaching elementary school engineering for several reasons. First, the curriculum design incorporates many specified opportunities for engaging in or reflecting on engineering practices. The FOSS curriculum designers have recognized the advantages of supporting teachers to provide this learning opportunity for their students. Second, with the publication of NGSS, conscientious science educators will be looking for engineering instruction in the materials they select. Third, part of the responsibility on the plate of curriculum developers is to provide professional development for users of the curriculum. And with the Third Edition of the FOSS program, the FOSS staff and family of professional developers are committed to ensuring that that professional development will include guidance for how to use the curriculum effectively to at least start the journey needed to incorporate engineering education practices into the implementation of FOSS. FOSS is a science education program, but it has become clear to us that scientific knowledge is inextricably and seamlessly connected to engineering education.

References

National Research Council. (2012). *A framework for K–12 science education: Practices, crosscutting concepts, and core ideas.* Washington, DC: The National Academies Press.

NGSS Lead States. (2013). *Next Generation Science Standards: For states, by states.* Washington, DC: National Academies Press.

7

Seeds of Science/ Roots of Reading

Jacqueline Barber, The Learning Design Group: Lawrence Hall of Science, University of California, Berkeley

Students test the strength of glue that they made in designing mixtures.

Seeds of Science/Roots of Reading is an effective curriculum program for Grades 2–5 that offers students the opportunity for intensive engagement with high-level science and engineering concepts and practices through multiple modalities (firsthand investigations, student-to-student discussion, reading science texts, and writing—the "Do-it, Talk-it, Read-it, Write-it" model). An explicit focus of the curriculum is *disciplinary literacy,* the specialized skills involved in reading, writing, and talking about science.

The program is composed of 12 units—four units at each of three grade bands (Grades 2–3, Grades 3–4, and Grades 4–5). Each unit involves students in deep forays into learning about the natural and designed worlds by searching for evidence through firsthand experiences and text in order to construct more and more accurate and complete understandings. Students engage in written and oral discourse with the goal of communicating and negotiating evidence-based explanations and goal-based designs, and evaluating and revising their explanations and designs.

The Seeds/Roots program was designed to be a core science program (able to address all aspects of science proficiency) while simultaneously serving as a supplementary literacy program (focused on reading comprehension, vocabulary development, and fluency as it relates to nonfiction text). Unlike many science programs that claim to integrate literacy, the Seeds/Roots program takes on an equivalent number of learning goals in literacy and science, and provides students with explicit instruction, opportunities for practice, and increasing independence in using literacy strategies to make sense of and communicate about the natural world. In many school districts, teachers are able to situate a portion of each Seeds/Roots unit in time normally used for literacy.

Engineering design is incorporated into each of the 12 units. Because the Seeds of Science/Roots of Reading program is primarily a science program, each of the design challenges involves students in applying science concepts they have learned as they solve intriguing engineering challenges, such as inventing a Mars rover, an automatic sorting system, magnet inventions, and more. Such close integration of science and engineering is strongly advocated in the Next Generation Science Standards (NGSS) (NGSS Lead States, 2013). This chapter focuses on one of the units—Designing Mixtures, a 20-session unit for students in Grades 2–3.

Designing Mixtures

Designing Mixtures immerses students in investigating ingredients and making mixtures in order to design (a) a strong glue and (b) a fizzy, tasty soda. In addition to the opportunities to engage in engineering and design, the unit enables students to learn about properties of substances, mixtures, dissolving, and solubility and the cross-cutting concept of cause and effect. Because Designing Mixtures is part of the Seeds of Science/Roots of Reading curriculum program, the unit also provides students with explicit instruction and practice in the literacy skills that are necessary for participating in science learning, such as comprehension strategies for informational texts, writing procedural texts, and engaging in evidence-based discourse using the language of science. This chapter describes a portion of the Designing Mixtures unit focused on designing glue and explains how it addresses the NGSS (NGSS Lead States, 2013), specifically those related to the practices, disciplinary core ideas, and crosscutting concepts of engineering and design.

Glue Investigations— Round One

Students begin by reading *What If Rain Boots Were Made of Paper?*, one of five custom-written books that are part of the Designing Mixtures unit. In the book, students are asked to imagine a series of unusual objects—such as rain boots made of paper and frying pans made of rubber—in order to have them begin to think about the relationship between objects, the materials used to make those objects, and the properties of those materials. The book sets the stage for a discussion of what materials are good for particular uses. Students then observe and analyze the different materials used to make objects in the classroom—scissors, pencils, tables, and so on. From this sequence, students learn what properties are, that every material has different properties, and that these properties make certain materials good for some uses and not so good for others. Students learn that there are people whose job it is to design objects and mixtures and that these designers choose materials that have the properties they want their objects and mixtures to have.

Students are then provided with a design challenge—to make a great glue. They begin by

What If Rain Boots Were Made of Paper? is one of five student books in the Designing Mixtures unit.

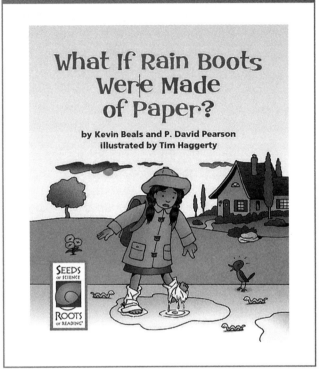

The student book *What If Rainboots Were Made of Paper?* engages the students in thinking about how the properties of different materials make them suitable for some products but not others.

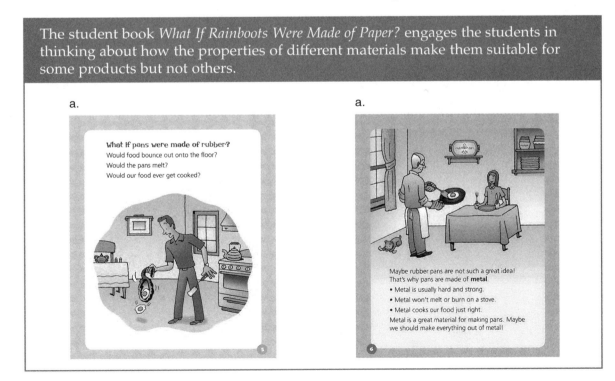

a.

What If pans were made of rubber?
Would food bounce out onto the floor?
Would the pans melt?
Would our food ever get cooked?

a.

Maybe rubber pans are not such a great idea!
That's why pans are made of **metal**.
• Metal is usually hard and strong.
• Metal won't melt or burn on a stove.
• Metal cooks our food just right.
Metal is a great material for making pans. Maybe we should make everything out of metal!

accessing their prior knowledge about glue and brainstorm a list of properties of glue. Through this discussion, and by examining what's said on the packaging of different glues, they realize that different glues are designed for use with different materials and in different situations. Students set out to make a glue that will stick an object to paper.

Students begin by observing the properties of four possible glue ingredients, first dry, then mixed with water, and see that different ingredients have different properties. Through discussion, the class decides on the most important property of any glue—that it is sticky! Students learn that while different kinds of glues have the same general properties (they are all used to stick something to something else), they can have different specific properties (sticking to different surfaces, different strengths, being waterproof, washable, removable, etc.).

Next students predict which possible glue ingredients will make the best glue and then test their predictions by setting up "sticky tests." A sticky test involves each pair of students using a dab of each wet glue ingredient to stick two beans to a class sheet of paper designated for that ingredient. The next day, after the ingredient mixtures have dried, the teacher holds the paper vertically and submits it to a shake-shake-shake. The class counts how many beans remain stuck to the paper and using this as a measure, orders the mixtures from least sticky to most sticky. The teacher introduces the idea of *scientific evidence* and explains that the results of the test provide evidence of how sticky each ingredient is. Students see how designers use evidence to revise their predictions and conclusions.

After testing the individual ingredients, each student gets to decide what ingredients they would like to mix together to make their own glue mixtures. They use the evidence from the sticky tests to make decisions about what ingredients to add to their glue mixtures. As they begin mixing students naturally begin to attend to other ingredient properties they are observing—the secondary properties of glue. It's common to hear students making comments like "The flour makes it really sticky, but it's super hard to spread. Let's add some corn starch and maybe it will be more spreadable." This firsthand experience leads students very authentically to the conclusion that specific

Students begin by observing the properties of possible glue ingredients.

Students display the results of their glue designs.

ingredients cause a mixture to have specific properties and that different combinations of ingredients may produce mixtures with different properties.

As students progress through the unit, they build knowledge of how designers work. Students understand that designers use tests to find out about the properties of a substance, that having a way to quantify the degree to which each ingredient exhibits a specific property makes comparing the properties of each ingredient much easier, and that evidence is very useful in making decisions about what ingredients to include.

Students also get firsthand experience with tradeoffs as they attempt to cut the gloppyness of the very sticky flour, with the other ingredients at hand, to make a more usable and easier-to-spread glue. This helps build their understanding that mixtures are useful when you want to design one thing that has several different properties.

At the end of this part of the instructional sequence, students explore and discuss the features of procedural text, an important genre of text for designers to master. They look through cookbooks and other how-to manuals to see the text structure used to communicate how to make something. Students then practice giving and receiving instructions for drawing a secret number, letter or shape, in preparation for recording the procedures for making their own glue recipe in a complete and precise way. Later the class will work together to write, test, and improve a procedure for making a sandwich, leading them to further reflect on the need for precise instructions. Students will have two more opportunities to write recipes in the Designing Mixtures unit, each time with increasing independence.

Glue Investigations—Round Two

Students return to designing glue after they have completed another design challenge that comprises the middle of the Designing Mixtures unit—creating a fizzy soda—where they build and apply knowledge about dissolving and solubility. With another design

Recording results of different design choices is an important part of the unit.

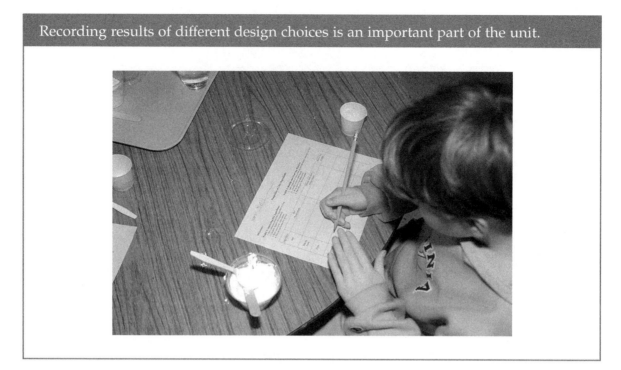

experience under their belts, students are ready for a more sophisticated challenge. The class first reads *Jess Makes Hair Gel*, a book that models how one boy approaches a design challenge, the obstacles he encounters, his missteps, and successes.

Jess sets out to make a hair gel that makes his hair shiny *and* able to stand up. After his first round of making hair gel, Jess has found substances that work to make his hair shiny *or* substances that work to make his hair stand up. When he finally finds one substance that works to do both, lime gelatin, he realizes that he needs to revise his design goals, because there are some properties he does *not* want his hair gel to have. He does *not* want his hair gel to be green and smell like fruit!

The class uses Jess's experience in designing hair gel as a model to launch them in Round Two of their glue investigations. Students already found in Round One that they could make glue that can attach an object to a piece of paper. For Round Two, they are challenged to expand their design goals, to make a glue that is really strong—that can remain stuck to the paper even when you pull on the object. Just like Jess, after designing their first glue, they will go back to the drawing board and expand the description of their goals for additional properties they want their glue to have.

Also in Round Two, the teacher begins to label the stages of the design process. The first glue design challenge and the soda design challenge provided students with a base of experience with the design process. As they proceed with the second glue design challenge in Round Two, the class talks about the stages of the design process, and the teacher posts and points out the following steps they are going through as they design their strong glue.

Important Steps for Designing Mixtures

1. Decide on the properties you want your new mixture to have.
2. Think of possible ingredients to make the mixture.

3. Test the possible ingredients to find out their properties.

4. Mix ingredients together to make a mixture with more than one property.

5. Compare the result to the list of properties to see if your mixture meets your goals.

6. Try again if the properties are not close enough.

7. Record a recipe that describes how to make the mixture.

The student reader *Jess Makes Hair Gel* introduces a more sophisticated challenge.

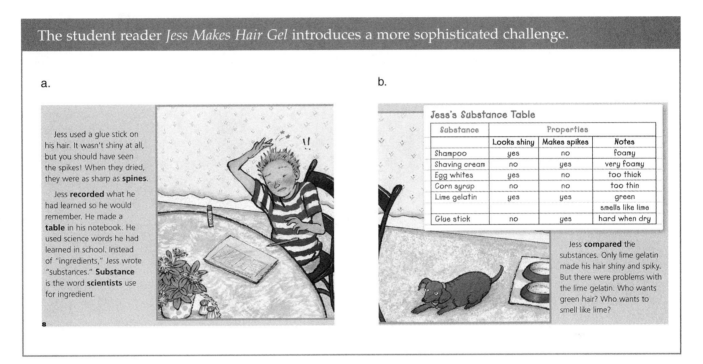

a.

Jess used a glue stick on his hair. It wasn't shiny at all, but you should have seen the spikes! When they dried, they were as sharp as **spines**.

Jess **recorded** what he had learned so he would remember. He made a **table** in his notebook. He used science words he had learned in school. Instead of "ingredients," Jess wrote "substances." **Substance** is the word **scientists** use for ingredient.

b.

Jess's Substance Table

Substance	Properties		
	Looks shiny	Makes spikes	Notes
Shampoo	yes	no	foamy
Shaving cream	no	yes	very foamy
Egg whites	yes	no	too thick
Corn syrup	no	no	too thin
Lime gelatin	yes	yes	green smells like lime
Glue stick	no	yes	hard when dry

Jess **compared** the substances. Only lime gelatin made his hair shiny and spiky. But there were problems with the lime gelatin. Who wants green hair? Who wants to smell like lime?

The class reflects on the steps Jess went through in his design of hair gel, and they read the next custom-written book in the Designing Mixtures unit, *Jelly Bean Scientist*, which tells the story of Ambrose Lee, a flavor chemist who designs jelly bean flavors. The students learn from their reading that although each step in the design process is important, not all designers follow the steps in the same exact order.

Continuing their investigations, students have evidence about four ingredients they tested in Round One. They proceed to gather evidence on additional promising ingredients to use in their new strong glue mixture. They do this by using both first- and second-hand information. Their own investigations provided firsthand information. To gather secondhand evidence that was collected by someone else, they are invited to search in a reference book called *Handbook of Interesting Ingredients*. This custom-written reference book, which is accessible by young readers, was modeled on the *Handbook of Chemistry and Physics*, a resource that scientists and engineers keep at hand to find information they can use in their work.

Students learn that they can look in the table of contents to find an ingredient they think might work in their glue mixture. In the table of contents, they'll see that the handbook includes information on substances such as cornstarch, corn syrup, egg white, flour, gelatin, and so forth. They also learn that they can look in the index of the handbook to find a property, such as sticky, slippery, thick, thin, etc., and use the page numbers listed to find which ingredients have that property.

The student book *Handbook of Interesting Ingredients* was modeled on the *Handbook of Chemistry and Physics.*

In reading about the *uses of ingredients,* the students might discover that crayon wrappers are glued with cornstarch, that egg whites were used as glue many, many years ago, and that gelatin was used more recently on postage stamps! Also, in reading about the *properties of ingredients,* students might get some ideas of which ingredients can thin or thicken a mixture and which ingredients are sticky.

In addition to gathering this secondhand evidence, students continue to gather firsthand evidence by subjecting the four new possible glue ingredients to the strength test. The strength test works like this: pairs of students stick a bent metal paper clip into a dab of the wet ingredient on an index card. When the ingredient dries, they can see how well the paper clip is attached to the card by hanging washers on the paper clip one by one until the paper clip pulls off the card. The more washers the dried glue ingredient holds, the stronger it is.

This part of the instructional sequence helps students learn that when trying to answer questions, scientists search for evidence from their own investigations as well as from books that other scientists have written.

The class then compiles the evidence from the handbook and from the strength test to create one class set of evidence of good glue properties.

The teacher leads the class to carefully review and evaluate the evidence to see what conclusions can be drawn. As a first step, the students revisit Jess's Substance Table from the book *Jess Makes Hair Gel.* The teacher points out how the table is organized, with ingredients (substances) down the left column, properties across the top of the table, and a place to write notes.

The teacher also points out how Jess recorded his evaluation of the evidence—with a yes or a no. This showed whether or not an ingredient had the property he was looking for.

Next, the teacher shows a Class Substance Table that is just like Jess's Substance Table. Across the top, there is room for three properties (design goals). The first is filled in for

The students look back at the data table from *Jess Makes Hair Gel.*

Jess's Substance Table

Substance	Properties		
	Looks shiny	Makes spikes	Notes
Shampoo	yes	no	foamy
Shaving cream	no	yes	very foamy
Egg whites	yes	no	too thick
Corn syrup	no	no	too thin
Lime gelatin	yes	yes	green
			smells like lime
Glue stick	no	yes	hard when dry

the students: "Is strong." The teacher leads the class in deciding what other properties on which they would like to evaluate the evidence. Typical choices include "Easy to spread," "Dries clear," and "No odor."

Then, the teacher leads the class through the evaluation of each ingredient, property by property, by asking a series of questions:

- Can someone summarize our evidence for cornstarch from the strength test?
- How could different groups doing the same test on the same ingredient get different results?
- How sure are we of this evidence?
- What conclusions can we draw from this evidence?

By seeing that different groups can get different results when doing the same test on the same ingredient mixture, they learn that evaluating evidence involves deciding how confident they are that the evidence is accurate. When everyone gets the same test result, we can be more confident that the evidence is accurate than if test results don't agree.

Finally, students decide on multiple ingredients they want to use in their own glue mixtures. Each pair of students works together to make two test glue mixtures: Test Glue 1 and Test Glue 2. Together they discuss ingredient choices and why they are choosing the ingredients they are. Students then make the two test glue mixtures and set up a strength test.

The next day, when the test glues have dried, students conduct strength tests for their two glue mixtures, evaluate the test results for both glue mixtures, compare the two glue mixtures, and then draw conclusions about which glue best met the design goals.

Again, the teacher uses a model from *Jess Makes Hair Gel* to model and scaffold students' comparison of these two test glues. Students are given a table organized in the same way, but students must add the properties that they want *their* glue to have. While last time, the teacher led the class in evaluating the evidence for each glue ingredient, this time students work in pairs to evaluate Test Glue 1 and Test Glue 2 themselves.

After they evaluate the two test glues, students discuss the results of their tests and discuss what changes they want to make. The teacher guides this by asking the following:

- How might you change your recipe?
- What evidence do you have that makes you think this will be a good change?

The class's completed data table indicates which evidence is from the students' firsthand investigations and which evidence is from the secondhand information available in the *Handbook.*

Evidence of Good Glue Properties

Ingredient	Evidence from Handbook	Evidence from Strength Test
egg whites	page 17- can stick things together / page 17- used as a glue	0, 0, 6, 0, 0
flour	page 19- sticky when mixed with water / page 18- hard when dry	11, 12, 9, 10, 13
corn syrup	page 15- can make a mixture sticky when dry	7, 9, 13, 10, 9
gelatin	page 21- can hold ingredients together	9-11, 8-11, 7, 9, 13

Students continue to work in pairs to make their final glue recipes that they test and evaluate as before. Students talk together in small groups to reflect upon their glue mixtures and how well they met the strong glue design challenge. Having designed, made, and tested their final mixtures, students review features of procedural text, then write and illustrate a recipe for their final glue mixture.

The class reflects on how the design process is iterative—you make a recipe, evaluate it, revise it based on evidence, and then make and evaluate it again. They also reflect on how designing mixtures to have certain properties can be a long process—and that designers who design mixtures need to be persistent.

Meeting the NGSS Design and Engineering Standards

The instructional sequence described earlier, from the Designing Mixtures unit, provides students with rich experiences that reflect the vision of the National Research Council's (NRC) *A Framework for K–12 Science Education and Next Generation Science Standards* as summarized below.

Science and Engineering Practices from *A Framework for K–12 Science Education: Practices, Crosscutting Concepts, and Core Ideas* (NRC, 2012).

In Designing Mixtures, students:

Brainstorm properties of good glue. Engineering begins with a problem, need, or desire that suggests an engineering problem that needs to be solved. Engineers ask

The students create a table like the one from *Jess Makes Hair Gel* to evaluate test glues.

Jess's Substance Table 2

Substance	Properties			
	Shiny	Makes spikes	Color	Smell
Lime gelatin	yes	yes	green	smells like lime
Plain gelatin	yes	yes	none	none

Students write and illustrate a recipe for their final glue mixture.

questions to define the engineering problem, determine criteria for a successful solution, and identify constraints. (p. 50)

Use washers as weights to test the strength of the different glue mixtures. Engineering makes use of models and simulations to analyze existing systems so as to see where flaws might occur or to test possible solutions to a new problem. (p. 50)

Conduct sticky tests and strength tests to compare single ingredients as well as mixtures. Engineers use investigation . . . to test their designs. Like scientists, engineers must identify relevant variables, . . . and collect data for analysis. (p. 50)

Evaluate data from firsthand investigations and secondhand sources to determine which mixtures best meet the design goals. Engineers analyze data collected in the tests of their designs and investigations; this allows them to compare different solutions and determine how well each one meets specific design criteria—that is, which design best solves the problem within the given constraints. (p. 51)

Gather quantitative data of stickiness and strength and use these values to determine the relative effectiveness of different ingredients and mixtures. In engineering, mathematical and computational representations of established relationships and principles are an integral part of design. (p. 51)

Systematically test a variety of ingredients and mixtures to iteratively work to achieve the best and strongest glue. Engineers use systematic methods to compare alternatives, formulate evidence based on test data, make arguments from evidence to defend their conclusions, evaluate critically the ideas of others, and revise their designs in order to achieve the best solution to the problem at hand. (p. 52)

Read and interpret science text and visual representations, search through reference text for a purpose, engage in peer-to-peer talk about their designs and design processes, and share their final designed recipes by writing procedural text. Engineers need to be able to express their ideas, orally and in writing, with the use of tables, graphs, drawings, or models and by engaging in extended discussions with peers. Moreover, as with scientists, they need to be able to derive meaning from colleagues' texts, evaluate the information, and apply it usefully. (p. 53)

Disciplinary Core Ideas from the *Next Generation Science Standards: For States, by States* (Volume 1) (NGSS Lead States, 2013).

In Designing Mixtures, students:

Learn that designers create solutions to problems using a specific goal-driven process. K-2-ETS1–1. A situation that people want to change or create can be approached as a problem to be solved through engineering. (p. 23)

Spend time considering the properties of different glues and coming to understand that glues designed for different purposes need different properties. K-2-ETS1–1. Before beginning to design a solution, it is important to clearly understand the problem. (p. 23)

Gather information from firsthand observations as well as secondhand science references. K-2-ETS1–1. Asking questions, making observations, and gathering information are helpful in thinking about problems. (p. 23)

Describe their successful designs by writing procedural text that enables others to know how to create glue mixtures. K-2-ETS1–2. Designs can be conveyed through sketches, drawings, or physical models. These representations are useful in communicating ideas for a problem's solutions to other people. (p. 23)

Gather, analyze, and compare data from several glue ingredients and glue mixtures. K-2-ETS1–3. Analyze data from tests of two objects designed to solve the same problem to compare the strengths and weaknesses of how each performs. (p. 23)

Focus closely on the properties of various glue ingredients to determine which ingredients have the properties they want in the glue mixtures. 2-PS1–1. Plan and conduct an investigation to describe and classify different kinds of materials by their observable properties. (p. 16)

Experience the power of designing glue using their prior knowledge, information from text, and information for firsthand investigations. 2-PS1–2. Analyze data obtained from testing different materials to determine which materials have the properties that are best suited for an intended purpose. (p. 16)

Crosscutting Concepts from the *Next Generation Science Standards: For States, by States* (Volume 2) (NGSS Lead States, 2013).

In Designing Mixtures, students:

Observe and test the effect of adding specific ingredients to a mixture. Cause and Effect—In Grades 3–5, students routinely identify and test causal relationships and use these relationships to explain change. (p. 83)

Compare and determine the relative stickiness of different glue ingredients and mixtures. Patterns—In Grades 3–5, students identify similarities and differences in order to sort and classify natural objects and designed products. (p. 82)

Important Elements of Engineering Curricula for Elementary Students

Visitors to a classroom where students are engaged in the Designing Mixtures unit typically exclaim over the expertise of Grade 2 and 3 students as they observe, test, talk about evidence, and reason their way to designing effective products. There are several important elements that make these activities accessible to students in this young age group.

Provide Models. Knowing how to engage with a design challenge like an engineer takes instruction, modeling, and opportunities to practice. In Designing Mixtures, the book *Jess Makes Hair Gel* serves as a model, not just of the design process, but of ways of recording data, how data tables can be designed, how to make sense of data, what to do when you encounter a failure, how to evolve and refine design goals over time, as well as providing models of dispositions, like curiosity and persistence. The ideas in the book are revisited multiple times over the course of the unit, as students take on different steps of the design process. Don't assume that young students know what it means to engage in engineering practices. Point these practices out explicitly as they arise during the activities.

Guide With Questions. While open-ended design challenges offer wonderful freedom and a chance for students to demonstrate their grasp of engineering and design processes, often times younger students lack the experience needed to know how to proceed. Guiding students with questions can make all the difference. For instance, prompting students with What do you think? Why do you think that? What's your evidence? goes a long way to helping students know how to talk like a scientist or engineer. Similarly, asking questions such as How sure are we of this evidence? How could we be more sure? or What conclusions can we draw from this evidence? help students begin to know how to make sense of data. Repeated use of these questions and even providing sentence starters can make all the difference for young students.

Provide Scaffolds. As students engage for the first time with a science or engineering practice, or for that matter, a literacy practice, make sure to scaffold their success. For instance, in Designing Mixtures, students are given the design challenge (design a glue; then design a strong glue), given the procedures for measuring success (the sticky test and the strength test), and given ways to organize their data (from *Jess Makes Hair Gel*). While eventually we will want students to be able to come up with their own ways of gathering data, organizing it, and even come up with their own design challenges to solve a broader problem, there is a great deal that's new for a 7- or 8-year-old, and lots they need to figure out and learn in this scaffolded situation. It's important that students have successful early design experiences from which they can learn and gain knowledge.

Release Responsibility Gradually. The first time students record their glue recipes, it is on a highly scaffolded student sheet that provides the instructions and the ingredients; students are prompted to put in the amounts. After students have explored the common text structure in cookbooks, how-to manuals, and other examples of procedural text, the teacher leads the class in writing the procedures for making a sandwich. She enacts (and points out that enactment) of a common procedural text structure, starting with the title (a short phrase describing what the recipe is for), a what-you-need section, and a what-you-do section. When it's time for students to write the procedure for making the soda they designed, they have a fairly loose scaffold. On page 1, they write both ingredients and amounts in the what-you-need section. On pages 2 and 3, they have a template that prompts them to write the procedure, step by step, and to make a drawing to illustrate each step. The teacher gives them sentence stems from which they can choose. Students then test their procedural text by trading recipes and following their buddy's procedure themselves (exactly as written) to make the soda and give each other feedback about what was unclear. When students write their final procedure for making strong glue, they are able to proceed without instruction (although they still use a loose template). By gradually releasing responsibility to the student and providing them with increased opportunities for independence, all students can be successful in communicating their designs with others.

Provide Repeated Opportunities. Students need repeated opportunities to engage in the design process before they will start to understand that the process is a general and powerful set of steps that can be used flexibly to solve many different problems. In Designing Mixtures, students are given firsthand experience with three large design challenges (make a good glue, make a tasty bubbly soda, and finally make a strong glue). In addition, they have the experience of learning secondhand about two other design challenges in two of the unit's books (*Jess Makes Hair Gel* and *Jellybean Scientist*). It is through these repeated opportunities to experience the design process that students will come to internalize the steps and their purpose.

Metacognitive Talk. Last but far from least is the importance of engaging in regular metacognitive talk. Throughout the last design challenge in the unit—strong glue—the teacher regularly connects what students are doing with steps of the design process. When reading informational text, the teacher talks aloud, making her thinking visible, as she demonstrates accessing her own prior knowledge as a way to make sense of text.

Conclusion

Seeds of Science/Roots of Reading offers many solutions for a variety of schools and classroom settings. It can be used during science, English language arts, and English language development time, and in summer school and other supplementary educational settings. We hope that you will find Seeds of Science/Roots of Reading to be an effective and flexible tool for increasing your students' achievement in both science and literacy.

References

National Research Council. (2012). *A framework for K–12 science education: Practices, crosscutting concepts, and core ideas.* Washington, DC: The National Academies Press.

NGSS Lead States. (2013). *Next Generation Science Standards: For states, by states.* Washington, DC: The National Academies Press.

8

Tangible Kindergarten

Learning How to Program Robots in Early Childhood

Marina Umaschi Bers,
Eliot Pearson Department of Child Development,
Tufts University, Medford, Massachusetts

Collaboration is an important goal of the Tangible Kindergarten project.

Image courtesy of Marina Bers.

As shown on the previous page, during Tangible Kindergarten® (Tangible K) classes each child receives a personalized printout with his or her photograph in the center of the page and the photographs and names of all other children in the class arranged in a circle. The children use this image to keep track of their collaborations with other children during the day so that at the end of the week they can write or draw "thank-you cards" to the children with whom they have collaborated.

Tangible K is a curriculum that promotes powerful ideas from computer science, in particular robotics, among children in Grades preK–2. Tangible K is specifically designed to engage young children in computational thinking and engineering design while integrating relevant concepts and skills with other areas of the early childhood curriculum. The curriculum promotes positive uses of technology and technological fluency. With an emphasis on the concept of sequencing as a core idea of computer programming that is relevant in the early years as a major predictor for academic success in literacy and math, the Tangible K curriculum also supports 21st century skills. Students engaged with the Tangible K curriculum work individually, in pairs, and in teams to program a robot's behaviors. In the process, they apply knowledge of mathematics, use inquiry and problem-solving skills, and develop their creativity by using the engineering design process.

The Tangible K curriculum is interdisciplinary and specifically designed to address the developmental stage of children in Grades preK–2. It integrates powerful ideas, concepts, and skills from the fields of computer science and engineering with traditional curricular areas such as math, science, literacy, social sciences, and the arts. The research shows that the curriculum helps children develop engineering and computer science practices while they build and program their robots. It also shows that children increase their sequencing skills, a foundational concept that is a predictor of later academic success. Furthermore, the Tangible K curriculum was designed to promote positive uses of and attitudes toward technology.

To date (September 2013), the Tangible K curriculum has been used by more than 250 early childhood teachers and has reached more than 2,000 students.

Six Powerful Ideas

In order to engage children in computational thinking, the Tangible K curriculum focuses on six powerful ideas, communicated to young children through activities.

Robotics is the engineering discipline that focuses on the creation and programming of robots, which are machines that can follow instructions and move on their own to perform tasks.

Activity: *What Is a Robot?* After an introduction to robotics by looking at different robots and talking about the functions they serve, children build their own robotic vehicles and explore their parts and the instructions they can use to program them.

The engineering design process is used to develop products to solve a need or problem. It has several iterative steps: identifying a need or defining the problem, doing research, analyzing possible solutions, developing the product, and communicating and presenting the product.

Activity: *Sturdy Building:* Children build a nonrobotic vehicle to take small toy people from home to school. The vehicle needs to be sturdy as well as perform its intended functions.

Sequencing, control, and flow. A sequence of instructions can be described in a program and acted out in order by a robot. Each block has a specific meaning. The order of the blocks is important.

Activity: *The Hokey-Pokey:* Choose the appropriate commands and put them in order to program a robot to dance the Hokey-Pokey.

Loops and parameters. A sequence of instructions can be modified to occur over and over again. Control flow commands can be qualified with additional information. For example, loops can be modified to repeat forever or a concrete number of times.

Activity: *Again and Again Until I Say When:* Students use a pair of loop blocks ("repeat"/"end repeat") to make the robot go forward again and again, infinitely and then just the right number of times to arrive at a fixed location.

Sensors. A robot can use sensors, akin to human sense organs, to gather information from its environment. Sensor information can be used to control when the robot follows given commands.

Activity: *Through the Tunnel:* Children use light sensors and commands to program a robot to turn its lights on when its surroundings are dark and vice versa.

Branches. At a branch in the program, a robot can follow one set of commands or another depending on the state of a given condition.

Activity: *The Robot Decides*: Students program their robot to travel to one of two destinations based on light or touch sensor information.

Overview of the Tangible K Curriculum

The Tangible K curriculum is designed for a minimum of 20 hours of classroom work, divided into the following structured sessions based on the six powerful ideas identified earlier:

1. Sturdy Building (the engineering design process)

2. What Is a Robot? (robots have special parts to follow instruction)

3. Hokey-Pokey·sequence of commands (the sequence or order of commands matters)

4. Again and Again Until I Say When (loops and number parameters)

5. Through the Tunnel (sensors and loops)

6. The Robot Decides (sensors and branches)

The curriculum unit is designed to take place over the course of one intensive week of work or over the course of several months, with several short sessions per week. Depending on children's developmental levels and prior experience with digital technology, programming, and robotics, students might need more or less time. One issue for each teacher to resolve is how long to allot for each of the six lessons. Each can be spread out over several sessions to accommodate the classroom schedule and students' attention spans for this work.

Tangible K involves children in making their own projects (i.e., creating content) by engaging them in making a robotic artifact and in programming its behaviors. Following is an overview of the six sessions. Themes vary in the pilot versions of this curriculum—transportation, community, animals—but the powerful ideas of computer science and robotics remain the same. The transportation curriculum is used here as an example.

Lesson 1. Sturdy Build (introduction to engineering design). Students build a sturdy, nonrobotic vehicle using LEGO bricks and other materials, and they use design journals to learn the engineering design process. As a result of this activity, students will understand that LEGO bricks and other materials can fit together to form sturdy structures, and the engineering design process is useful for planning and guiding the creation of artifacts.

Lesson 2. What Is a Robot? Students describe the components of a robot, including the brain, motors, and wires. They upload a program to a robot via the tangible blocks or computer interface and build a sturdy, robotic vehicle using LEGO bricks and other materials. Through these activities, the students come to understand that robots need moving parts, such as motors, to be able to perform behaviors specified by a program. The robotic brain has the programmed instructions that make the robot perform its behaviors; and it must communicate with the motors for them to function.

Lesson 3. Hokey-Pokey (sequence of commands). The students select the appropriate block corresponding to a planned robot action, then connect a series of blocks. The students then upload a program to the computer and transmit it to a robot. From these activities, students learn that each icon corresponds to a specific command; a program is a sequence of commands that is followed by a robot; and the order of the blocks dictates the order in which the robot executes the commands.

Lesson 4. Again and Again Until I Say When (loops and number parameters). The students recognize a situation that requires a program to use loops. They then write a program that loops and use parameters to modify the number of times a loop runs before the program stops. Students learn that a command or sequence of commands may be modified so that they repeat. Some programming commands, like "Repeat," can be modified with additional information. Also, a simple program that uses fewer blocks is better than a complex one that accomplishes the same goal.

Lesson 5. Through the Tunnel (sensors and loops). Students connect a light or touch sensor to the correct port on the robot. They then write a program that includes waiting for a specific condition. They learn that a robot can "feel" and "see" its surroundings through the use of sensors, and a robot can react to collected data by changing its behavior. Also, a robot can be programmed to remain on a certain task until a specific condition is met.

Lesson 6. The Robot Decides (sensors and branches). The students connect a light or touch sensor to the correct port on the robot and identify a situation that calls for a branched program. They then write a program that uses a branch. They learn that a robot can "choose" between two sequences of commands depending on the state of a given condition.

Each session follows a similar format: (1) warm-up games to introduce the new concept or powerful idea in a playful way, (2) a building and/or programming task to reinforce the powerful idea underlying the lesson, (3) working on a small project (individually or in pairs) that uses the powerful idea in a new context, (4) participate in a technology circle to share learning process and products, and (5) assessment.

After the six Tangible K sessions, the class creates a final project focusing on a particular theme. This is an opportunity to revisit the learned concepts and skills, applying them to a project related to other curricular content. The length of time for these projects varies according to the group of students and the teachers' goals, expectations, and curricular demands. These final projects are to be shared in an open house for the wider community.

Examples of children's Tangible K final projects include a robotic city, a zoo with moving animals, a dinosaur park, a circus, and a garden with robotic flowers responsive to different sensors. These projects incorporated the use of inexpensive recyclable materials. For example, one kindergarten classroom in Boston, after a field trip to the old city, constructed a robotic Freedom Trail, using cardboard boxes to recreate the historical buildings of the city and embedding light sensors and motors into the boxes to bring their buildings to life.

To supplement the structured challenges, two to three hours of free exploration are allotted throughout the curriculum. These open-ended sessions are vital for children to fully understand the complex ideas going on with their robotic creations and programs. The free-exploration sessions also serve as a time for teachers to observe students' progress and understandings. These sessions are as important for learning as the lessons themselves! In planning and adjusting the time frame of this curriculum, free-exploration sessions should not be left by the wayside. Rather, if time is tight, teachers can consider leaving out a particular lesson altogether, giving children enough time to really understand and work with the ideas they are introducing rather than skimming over all the lessons presented in this curriculum. Free exploration provides opportunities for playing with materials and ideas. This will help build a solid foundation.

A Long Sequence of Programming Commands for a Robot

Image courtesy of Marina Bers.

To date, the DevTech group at Tufts University has developed several curriculum units for use with a variety of robotics kits such as LEGO Wedo, LEGO Mindstorms, and KIWI, a developmentally appropriate robotic kit that my team and I designed for early childhood education. The units have been piloted by children in Grades preK–2.

Using the KIWI system, children program their robots by connecting together wooden blocks that are then read by the robot. Each block corresponds to one action that can be performed by the robot. Thus, programming the robot's behavior involves arrangement of a logical sequence of actions represented by wooden blocks. The curricula provide a hands-on introduction to a selection of computer programming and robotics concepts and powerful ideas that are integrated with mathematics, science, social studies, and language arts core curriculum framework.

The curriculum development work described earlier has been described in a number of publications, including Bers (2008, 2010), Bers, Seddighin, and Sullivan (2013), Sullivan, Kazakoff, and Bers (2013), and Kazakoff, Sullivan, and Bers (2013).

Instructional Considerations

Modifications. Some students may benefit from further division of the activities into smaller steps or from more time to explore each new concept before moving onto the next, either in the context of free exploration or with teacher design challenges. Each of the powerful ideas here can easily be expanded into a unit of study. For instance, students could explore a range of different activities and challenges with sensors to learn how they work in more depth.

Teacher as Facilitator. The theory of constructionism developed by Seymour Papert shows that children learn best when they construct digital artifacts and knowledge by playing with and exploring concrete materials. The social context of these explorations is also crucial, and teachers can provide scaffolding by creating a learning environment that supports children's explorations and experimentation. Through questions and observations, the teacher engages students in articulating and extending their own observations, thought processes, and explorations. The teacher may not directly answer students' questions but rather show them how to find it themselves. This kind of exploration fosters an environment in which what we often see as "failure" is a natural step of the learning process, a signal to ask questions and explore further.

The Design Process. The engineering design process of building and the computational thinking involved in programming foster *competence* in computer literacy and technological fluency. The classroom practice of having children keep design journals during the process of creating robots helps make transparent to the children (as well as teachers and parents) their own thinking, their learning trajectories, and the project's evolution over time. Like the scientific method, the formal steps of the engineering design process—posing a problem, doing research, planning, developing a prototype, testing, redesigning, and sharing solutions—give students a tool for systematically addressing a problem.

Journals and Learning Style. Tangible K design journals may provide more or less structured paths for children to navigate the process from idea to product by scaffolding these formal steps. A journal may have worksheets to address all steps of the design process or simply white pages to invite imagination; at best, they have a combination of both. This individualization is important. Some children need constraints and top-down planning in order to work effectively. Others do not like to plan in advance. They might belong to a group of learners characterized as "tinkerers" who engage in dialogues and negotiations with the technology. They enjoy working bottom up, messing around with the materials to come up with ideas as they create, design, build, and program. Both learning styles are conducive for building competence in the technological domain.

Creativity. The Tangible K approach is based on the promotion of creativity, as opposed to efficiency, in problem solving. The approach is informed by the original meaning of the word *engineering,* which derives from the Latin *ingenium* meaning "innate quality, mental power, clever invention." The program integrates media such as LEGO pieces, motors, sensors, recyclable materials, arts and crafts materials, and graphical elements from the programming language. In the process of solving technical problems in creative ways with these media, children develop *confidence* in their learning potential.

Managing Frustration. However, clever or creative projects may be difficult to make, and the process can be frustrating. After many tries, the jaw of a child's robotic crocodile still may not open or her car may break every time it turns to the left. To avoid frustration, some teachers carefully choose the projects for children to work on or provide step-by-step directions. Such a strategy may shelter children from what Alan Kay calls the "hard fun" of creative learning. Instead, the Tangible K approach aims to help children learn to manage frustration—an important step toward the development of confidence in one's ability to learn. The learning environment is set up to create a culture in which it is expected that things may not work and in which succeeding the first time is seen as a rarity, perhaps as a sign that the child might not have challenged herself. As children go through the program, they gradually realize their ability to find solutions by trying multiple times, by using different strategies, or by asking for help.

Collaboration. Most educational robotic programs for older children, such as the National Robotics Challenge and FIRST (For Inspiration and Recognition of Science and Technology), are set up as competitions in which robots have to accomplish a given task, usually with the goal of outperforming other robots. However, research has shown that most females do not respond well to teaching strategies that stress competition; such strategies also might not always be appropriate in the early childhood setting. The Tangible K learning environment, instead of focusing on competition, promotes sharing resources and *caring* about each other.

The use of collaboration webs fosters collaboration. At the beginning of each day of work, each child receives, along with the design journal, a personalized printout with his or her photograph in the center of the page and the photographs and names of all other children in the class arranged in a circle surrounding that central photo (see p. 133). Throughout the day, at the teacher's prompting, each child draws a line from his or her own photo to the photos of the children with whom he or she has collaborated. (Collaboration is defined as getting or giving help with a project, programming together, lending or borrowing materials, or working together on a common task.) At the end of the week, children write or draw "thank-you cards" to the children with whom they have collaborated the most.

Communication. Communication is an important feature of the Tangible K curriculum, which includes mechanisms that promote a sense of *connection* between peers or between peers and adults. One feature that encourages communication is technology circles. During technology circles, children and adults stop their work, put their projects on the table or floor, sit down in a circle together, and share the state of their projects. This is similar to other circle times that children are exposed to in kindergarten.

Technology circles present an opportunity for debugging as a community—that is, for solving technical problems in programming or building. The teacher starts the technology circle by asking children to show their projects and asking questions such as "What worked as expected and what didn't?" "What are you trying to accomplish?" "What do you need to know in order to make it happen?" The teacher then uses children's projects and questions to highlight powerful ideas illustrated by the projects. The curriculum emerges based on what this particular learning community needs to know. This approach provides technical information on demand, based on emerging needs, and is an alternative to lectures. Technology circles can be called as often as every 20 minutes at the beginning of a project or only once at the end of a day of work, depending on the needs of the children and the teacher's need to introduce new concepts.

Community Building. Community-building techniques in Tangible K programs scaffold support networks that promote each child's *contribution* to the learning environment and community. In the spirit of the Reggio Emilia approach (started in municipal infant-toddler centers and preschools of Reggio Emilia, Italy, after World War II), the children's projects are shared with the community via an open house, demonstration day, or exhibition. An open house provides authentic opportunities for children to share and celebrate the processes and tangible products of their learning with others who are invested in their learning, such as family, friends, and community members. These public displays make learning visible to others and to the children themselves.

Choices of Conduct. Tangible K activities provide opportunities for children to experiment with "what if" questions and consider potential consequences of their own choices. Choices of conduct are not only made by children. Teachers also make important decisions that affect what the children do. For example, if the LEGO building pieces are sorted by types and placed in bins in the center of the room (instead of given to each child or group as a presorted robotic kit), children learn to take what they need without depleting the bins of the "most wanted" pieces, such as special sensors or the colorful LEGO minifigures. They also learn how to negotiate for what they need.

For teachers using the Tangible K program, helping children develop an inner compass to guide their actions in a just and responsible way is as important as the focus on learning about robotics. The program's emphasis on choices of conduct may provoke examination of values and exploration of *character traits*. Differentiation of roles can be important to the growth of a responsible learning community. In any classroom, for example, one child may learn very quickly about mechanics, while another may become a programming expert, and still another may easily problem-solve or skillfully mediate conflicts among group members. Such children may be assigned "expertise badges" by teachers or by the other children. Those children who are seen as especially skilled at something can make the choice to help classmates build a bigger structure or address other challenges. Children are also encouraged to take on new roles and be flexible; there is a badge for "expert on trying new things."

The research that supports the instructional methods described in this section has been documented in a number of publications, including Papert (1980, 1991), Bers (2008), and Lee, Sullivan, and Bers (2013).

Connections to the Next Generation Science Standards

The powerful ideas underlying the Tangible K curriculum were developed to support *Standards for Technological Literacy* (ITEA, 2000, 2005, 2007) and the *Massachusetts Science and Technology/Engineering Curriculum Framework* (Massachusetts Department of Education, 2006). However, the curriculum is also well aligned with all three dimensions of the NGSS (NGSS Lead States, 2013): science and engineering practices, core ideas, and crosscutting concepts.

Science and Engineering Practices. Appendix F in the NGSS describes the eight practices of science and engineering that are appropriate for students in Grades K–2. In our opinion, the Tangible K curriculum provides an environment and series of challenges to meet all eight performance expectations at the K–2 level. That is, students define the problems they wish to solve (with assistance), develop and use computational models, design solutions, argue from evidence, and so on. However, regarding the practice of mathematics and computational thinking, the Tangible K curriculum enables students to meet the following expectations defined at the middle school level, albeit at a level that is less sophisticated than would be expected of middle school students.

- Create algorithms (a series of ordered steps) to solve a problem
- Use digital tools and/or mathematical concepts and arguments to test and compare proposed solutions to an engineering design problem

Core Ideas. Three core ideas in engineering design are defined in the NGSS for Grades K–2:

K-2-ETS1–1. Ask questions, make observations, and gather information about a situation people want to change to define a simple problem that can be solved through the development of a new or improved object or tool.

K-2-ETS1–2. Develop a simple sketch, drawing, or physical model to illustrate how the shape of an object helps it function as needed to solve a given problem.

K-2-ETS1–3. Analyze data from tests of two objects designed to solve the same problem to compare the strengths and weaknesses of how each performs.

The powerful ideas underlying the Tangible K curriculum are essentially problem-defining and problem-solving tools that enable students to accomplish the above in the context of computational thinking. For example, in order to program a robot, the students need to first define the problem they are attempting to solve. The robots are physical models that are put through their paces to test the students' creative solutions. And the students frequently test their creations and compare their results with those of other students who were attempting to solve the same (or a similar) problem.

Crosscutting Concepts. Appendix G in the NGSS describes seven crosscutting concepts that are appropriate for students in Grades K–2. Here too the Tangible K curriculum helps students develop their understanding of crosscutting concepts. For example, programming computers helps students recognize patterns, especially when using loops and sequences. The crosscutting concept of cause and effect is reinforced as students program their robots to respond autonomously to input from their sensors. The crosscutting concept of systems and system models is also evident in the Tangible K curriculum because the robot is both a system of interacting parts and a model of a system, as it mimics the ability of a person to react autonomously to the input from our senses.

Connections to Other Areas of the Curriculum

The Tangible K robotics program is explicitly designed to address "the missing middle letters" of STEM in early childhood education—the T (technology) and the E (engineering). However, for the program to be successfully adopted in classrooms, it must integrate and facilitate the introduction of other curricular content, both in terms of themes and disciplinary concepts and skills (Bers, Ponte, Juelich, Viera, & Schenker, 2002). Following are several clear connections between powerful ideas from the Tangible K curriculum and other domains of knowledge.

Sequencing, Control, and Flow. A sequence of instructions can be described in a program and acted out in order by a robot. Disciplinary connections: literacy: storytelling, "how-to" books, symbolic system, setting up controlled experiments, basic explorations of geometry, cause and effect.

Loops. Sequences of instructions can be modified to repeat indefinitely or in a controlled way. Disciplinary connections: expanded geometry explorations, time, cycles, symbols used to communicate a message.

Parameters. Some instructions can be qualified with additional information. Disciplinary connections: expanded geometry explorations, number sense, timing and control.

Sensors. Devices measure a change in the environment and convert it into a signal that can be read by an observer, an instrument, or a robot. Disciplinary connections: natural and human-made world; biology: sensing in animals and humans.

Branches. Some instructions in a program ask questions and, depending on the answer, have a robot do one thing or another. Disciplinary connections: cause and effect, logic, expanded scientific observations, executive, function skills, decision making.

Theory

Computational Thinking. The Tangible K curriculum introduces young children to *computational thinking*, which can be defined as a type of analytical thinking that shares many similarities with mathematical thinking (e.g., problem solving), engineering thinking (designing and evaluating processes), and scientific thinking (systematic analysis). The foundation for computational thinking is abstraction—abstracting concepts from cases and evaluating and selecting the "right" abstraction. It relies on selection of inputs (manipulation of variables and computational instructions), observation of outputs (outcome data), and decomposition of what happens in between. Computational thinking involves the ability to abstract from computational instructions (programming languages) to computational behaviors, to identify potential "bugs" or errors to fix, to decide what details among the input-computation-output algorithm to highlight and retain and what details to discard. Wing (2006) describes computational thinking as a fundamental skill for everyone, not just for computer scientists.

The term computational thinking grew out of the pioneer work of Seymour Papert and colleagues on design-based constructionist programming environments; the term was used to refer to ways to algorithmically solve problems and to acquire technological fluency (Papert, 1980, 1991). Previous work on elementary school children and computational thinking can be found in the research literature on constructionist programming environments (Clements, 1999; Flannery & Bers, 2013; Repenning, Webb, & Ioannidou, 2010; Resnick et al., 2009).

Theoretical Framework. The theoretical foundation that guided the development, implementation, and evaluation of this robotics curriculum is called Positive Technological Development (PTD). The PTD framework is a natural extension of the computer literacy and the technological fluency movements that have influenced the world of education but adds psychosocial and ethical components to the cognitive ones. PTD is an interdisciplinary approach that integrates ideas from the fields of computer-mediated communication, computer-supported collaborative learning, and the Constructionist theory of learning developed by Seymour Papert, and views them in light of research in applied development science and positive youth development. Development of the PTD has been documented by Bers (2010, 2012).

PTD provides a model for developing and evaluating technology-rich programs by focusing on the positive ways that children can interact with technology. The model is illustrated and briefly described below.

Assets of youth development identified by decades of research on positive youth development (Bers, Doyle-Lynch, & Chau, 2012; Lerner, Almerigi, Theokas, & Lerner, 2005) are listed in the left-hand column: caring, connection, contribution, competence, confidence, and character.

Positive behaviors that should be supported by educational programs that use new educational technologies such as robotics are listed in the center column. These include communication, collaboration, community-building, content creation, creativity, and choices of conduct.

Classroom practices that support and encourage positive behaviors and assets of youth development are listed in the right-hand column. These include tech circles, the collaboration web, open house, design processes, final projects, and expertise badges.

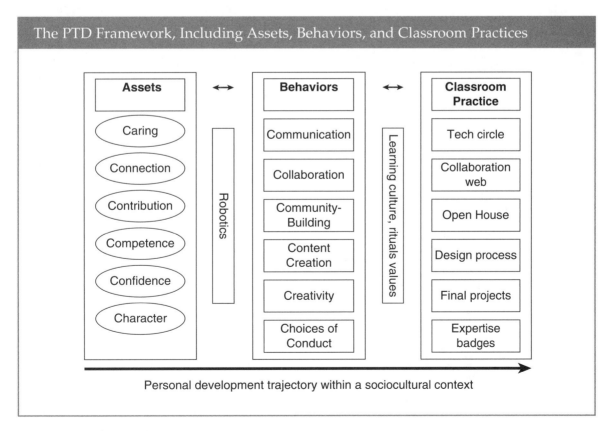

Image courtesy of Marina Bers.

PTD takes into consideration the learning environment and the pedagogical practices, cultural values, and rituals that mediate teaching and learning, and therefore the introduction of a robotics curriculum such as Tangible K (Rogoff, Goodman Turkanis, & Bartlett, 2001).

Assessment

The PTD framework shown on the previous page provides guidelines both for designing the educational program and for evaluating children's learning and development. *Content creation* and *creativity* (the first two "Cs") are evaluated in terms of competence (or level of understanding) and confidence in the domain. The following are used to assess content creation and creativity:

- **Student's portfolios** are composed of student's design journals, their programming samples (code), and robotic projects. Change over time in the level of sophistication and complexity is assessed.
- **Video journals** are recordings made at least three times during the program (e.g., beginning, middle, and end) showing what the children have been working on and explaining their activities.
- **A rubric of levels of understanding** is a set of questions for the teacher or researcher to complete at the end of each session to assess each child's level of understanding on a scale of 0 to 5 for each learning objective.

Children's collaboration and communication skills are evaluated in terms of the levels of caring and connection achieved by the children by analyzing the collaboration webs over time (Lee et al., 2013) and the children's participation in the technology circles.

Finally, community building and choices of conduct are evaluated by looking at a child's overall participation and engagement in the Tangible K program and her *contributions* to the learning environment, in particular during the final project presented at the open house. Expertise badges are seen as representative of the child's character traits. Change over time is analyzed.

Assessment in the Tangible K program, unlike most programs focused on technological literacy, addresses not only the cognitive dimension but extends also to the social and the moral dimensions of the child's experience through and with the technology, toward a goal of helping the child develop in an integrated and holistic way.

In terms of research, the evaluation goals guiding the Tangible K robotics program are twofold. The first goal is to provide an evidence-based systematic account of children's learning of components of the PTD framework. The second goal is to establish potential learning trajectories of design tasks with incremental levels of difficulty, matched to the children's levels of understanding (Clements & Sarama, 2009). Future work related to Tangible K robotics will focus on developing new curriculum modules, implementing a less costly robotics system that uses everyday materials, and constructing a solid theoretical model for learning trajectories in this area.

Conclusion

The Tangible K curriculum presented in this chapter brings engineering and computational thinking to the early childhood classroom. It does so by focusing on six powerful ideas: robotics; the engineering design; sequencing, control, and flow; loops and parameters; sensors; and branches. Following the PTD theoretical framework, this curriculum emphasizes not only the cognitive aspects of learning how to build and program a robot but also the psychosocial and ethical dimensions of teamwork.

References

Bers, M. U. (2008). *Blocks, robots and computers: Learning about technology in early childhood.* New York, NY: Teacher's College Press.

Bers, M. U. (2010). The Tangible K robotics program: Applied computational thinking for young children. *Early Childhood Research and Practice, 12*(2).

Bers, M. U. (2012). *Designing digital experiences for positive youth development: From playpen to playground.* Cary, NC: Oxford University Press.

Bers, M. U., Doyle-Lynch, A., & Chau, C. (2012). Positive technological development: The multifaceted nature of youth technology use toward improving self and society. In C. C. Ching & B. J. Foley (Eds.), *Constructing the self in a digital world* (pp. 110–136). New York, NY: Cambridge University Press.

Bers, M. U., Ponte, I., Juelich, K., Viera, A., & Schenker, J. (2002). Teachers as designers: Integrating robotics into early childhood education. *Information Technology in Childhood Education, 123–145.*

Bers, M. U., Seddighin, S., & Sullivan, A. (2013). Ready for robotics: Bringing together the T and E of STEM in early childhood teacher education. *Journal of Technology and Teacher Education, 21*(3), 355–377.

Clements, D. (1999). The future of educational computing research: The case of computer programming. *Information Technology in Childhood Education Annual, 147–179.*

Clements, D., & Sarama, J. (2009). *Learning and teaching early math: The learning trajectories approach.* New York, NY: Routledge.

Flannery, L. P., & Bers, M. U. (2013). Let's dance the "Robot Hokey-Pokey!": Children's programming approaches and achievement throughout early cognitive development. *Journal of Research on Technology in Education, 46*(1), 81–101.

International Technology and Engineering Education Association. (2000, 2005, 2007). *Standards for technological literacy: Content for the study of technology.* Reston, VA: Author.

Kazakoff, E., Sullivan, A., & Bers, M. U. (2013). The effect of a classroom-based intensive robotics and programming workshop on sequencing ability in early childhood. *Early Childhood Education Journal, 41*(4), 245.

Lee, K., Sullivan, A., & Bers, M. U. (2013). Collaboration by design: Using robotics to foster social interaction in Kindergarten. *Computers in the Schools, 30*(3), 271–281.

Lerner, R. M., Almerigi, J. B., Theokas, C., & Lerner, J. V. (2005). Positive youth development: A view of the issues. *Journal of Early Adolescence, 25*(1), 10–16.

Massachusetts Department of Education,. (2006). *Massachusetts Science and Technology/Engineering Curriculum Framework.* Boston: Author.

NGSS Lead States. (2013). *Next Generation Science Standards: For states, by states.* Washington, DC: The National Academies Press.

Papert, S. (1980). *Mindstorms: Children, computers, and powerful ideas.* New York, NY: Basic Books.

Papert, S. (1991). What's the big idea: Towards a pedagogy of idea power. *IBM Systems Journal, 39*(3–4), 720–729.

Repenning, A., Webb, D., & Ioannidou, A. (2010). Scalable game design and the development of a checklist for getting computational thinking into public schools. *Proceedings of the 41st ACM Technical Symposium on Computer Science Education, 265–269.*

Resnick, M., Maloney, J., Monroy-Hernandez, A., Rusk, N., Eastmond, E., Brennan, K., . . . Kafai, Y. (2009). Scratch: Programming for all. *Communications of the ACM, 52*(11), 60.

Rogoff, B., Goodman Turkanis, C., & Bartlett, L. (2001). Learning together: Children and adults in a school community. New York, NY: Oxford University Press.

Sullivan, A., Kazakoff, E. R., & Bers, M. U. (2013). The wheels on the bot go round and round: Robotics curriculum in pre-kindergarten. *Journal of Information Technology Education: Innovations in Practice, 12,* 203–219.

Wing, J. M. (2006). Computational thinking. *Communications of the ACM, 49*(3), 33–35. Retrieved from http://www.cs.cmu.edu/afs/cs/usr/wing/www/publications/Wing06.pdf.

9

Engineering Adventures

Engineering for Out-of-School Time

Melissa Higgins and Christine Cunningham,
Engineering is Elementary,
Museum of Science, Boston, Massachusetts

Students figure out how to redesign their structure to prevent shearing during an earthquake.

Image courtesy of Engineering is Elementary.

Engineering Adventures (EA) is an engineering curriculum created specifically for out-of-school time (OST) afterschool and camp programs. Aimed at children in Grades 3–5, EA units introduce the engineering design process, guiding children to ask questions, imagine, plan, create, and improve solutions to real-world problems. Units consist of six to ten 45-minute activities. The engineering challenges presented in EA give children the opportunity to apply and reinforce the science and engineering practices put forth by the Next Generation Science Standards (NGSS), inviting children to further use and integrate the science, technology, engineering, and mathematics (STEM) concepts they learn during the school day.

EA has been developed by the Engineering is Elementary team and is published by the Museum of Science, Boston.

What Is Engineering Adventures?

Every day people all around the world are engineering. In Senegal, a boy visits the local scrap market and imagines designs for toy cars made from recycled materials. In Australia, a girl creates a humane trap to catch the cane toads in her backyard that nibble on her dog's food. In California, a boy blowing bubbles adds rings to the wand so he can make more bubbles faster.

The engineering tasks described here are just a few examples of the challenges presented in EA units. With help from India and Jacob (a pair of fictional teenagers who travel the world), children learn about engineering problems around the globe. Armed with the engineering design process (EDP) (see below) as a problem-solving tool, children are guided to successfully engineer innovative solutions to these real-world challenges.

EA units can be downloaded free of charge at www.engineeringadventures.org. Full units, evaluation reports, and comments from OST educators using EA are also available on our website and can help to paint a fuller picture of the program.

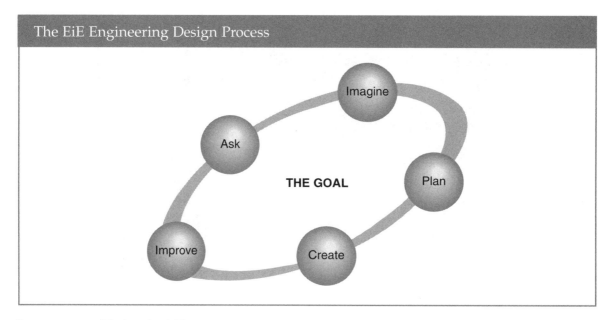

The EiE Engineering Design Process

Image courtesy of Engineering is Elementary.

Engineering is Elementary, created by the same team that developed EA, was designed for elementary-age children in school settings. Engineering is Elementary is featured in Chapter 7.

The EA curriculum development team has created units that are designed to bolster children's engineering skills through engaging challenges. *To the Rescue: Engineering Aid Drop Packages* guides children to engineer packages of much-needed supplies for residents of Thailand who have been isolated through flooding. The packages will need to keep supplies from breaking when dropped from an airplane and will also need to clearly communicate the contents to the intended user. *Shake Things Up: Engineering Earthquake Resistant Buildings* teaches children about the 2010 earthquake that destroyed many buildings in Haiti. Using models, children engineer earthquake-resistant buildings and develop a list of building codes. Other units incorporate the engineering problems from Australia, Senegal, and California that were mentioned above. The EA team has developed seven engineering units and plans to develop three more to complete the series. Information about the first seven EA units can be found in Table 9.1.

We have found that setting the context for an engineering challenge by using a real scenario helps children connect engineering to the world in which they live and makes them more invested in the problem. This investment, along with understanding of the engineering design process, leads to persistence, innovation, thoughtful problem solving, and, ultimately, to children identifying themselves as talented engineers.

The following section offers a closer look at one EA unit, *Shake Things Up: Engineering Earthquake Resistant Buildi*ngs, which helps to illustrate how the skills and challenges presented in a unit relate to the NGSS (NGSS Lead States, 2013).

Table 9.1 EA Units

Title	Engineering Field	Location
Hop to It: Safe Removal of Invasive Species	Mechanical	Australia & New Zealand
Bubble Bonanza: Engineering Bubble Wands	Materials	California, USA
To the Rescue: Engineering Aid Drop Packages	Package	Thailand
Shake Things Up: Engineering Earthquake Resistant Buildings	Earthquake	Haiti
Go Green: Engineering Recycled Racers	Green	Senegal
Liftoff: Engineering Rockets and Rovers	Aerospace	NASA's Jet Propulsion Lab and the International Space Station
Sky's the Limit: Engineering Flying Devices	Aeronautical	The Empty Quarter (Arabian Peninsula)

Prep Adventure 1: What Is Engineering? Tower Power

In this activity, children are challenged to engineer an index card tower that supports a stuffed animal. The activity is intended to introduce children to the EDP as a tool they can use to help solve problems. It also exemplifies the quick, iterative, team-based design work that will be used throughout the rest of the unit.

Because this activity is written as a broad introduction to engineering and the EDP, it allows children to engage in all Grades 3–5 performance expectations put forth by the NGSS. Children must define their problem and clarify the criteria and constraints by asking questions (3–5-ETS1–1). They work within their groups to discuss possible solutions (3–5-ETS1–2), choose one to plan and create, and finally test their towers and discuss possible improvements (3–5-ETS1–3).

Prep Adventure 2: What Is Technology? Technology Detectives

Children examine several technologies in this adventure, imagining ways to improve them. They are introduced to the ideas that technologies are any things created by people to help solve a problem or meet a need and that engineers are the people who design technologies.

This activity focuses primarily on the first two Grades 3–5 performance expectations. Children need to think carefully about the problem that a given technology was designed to solve (3–5-EST1–1) and then generate ideas about new technologies that might help to solve the problem in a different way (3–5-ETS1–2).

Adventure 1: A Shaky Situation

India and Jacob, the fictional characters who appear in each EA unit, introduce the earthquake engineering challenge to children by explaining that they have traveled to the country of Haiti and learned about the massive 2010 earthquake that destroyed many buildings. After watching a video about the earthquake, children build and experiment with a shake table that they will use to conduct testing throughout the rest of the unit (see opposite).

While EA units are primarily written to reinforce skills and practices, this adventure is an example of how lessons can be also written to introduce links to science content. When experimenting with the shake table, children are investigating how forces affect the motion of an object (3-PS2–1). They are also likely beginning to recognize patterns (3-PS2–2 and 3-PS2–3) related to use of the shake table and the resulting force (pulling back the shake table further results in a greater force—a stronger shake—that has a resulting stronger force on objects sitting on the shake table). A "magnitude meter" is used so comparisons can be made across groups (3–5-ETS1–3).

Adventure 2: Building Skeletons

In this adventure, children begin to focus on the crux of their challenge to engineer earthquake-resistant buildings. They first make building "units" or pieces that act as the interior skeletons for their buildings. Children think specifically about how the configuration (shape and size) in which they arrange the building units might impact the building's ability to resist earthquakes.

This adventure provides children with the chance to more precisely explore the effect of pushes and pulls on the models they will be working to stabilize throughout the unit. They will investigate how the possible configurations of their building units might make the model more or less balanced (3-PS2–1). Because they are easily able to change the configuration of their building models, they will likely start

Children Constructing Shake Tables

Image courtesy of Engineering is Elementary.

to recognize patterns in the types of arrangements that are most stable (3-PS2–2 and 3-PS2–3). They will be able to apply what they learn here as they design their earthquake resistant buildings later on.

Adventure 3: Stop the Slide

Just as the above-ground configuration of a building impacts its ability to withstand an earthquake, the way in which a structure is attached to the ground can also play a role in its stability. This activity asks children to experiment with engineered solutions for attaching their buildings to the "ground" (or in the case of their models, the shake tables) (See p. 152).

Focusing on one aspect of the design challenge (attaching their models to the ground), children can quickly iterate different solutions during this activity to determine an optimal way to keep buildings in place during an earthquake (4-ESS3–2).

Adventure 4: Getting Braces

The side-to-side shaking motion commonly created during an earthquake can cause the top and bottom of a given building to move in opposite directions at the same time. This is known as shearing. Bracing a building can help to prevent destructive shearing motions. In this adventure children experiment with different types and orientations of materials to engineer braces that prevent their model buildings from shearing.

Children are able to use and test a variety of bracing materials during this activity, with the goal of identifying braces that would reduce the shearing impact of the earthquake (4-ESS3–2).

(Continued)

(Continued)

Student Tests Her Building Unit on a Shake Table

Image courtesy of Engineering is Elementary.

Adventure 5: Creating an Earthquake-Resistant Building

The last three adventures in each EA unit follow a similar pattern. In one session, children create their technology, applying and combining all they have learned in the previous adventures. In another session, they improve their technology. Finally, children present their technology and knowledge of the EDP through an Engineering Showcase.

In the "Create" adventure for the *Shake Things Up* unit, children first work with their groups to choose a specific building type and structure they would like to work with (two-story school, one-story home, four-story skyscraper, etc.). They are then guided to focus on the Imagine, Plan, and Create steps of the EDP as they design a building that can withstand a 7.0-magnitude earthquake on their shake tables.

This activity requires children to incorporate much of the data they gathered from the previous lessons. While children are free to choose the type of building they would like to work on, each comes with its own unique set of criteria (an apartment building must have at least eight building units) and constraints on materials (no more than 50 other items can be used to stabilize the apartment building) (3–5-ETS1–1). Children should have time to do at least one test of their design and begin to generate improvement ideas for the next session (3–5-ETS1–2).

Adventure 6: Improving an Earthquake-Resistant Building

This adventure gives children a chance to revisit their design and address any issues they recognized while first creating and testing their earthquake-resistant buildings. Often a much-needed adventure for many groups, the Improve session underscores the idea that engineering is an iterative process, and creating something that is not quite perfect during the first try is in fact a common and useful part of engineering. Throughout previous adventures, children were asked to think about building codes they would recommend to create earthquake-resistant structures. In this adventure, children are also asked to finalize the list of building codes they have been creating throughout the course of the unit.

Engaging in the improve step of the design process is a critical part of engineering since it pushes children to try multiple solutions, allowing for continued learning and advancement rather than failure (4-ESS3–2).

Adventure 7: Engineering Showcase: Shake Things Up

We suggest inviting family, friends, and others from the OST program to attend the showcase. This is a time for children to present the engineering work that they have done—both the actual technology they created and the EDP they used to scaffold their work. As a "grand finale," children connect all of their shake tables and earthquake-resistant building designs in order to create a model city. Their final test is to create a 7.0-magnitude earthquake using all the shake tables at once to see how the city withstands the earthquake (below).

Buildings Connected to Make a Model City

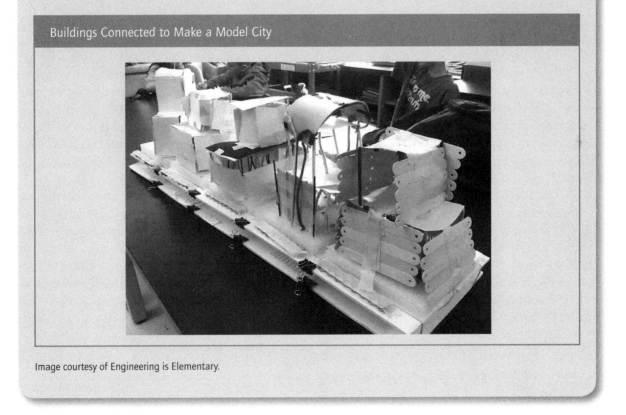

Image courtesy of Engineering is Elementary.

The Engineering Showcase provides a space for children to practice their engineering communication skills as they use evidence to justify their design decisions and communicate their results to others. Obtaining, evaluating, and communicating information is one of the practices from the NGSS. At the Grades 3–5 level, students are expected to "communicate scientific and/or technical information orally and/or in written formats" (NGSS Lead States, 2013, p. 65).

EA and the NGSS

The EA unit *Shake Things Up: Engineering Earthquake-Resistant Buildings* exemplifies the focus on engineering and science practices that EA developers believe lead to successful engineering curricula for OST. The *Shake Things Up* unit includes two preparatory activities and seven earthquake engineering-focused activities.

The EA team believes strongly that OST programs can and should strengthen children's engineering skills. Because EA focuses on skill building, we do not claim that an EA unit *teaches* a particular science or engineering content standard. Rather, we prefer to say that EA units teach engineering and science practices, and link to various science and engineering content. Children are not expected to be familiar with any particular science or engineering content prior to engaging in the unit—they should be able to glean all they will need from actively participating in the challenge.

The NGSS states that "the performance expectations in elementary school grade bands develop ideas and skills that will allow students to explain more complex phenomena in the four disciplines as they progress to middle school and high school" (NGSS Lead States, 2013, p. 2). By supporting the engineering performance expectations, EA units are creating a strong foundation for further engineering exploration both in and out of school as children grow.

The five-step EDP that forms the foundational structure for all EA units meshes well with the engineering practices. As a tool that scaffolds the critical thinking required to effectively reach a goal, the utility of the EDP extends beyond engineering lessons and into the larger world of children as problem solvers. While each EA unit touches upon a variety of science and engineering topics relevant to the specific design challenge outlined in the unit, the appearance of the EDP in each unit ensures reinforcement of the science and engineering practices put forth by the NGSS. The EDP presented in EA includes the following steps: Ask, Imagine, Plan, Create, and Improve. As shown in Table 9.2, these five steps reflect the Science and Engineering Practices for Grades 3–5 outlined in the NGSS.

Both the EDP from EA and the Science and Engineering Practices articulate a clear expectation for designing and improving multiple solutions. Implied in this expectation is a shift from framing failure as a negative outcome to embracing failure as an opportunity to learn from what did not work. Unexpected results provide chances to gather further information that will be applied in the next design iteration. The cyclical nature of the EDP and anticipation of multiple solutions help allay fears of failure. The focus on the process of engineering rather than a strict focus on the resulting product allow EA units to meet the goals of helping children gain confidence about their abilities and skills as engineers.

Criteria and Constraints for Engineering in OST

The Engineering is Elementary team at the Museum of Science, Boston, began development of the EA curriculum in 2010, shortly after development of the in-school Engineering is Elementary curriculum was completed. (For more information about the Engineering is Elementary curriculum, see Chapter 1.) When the Engineering is Elementary curriculum development team made this switch from creating in-school to afterschool and camp curricula, we were immediately presented with several new challenges—new criteria and constraints to put it in engineering terms. The value OST programs place on pursuing individual interests was a natural match for the social constructivist pedagogy that shapes both Engineering is Elementary and EA units. Both our in-school and out-of-school units allow children to create their own understandings with the help and support of peers.

Table 9.2 The EA EPD as Compared With the Grades 3–5 Science and Engineering Practices

Engineering Adventures Engineering Design Process	NGSS Grades 3–5 Science and Engineering Practices
Ask: • Children define the problem, including criteria and constraints. • Children generate questions they will need to answer in order to gather more information about the challenge. These might be questions about science phenomena, properties of materials, or how others have solved similar problems.	**Asking Questions and Defining Problems** Asking questions and defining problems in 3–5 builds on Grades K–2 experiences and progresses to specifying qualitative relationships. • 3-5-ETS1-1. Define a simple design problem that can be solved through the development of an object, tool, process, or system and includes several criteria for successes and constraints on materials, time, or cost.
Imagine: • Children brainstorm solutions (technologies) that could help solve the problem. **Plan:** • From the possible solutions imagined and using information gathered during investigations, children decide on one possible solution. They think carefully about what their research data and observations have revealed about attributes of successful solutions as they create a plan and materials list for their first design.	**Planning and Carrying Out Investigations** Planning and carrying out investigations to answer questions or test solutions to problems in 3–5 builds on K–2 experiences and progresses to include investigations that control variables and provide evidence to support explanations or design solutions. • 3-5-ETS1-3. Plan and conduct an investigation collaboratively to produce data to serve as the basis for evidence, using fair tests in which variables are controlled and the number of trials considered.
Create: • Children create and test their design based on their plan, identifying strengths and weaknesses. **Improve:** • Based on testing, group discussion, and observations of other designs that are working well, children improve their designs by cycling through some or all steps of the EDP.	Constructing Explanations and Designing Solutions Constructing explanations and designing solutions in 3–5 builds on K–2 experiences and progresses to the use of evidence in constructing explanations that specify variables that describe and predict phenomena and in designing multiple solutions to design problems. • 3-5-ETS1-2. Generate and compare multiple solutions to a problem based on how well they meet the criteria and constraints of the design problem.

But children and educators come to OST programs with myriad background experiences, science knowledge, and expectations. That creates unique requirements. Classroom curricula can be written assuming students have some shared science and engineering content learning. Testing shows that successful OST engineering curricula cannot make these assumptions. In addition, most OST program staff have expressed to us that they strongly prefer, and even expect, that successful curricula for OST programs be self-contained. All the knowledge that educators and children will need to successfully complete the challenge must be built within unit activities.

Given the complex realities of OST, stakeholders in the OST community have long debated what can reasonably be expected of afterschool and camp programs in regard to STEM. A recent study, Defining Youth Outcomes in Afterschool (Afterschool Alliance, 2013), begins to outline possible results. The findings echo the longstanding beliefs of the EA developers about valid goals and outcomes for OST. The study indicated OST programs can and should help children to

- develop an interest in STEM and STEM learning activities;
- develop capacities to productively engage in STEM learning activities; and
- come to value the goals of STEM and STEM learning activities.

The capacity to ask questions, plan and carry out investigations, and design solutions as outlined in the NGSS will undoubtedly help to meet the STEM goals for OST as outlined by the Afterschool Alliance. Actively and rigorously supporting the science and engineering practices in OST environments therefore seamlessly support the goals of educators and stakeholders in both formal and informal education environments.

Who Should Teach Engineering Adventures?

OST educators come from a wide variety of backgrounds. Near-peer educators enrolled in high school or college are frequent facilitators of OST activities. In some cases, educators have a background in youth development or the arts. Occasionally educators may have educational or job experience in STEM. The EA curriculum is designed to be easy to use for all educators.

EA units are written in a way that allows educators with no background in science or engineering to facilitate the activities. Although we assume EA educators will have some basic classroom management and pedagogical understandings about positive and successful ways to work with children, we do not assume any content-related background knowledge. In the introduction section of EA units, we suggest that educators may want to embark on the engineering challenge alongside the children in their program. This type of parallel work can in fact help to reinforce the idea that initial designs are rarely successful and the design process is iterative—no matter your age or experience!

Because EA activities focus on the development of engineering skills and 21st century skills, such as teamwork and collaboration, anyone can facilitate these activities. EA challenges allow a multitude of possible solutions instead of a single "right answer." So educators do not have to guide children to a predetermined end point. The open-ended nature of EA units can be just as liberating for educators as for children.

Instructional Materials

The EA curriculum developers strongly believe in creating materials that are rooted in the reality of OST programs. For many OST programs, funding is a significant constraint. The EA curriculum was designed with this in mind. EA units (which include an educator guide and engineering journals for children) can be downloaded at no cost. The hands-on materials required to complete each challenge are chosen with cost and ease of access in mind. Educators can purchase full materials kits or gather their own materials with the help of a complete shopping list included in the introductory section of each educator guide.

The educator guide contains all the information that an educator needs to facilitate the unit's activities. Each activity begins with a message from two fictional characters named India and Jacob (below). Referred to as the EA "duo," this brother and sister pair travels the world, finding engineering problems wherever they go. The duo help set the context and goals for each day's activity by sending information to the children in EA programs. This method for creating a context motivates children and helps them understand why they are working on a specific investigation or engineering challenge. It also takes the onus off of the OST educator to be the sole source of activity facilitation. The goals for the day's activity can be reinforced through multiple methods, since the educator can share a written e-mail from India and Jacob and/or play a recorded audio message. The hands-on activities that follow encourage children to carefully observe findings and to share and reflect on what they have found to be successful. The educator guide also provides suggested questions to help the educator prompt kids to think critically about their design choices.

India and Jacob are fictional characters who introduce EA challenges.

Image courtesy of Engineering is Elementary.

Each EA unit includes a series of activities (called "adventures") that culminate in a design challenge. The number of adventures in a unit varies (normally between 6–10). EA staff develop the adventures to provide children with the investigative and data-gathering experiences they will need to make successful design choices to complete their challenge. Each of the adventures in a unit takes about 45 minutes to complete, which we have found fits well within most OST program schedules.

Each unit includes two preparatory lessons; one to introduce the work of engineers and the EDP, and the other to introduce the term *technology*. In most units, students investigate the properties of materials available to use during the design challenge.

The engineering journal includes information children will need for the day's activity, as well as space to record ideas, findings, and reflections. Persuading children to record their thoughts using words or sketches can be difficult in the OST setting. Having spent a full day in school being asked to complete many paper-based tasks, some children are loathe to pick up a pencil after the final school bell has rung. For other children, though, having a place to record their ideas, draw plans, and reflect helps engage them more deeply in the engineering challenge. The curriculum development team tested and revised the EA engineering journals many times, with each revision aimed at better enticing children to track their work, record designs, and use notebooks as professional engineers might. We suggest that educators provide an engineering journal for each participating child and require or encourage completion at their discretion.

A Rubric of Success is included in the overview section of the educator guide for each unit. Given the incredibly varied backgrounds of OST educators, it is safe to assume that many have never facilitated hands-on, open-ended science or engineering activities with children. It is therefore important to give them a sense of the types of interactions or developments they might notice that would indicate the activity is successfully engaging kids as engineers. A group of children in the midst of an engineering design challenge might not look that different from a group of children creating chaos! Pointing out some key indicators to educators (such as the kids sharing ideas, persisting through difficulties, or valuing the EDP) helps educators to differentiate between the disorder of children off-track and the natural commotion of child engineers at work.

Assessment tools for EA take into consideration the reality of OST environments and the goals common to OST programs. An engineering attitudes assessment is one of the primary tools that our research and evaluation team has used to ascertain whether units are meeting the goals set by the curriculum developers. When we first began testing EA units, we included several science and engineering content questions on the assessment. Since children bring diverse backgrounds to afterschool programs, it was difficult to show reliable gains on these questions and even harder to directly link these gains with participation in EA units. We have had much more success collecting and analyzing children's writing and drawings in the engineering journals.

An engineering attitudes assessment is available on our website for educators to download, but the EA development and research teams believe educators will be able to glean all they need to know from the embedded assessments of the engineering journals and the Success Rubric included in the educator guide. These pieces help tell the full story of the skills children are building, including persistence, critical thinking, and communication.

Complete materials kits that include all of the "stuff" children need to engage in hands-on EA can be purchased, but the educator guide also includes a detailed materials list for educators who prefer to source the materials on their own. EA curriculum developers were careful to keep the cost of materials as low as possible and chose items that were easy to purchase locally (e.g., at an office supply, grocery, or hardware store). Some lessons include suggested online video links. However, since many OST programs do not have access to computers or the Internet, any critical information in the videos is also provided in children's engineering journals or through other paper-based handouts.

Impacts on Children

Evaluations completed during pilot testing of EA units have shown that the units are successfully meeting our goals to improve children's attitudes about engineering (Higgins, Hertel, Cunningham, & Lachapelle, 2013). Using a pre-post assessment, children are asked to rank their level of agreement with several statements. Children reacted more positively to the following statements after completing an EA unit than before:

> *"I would enjoy being a scientist when I grow up."*
>
> *"I would enjoy being an engineer when I grow up."*
>
> *"Engineers help make people's lives better as part of their job."*

More data about the types of gains made by children participating in EA units are found in children's engineering journals. The figure below shows two models from the journal of a child participating in the *Shake Things Up* unit. Comparing drawings from the early "create" and subsequent "improve" step of the EDP evinces the child's increased understanding of the importance of bracing against a push or pull. To engineer an earthquake-resistant building, this child changed the design and the materials used (switching from straws and pipe cleaners to craft sticks). Through testing of the initial design and re-engineering to make improvements, this child demonstrated many of the learning goals of EA, including her ability to use the design process to solve problems. This drawing also reflects the need to design multiple solutions as outlined through the performance expectations for engineering design as set forth by the NGSS.

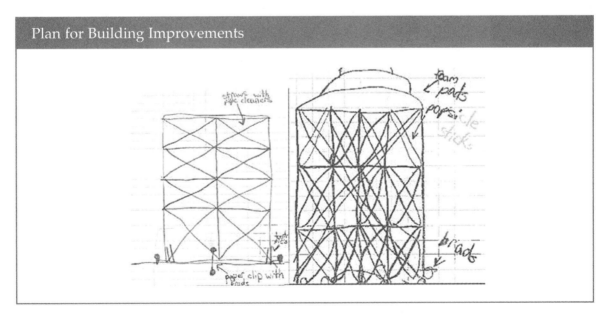

Image courtesy of Engineering is Elementary.

Evidence that EA is helping children effectively use the EDP is reinforced by asking children to reflect on their experience. The figure below shows how a child used the lens of the EDP to consider a group decision during the *Shake Things Up* unit to use toothpicks to secure the building.

This child was able to communicate the questions asked to begin her engineering investigation, the type of planning and testing her group completed, and the final improvement choices made to her model. These examples of children effectively meeting engineering design performance expectations are very encouraging.

Future Improvements to the EA Program

With publication of the NGSS, there are many opportunities to introduce OST educators and children to the science and engineering practices. The EA team is currently undertaking several initiatives:

Develop engineering professional development for OST educators. The EA team strives to meet educators where they are. Part of working in OST is understanding that OST educators come with many different backgrounds, and many have never before facilitated science or engineering activities. Helping OST educators become comfortable teaching these activities involves clearly articulating how the EDP and the NGSS practices dovetail with

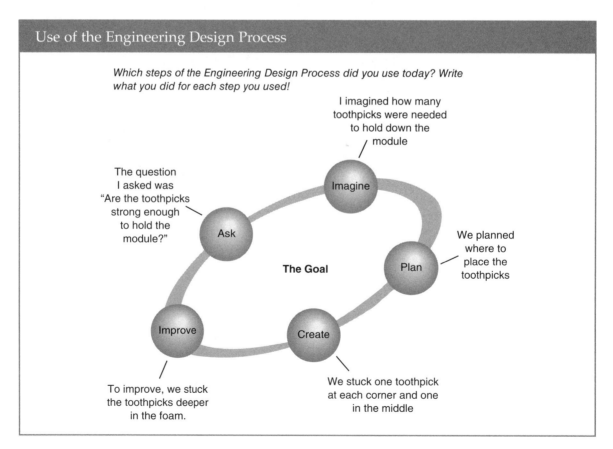

Image courtesy of Engineering is Elementary.

the skill building they are likely already reinforcing in their programs. The EA team has developed, pilot-tested, and revised several iterations of professional development workshops designed to make OST educators feel comfortable and confident teaching engineering in their programs. Further, the team has created a professional development guide to support program directors or lead educators from OST sites around the country as they facilitate these professional development workshops. The EA professional development guide is undergoing testing and will likely be released in early 2014.

Create online OST professional development videos that connect to the NGSS science and engineering practices. As stated earlier, a large part of engineering professional development for the OST setting is helping educators feel comfortable and confident. Allowing educators to see what activities look like in an OST setting can help them visualize how activities might look in their own programs. The EA team plans to create short video supports for educators interested in facilitating EA. These videos would reinforce constructive ways to scaffold the science and engineering practices.

Develop and test several smartphone apps. The availability of digital technology and level of use varies widely across OST programs. Some sites have iPads or other tablets available for nearly all children, while others do not even have Internet access. However, the EA team has observed that almost all OST educators and many of their child participants do have (and frequently use) personal smartphones. We are developing several smartphone apps that can be used as supplemental supports and activities for EA units. Because access to these types of technologies cannot be ensured, the apps are not a required part of any given EA unit, but rather a reinforcement of content that is also delivered in another way.

For example, one app allows children to scan a QR code to listen to the audio message from India and Jacob. Children who don't have the ability to scan the code can read the hard-copy version of the message or listen to the audio from a CD included in the educator guide. Another app is a technology flashcard game that asks children to decide whether the object shown on the flashcard is a technology. The same content is delivered through the second prep adventure ("What Is Technology") in each EA unit. The development team plans to conduct a research study about possible differences in learning and retention of content for children who complete the adventure versus those who play the game using the app.

Map NGSS links for educators. The introductory section of each EA guide lists links to a variety of standards touched upon by the unit, including applicable National Science Education Standards and International Technology and Engineering Educators Association Standards. These standards charts will be revised to also include applicable NGSS standards.

Conclusion

OST programs have long done impressive work focusing on character development of youth, and the STEM skill development being widely embraced by the field is an important, logical progression. The inclusion of engineering design as a core idea and scientific and engineering practices in the NGSS create a clear vision for building STEM capacity in OST.

Since the Engineering Adventures curriculum helps children gain engineering skills, become strong critical thinkers, and feel confident about their ability to solve problems, it can be a very useful means for introducing and expanding STEM in out-of-school settings. These skills, valued by the OST community as well as the engineering community, overlap very well with the core ideas and engineering practices in the NGSS.

Along with the hundreds of OST educators who have helped pilot-test units under development, more than 3,000 educators have downloaded completed EA units. The EA team looks forward to growing this number in the coming years by offering professional development supports to OST educators.

References

Afterschool Alliance. (2013). *Defining youth outcomes for STEM learning in afterschool.* Retrieved from http://www.afterschoolalliance.org/stem_outcomes_2013.pdf.

Higgins, M., Hertel, J. D., Cunningham, C. M., & Lachapelle, C. P. (2013). *Engineering Adventures curriculum development grant.* Boston, MA: Engineering is Elementary. Retrieved from http://www.eie.org/sites/default/files/bechtelreportforweb.pdf.

NGSS Lead States. (2013). *Next Generation Science Standards: For states, by states.* Washington, DC: The National Academies Press.

10

Engineering by Design TEEMS™ and I³

For Grades 3, 4, 5, and 6

William Giese, School District of the
Menomonie Area: Menomonie, Wisconsin

The Engineering Design Process for Upper Elementary Grades

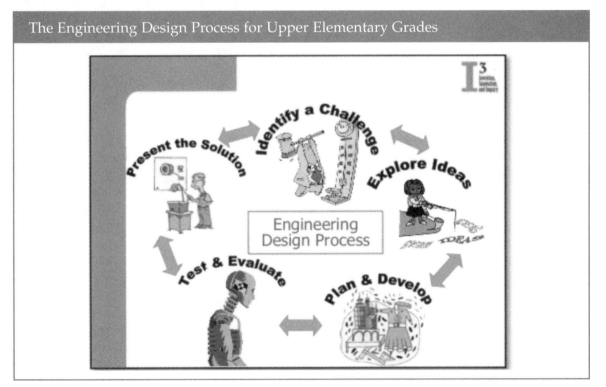

Image courtesy of ITEEA.

For the past 20 years, I have had the pleasure of incorporating and integrating elementary science, technology, engineering, and math (STEM) initiatives into my fifth-grade classroom. That experience has strengthened my belief that students react positively to hands-on and minds-on project-based learning. This chapter will discuss ways that you could strengthen your upper elementary STEM curriculum by allowing children frequent opportunities to learn and experience the engineering design process with the following curriculum materials:

- **EbD-TEEMS**™ is an integrated K–5 curriculum developed by the International Technology Education and Engineering Association (ITEEA, 2013).
- **Invention, Inquiry, and Innovation** (I[3]) for Grades 5–6 includes 10 units that promote a STEM learning model for upper elementary students. I will outline all 10 units and offer helpful hints from a teacher who has taught the Whispers of Willing Wind, a unit on energy and power.

EbD-TEEMS™ and I[3] are accessible at www.iteea.org/EbD/ebd.htm or through the ITEEA's Consortium of States as described later in this chapter.

Additionally, I will provide helpful classroom hints and tips that I have found successful throughout my career.

Power and Energy: The Whispers of Willing Wind

The Whispers of Willing Wind, a unit in the I[3] curriculum, provides an excellent example of the instructional materials available from the ITEEA for the upper elementary grades. The unit begins by assigning student teams to research the positive and negative effects of a particular source of energy, such as nuclear energy, hydroelectric energy, coal/oil/petroleum energy, solar energy, and wind energy. Teams are asked to find out how it is produced, how it gets to their homes, and to illustrate their findings by creating an energy cycle poster showing how the energy is produced and brought to market.

Next, students are assigned to monitor and record their family's home energy habits. At this point, the instructor defines renewable versus nonrenewable energy resources and engages the students in a discussion about these alternative forms of energy production. This phase of the unit helps children realize how they depend on energy production and find out where the energy they enjoy is coming from.

Next, students are challenged to design and build a working wind turbine, the tower to support the turbine, and a device to connect the two. There are criteria and constraints that the young engineers must meet. The students learn about scale and ratio as they draw conceptual designs for their turbine. The results of this phase depend on the students' creativity and availability of materials.

As students design their turbines, they take notes in their engineering design journals about daily progress, discoveries, false starts, materials, and changes made along the way. This is an important part of the whole unit as it forces children to write in a technical manner.

The unit culminates in a competition to see who can "draw water from the well," which involves quickly wrapping up 36 inches of string using wind power. Excitement is high as children use stopwatches, run tests, record results, and try to make improvements in their designs. Wind is supplied by a shop vacuum, box fan, or hair dryer, and the students are responsible to appropriately apply the wind speed and direction.

This event is a great way to showcase the technology education occurring in your classroom. Invite parents to attend the windmill competition. They will be impressed by the variety of designs and ingenuity on display. Believe it or not, students have wrapped up the string in my classroom in under 2 seconds!

Teaching the Engineering Design Process

For both of the curriculum projects described in this chapter, it is important to present the steps of the engineering design process very clearly. It may be helpful to make a bulletin board of the engineering design process, as shown previously on p. 163, to reference during class work and to provide a template in the students' journals so they have a visual reminder of where they are in the process.

When teaching the engineering design process, it is useful to correlate how this same process is used in the business world and touches everyone. Somewhere, someone needed to follow an engineering design process for anything that is created or produced. Children can relate to that!

Connections to the Standards

This unit and the others described in this chapter satisfy the *Grades 3–5 Engineering Design Performance Expectations* in the Next Generation Science Standards (NGSS) (NGSS Lead States, 2013):

3–5-ETS1–1. Define a simple design problem reflecting a need or a want that includes specified criteria for success and constraints on materials, time, or cost.

3–5-ETS1–2. Generate and compare multiple possible solutions to a problem based on how well each is likely to meet the criteria and constraints of the problem.

3–5-ETS1–3. Plan and carry out fair tests in which variables are controlled and failure points are considered to identify aspects of a model or prototype that can be improved.

The Whispers of Willing Wind also satisfies the following performance expectations for the fourth-grade level:

4-PS3–1. Use evidence to construct an explanation relating the speed of an object to the energy of that object.

4-PS3–2. Make observations to provide evidence that energy can be transferred from place to place by sound, light, heat, and electric currents.

4-PS3–3. Ask questions and predict outcomes about the changes in energy that occur when objects collide.

4-PS3–4. Apply scientific ideas to design, test, and refine a device that converts energy from one form to another.

4-ESS3–1. Obtain and combine information to describe that energy and fuels are derived from natural resources and their uses affect the environment.

All of the I³ units also correlate extremely well with the following Common Core State Standards (CCSS) in English language arts that demand technical writing and nonfiction reading, both skills that are necessary to complete design challenges. CCSS mathematics practices are also addressed, specifically measuring and developing number sense and number use (NGA & CCSSO, 2010).

> RST.11–12.7. Integrate and evaluate multiple sources of information presented in diverse formats and media (e.g., quantitative data, video, multimedia) in order to address a question or solve a problem.
>
> RST.11–12.8. Evaluate the hypothesis, data, analysis and conclusions in a science or technical text, verifying the data when possible and corroborating or challenging conclusions with other sources of information.
>
> RST.11–12.9. Synthesize information from a range of sources (e.g., texts, experiments, simulations) into a coherent understanding of a process, phenomenon, or concept, resolving conflicting information when possible.
>
> RI.4.3. Explain events, procedures, ideas, or concepts in a historical, scientific, or technical text, including what happened and why, based on specific information in the text.
>
> W.4.2. Write informative/explanatory texts to examine a topic and convey ideas and information clearly.
>
> W.4.7 Conduct short research projects that build knowledge through investigation of different aspects of a topic.
>
> W.4.9. Draw evidence from literary or informational texts to support analysis, reflection, and research.
>
> Mathematics Practice MP.2. Reason abstractly and quantitatively.
>
> Mathematics Practices MP.4. Model with mathematics.

Invention, Innovation, and Inquiry

The I[3] Project provides professional support for teachers interested in technological literacy in the upper elementary years. This project is supported, in part, by the National Science Foundation (NSF) and is being disseminated by ITEEA and the California University of Pennsylvania.

I[3] is short for Invention, Innovation, and Inquiry: Units for Technological Literacy, Grades 5–6. The project is so named because invention and innovation are the hallmarks of technological thinking and action. Each unit has standards-based content, suggested teaching approaches, and detailed learning activities including brainstorming, visualizing, testing, refining, and assessing technological designs. Students learn how inventions, innovations, and systems are created and how technology becomes part of people's lives.

Each unit comes complete with the printed material in PDF format. Units follow a similar design but are built around different science concepts. Teacher materials have everything a novice elementary teacher in technology education would need to conduct the investigation. Background, content-level explanations in science, math, social studies, technology, and engineering, a complete student materials section that includes an engineering design journal, project rubrics, and pre-post unit assessments are included in all units.

There are 10 units of instruction in the I³ lessons. Each unit teaches a unique area of science instruction, but all of the units are organized the same. The 10 units are briefly described here.

Innovation: Inches, Feet, and Hands is about innovation, measurement, and anthropometrics, which is the study of the size of human form. Students will be using an engineering design process to design and develop an improved product that is used by the human hand. They will be studying the sizes of the human hand and using these measurements to estimate sizes of various objects. They will also be improving their measurement ability through various activities. Learning goals are for students to

- demonstrate an understanding of basic design concepts as they relate to measurement and human form;
- explain and demonstrate how an engineering design process can be used to improve technological devices;
- describe limitations for a given device or design; and
- realize that with innovation, technological devices can be improved in different ways.

Invention: The Invention Crusade will help students in Grades 5 and 6 to explore the process of developing an idea into an invention. Students are asked to invent and construct a working model or prototype of a gadget that will help a small child do a household task. The culminating event is a "Kids Better Living Home Show," where the young inventors explain the ideas behind their gadget and give other elementary students an opportunity to try the new invention. Learning goals are for students to

- explain and demonstrate how ideas can become inventions by using an engineering design process;
- recognize that products are invented to meet specific needs and wants;
- describe the general characteristics of famous inventors and their inventions; and
- document their inventive thinking with sketches and notations in an inventor's journal.

Manufacturing: The Fudgeville Crisis invites students to explore and identify how the process and preservation of food has changed over time and will see how raw materials can be processed into fudge. Throughout the unit, students will be divided into four different teams, and each team will become a different company. Each company will experiment with how material can be formed to keep a desired shape, how food can be packaged to keep it fresh, and the importance of cleanliness in a food production environment. As a culminating activity, each team will mass-produce and package their fudge for a fudge festival. Learning goals are for students to

- analyze the causes of change in food quality over time;
- design a package that can extend the freshness of a food product;
- design a production system for a food product and use it to produce shaped fudge; and
- recognize the importance of following and maintaining cleanliness when handling food products.

Construction: Buildings and Beams engages students in acting as structural engineers. The students design and construct at least two laminated paper beams. They explore forces that act on structures and discover that the strength of a beam varies with height, shape, and thickness. Lastly, they test, evaluate, and revise their beams using feedback from testing to refine their designs. Learning goals are for students to

- describe forces that act on structures;
- explain how the size and shape of a beam affect its ability to resist loads;
- calculate the efficiency of a constructed beam; and
- design, construct, and test a variety of beams to determine which can support the most weight.

Transportation: Across the United States invites students to explore transportation technology by understanding transportation environments (land, water, air, and space) and transportation systems. They will be able to experience how ideas for inventions and innovations are modeled and recognize how transportation has played an important role in the development of the United States. Learning goals are for students to

- explain the significance of transportation in the westward expansion of the United States;
- describe how inventions and innovations in technology can be modeled;
- recognize that transportation systems are comprised of several subsystems; and
- design, construct, and test a prototype of a transportation vehicle by following the engineering design process.

Communication: From Print to Radio illustrates to students that few things have changed our world as drastically as communication technologies, such as the telephone and television. They have changed our homes, our workplaces, and our buying choices. Designing, creating, and producing commercials will show students how to work within the communications environment to create a unique and appealing commercial to promote school spirit. In this unit, students explore communication processes and mediums by designing, developing, and implementing different types of commercial projects promoting school spirit. In teams of three or four, students create an advertising firm. Each team creates an identity for their firm and meets their school's advertising needs to encourage students to support their school and show school spirit. Learning goals are for students to

- describe how to assess the design of technological products by asking good questions;
- explain the concepts of risks, benefits, and trade-offs; and
- use the findings of an inquiry process to design and produce an improved school bag by following an engineering design process.

Power and Energy: The Whispers of Willing Wind is described in some detail at the beginning of this chapter. The unit presents an alternative form of energy that is both available and inexhaustible. Students construct a device that will capture wind energy and convert it into mechanical energy. The students also design and build a structure that will support their wind energy device. The students research and compare the energy cycles of the most common resources used to produce electricity in an attempt to gain an understanding of how those systems work. The students also examine the ways energy is used for technological devices in their home. Learning goals are for students to

- explain how energy is created, transmitted, and utilized in a home;
- describe benefits and drawbacks of utilizing renewable energy; and
- design and develop a device that will harness wind and convert it into mechanical energy.

Inquiry: The Ultimate School Bag asks students to assume the role of design engineers for a company called Sensible School Supplies. They will use inquiry skills to investigate and evaluate the school bags they currently use and apply what they discover to design and construct a model of their version of the ultimate school bag. The students will then present their school bag designs to students from other classes. Learning goals are for students to

- learn to assess the design of technological products and systems;
- understand the concepts of risk, benefits, and trade-offs;
- use the findings of an inquiry process to design and produce an improved product by following an engineering design process; and
- recognize the widespread use of technology in our society.

Technological Systems: Creating Mechanical Motion involves students in exploring simple machines and linkage mechanisms. After seeing what these can accomplish, students will be challenged to design a toy that uses these mechanical devices to create movement. Since everyone thinks of toys and games as fun, this is an ideal medium for learning. As students turn their ideas into models, learning occurs. Students will design, build, test, and improve their designs. Learning goals are for students to

- explain mechanical linkage function and movement;
- explain how the engineering design process is used when creating mechanical devices; and
- recognize that simple machines can be used with linkage mechanisms to create a mechanical system.

Design: Toying With Technology shows students how to take an idea from brainstorming to sketching to prototyping. Students will see how creative designs, unique logos, vivid color schemes, and celebrity endorsements can affect how many people may buy, sell, and play with board games. Students explore two-dimensional and three-dimensional visualization processes and media by designing, developing, and building a board game. Students design and create a game for the Happyland Toy Company, a fictitious board game company. Learning goals are for students to

- describe and demonstrate how visualization and drawing techniques are used to document ideas using two- and three-dimensional representations;
- explain how the engineering design process may be used to develop a new product such as a game; and
- recognize that effective marketing techniques can increase product success.

EbD-TEEMS™: Grades K–5

Engineering byDesign™ (EbD) is a fully articulated sequence of courses for Grades K–12 aimed at helping students develop technological literacy in a STEM context. EbD was developed by the STEM Center for Teaching and Learning™ of the International Technology and Engineering Education Association (ITEEA).

EbD is based on the *Standards for Technological Literacy* (ITEEA, 2000/2002/2007) and is aligned with the *Principles and Standards for School Mathematics* (NCTM, 2000) and the *Benchmarks for Science Literacy* (AAAS, 1993, 2008). Additionally, the program has been mapped to the National Academy of Engineering's *Grand Challenges for Engineering* (NAE, 1997–2010).

EbD-TEEMS™ is the K–5 portion of EbD. EbD-TEEMS gives elementary students a developmentally appropriate scaffolding of engineering concepts throughout their developmental years. TEEMS stands for Technology, Engineering, the Environment, Mathematics and Science. The study of environmental issues and concerns are integrated into each building block of lessons.

A separate chapter in this volume by Diana Cantu describes the EbD-TEEMS™ curriculum for Grades K–2. The curriculum building blocks for Grades 3–5 are shown in Table 10.1.

Following are special features of the curriculum for the upper elementary level.

Media Rich—EbD-TEEMS™: Grades 3–5 are media rich, meaning they have embedded links to resource material throughout the lesson. Students can meet real engineers and learn about their work, access necessary resources in order to complete assigned tasks, and watch videos related to the design challenge. Additionally, instructors can receive student work electronically.

Online Assessments—EbD-TEEMS™: Grades 3–5 allow for teachers to administer assessments online. This feature is extremely teacher friendly, and it very quickly assesses how well each student mastered the concepts. Teachers can use this feature to guide future instruction, review missed content, and validate student learning with specific data.

6E Learning Strategy—All lessons in the EbD-TEEMS™: Grades 3–5 curriculum follow the 6E Learning Strategy that consists of (Pre)Evaluation, Engagement, Exploration, Explanation, Elaboration, and (Post)Evaluation. This model assures fidelity in concept development and articulation.

Building Blocks—Each grade level is organized around a cohesive building block of learning related to an environmental theme. Though building blocks are grade-level unique and specific, the vocabulary and STEM concepts developed are similar and follow a developmental sequence. By integrating the environmental themes, students will become aware and cognizant of the environmental challenges facing future generations.

STEM Notebooks—Each unit demands that the student create a STEM Notebook. This opportunity to engage in technical writing is an important part in learning to think and

Table 10.1 EbD-TEEMS™ Building Blocks for Grades 3–5

Grade	EbD-TEEMS™ Building Blocks
Third Grade	Every Drop Matters. Students are challenged to develop systems to conserve and reuse water as they explore the scarcity of water resources on Earth.
Fourth Grade	The Power of Solar. Students are challenged to build and test models as they explore solar energy as a sustainable source of power for structures.
Fifth Grade	Community Connections. Students are challenged to plan improvements to community infrastructure as they explore transportation and public services.

act as an engineer. Assessment Rubrics are included so the student is clear on expectations and teachers can evaluate their students' notebooks based on set criteria.

Language Arts Integration—Every unit has authentic literature embedded within it. For example, in the fifth-grade unit, students read the book *A Street Through Time: A 12,000-Year Walk Through History* by Dr. Anne Millard (1998). Incorporating children's literature is a key component in all of the grade-level building blocks. This was an intentional component in developing TEEMS, as elementary teachers demand literacy integration.

Real-World Connections—EbD-TEEMS™ provides connections to real-world scientists, inventors, engineers, and entrepreneurs. Web-based links are provided and used within lessons. Children learn an appreciation for the engineering challenges these professionals face at their work every day.

Each unit is designed for a 6- to 8-week commitment by the teacher. Lessons vary in length, and there is flexibility in administering the lessons based on individual time constraints. The integrative nature of this curriculum lends itself to not being a "stand-alone" project but rather an inclusive supplement to what is already being taught in the classroom. School leaders can decide when and how the curriculum is administered throughout the system.

Classroom Tool Kits

In order to complete the design challenges in I³ and EbD-TEEMS™, children will need access to simple hand-held tools that are safe and easy to manage. In my classroom, I have created five tool kits in bins that contain the following:

Tools

- 2 hammers
- 6 hand clamps
- 4 coping saws
- 2 hand-drills with ¼" and 3/16" drill bits
- 5 safety glasses
- assorted nails

Supplies

- wood cut to 3/8" × 3/8" × 3"*

*Parents are a good resource for cutting this wood. Usually there is someone who enjoys woodworking and has the means to cut wood to these specifications.

- wooden dowels in 1/4", 3/16" diameters
- recycled materials that assist in specific projects
- cool-type hot-glue guns and glue sticks

It is mandatory that ALL students wear safety glasses whenever tools are in use. Time must be dedicated to teach children how to use the tools appropriately. Early in the year, full lessons using a "guided-discovery" approach will help to ensure that tools are being used appropriately. I have found that these opportunities lend themselves to a review of "Simple Machines" that they have probably learned in an earlier grade. For example, identifying the hammer as a form of a lever is a connection children may be able to make. Frequent reminders and review of rules for tool use happen often throughout the year and whenever tools are in use.

Engineering Design Journals

Engineering design journals are a vehicle for students to keep track of their progress when involved in a design-build initiative. It also forces children to pay attention to, and actually do, the design portion of their project. Too often, children will want to jump in and build something with whatever materials are being provided. Skipping the design portion of the engineering design process tends to produce poor results. It is important for students to realize that the engineering design process was followed for every technological advance in our society.

Rubrics can help students track expectations and completion of tasks as they proceed throughout the process. Table 10.2 shows how a teacher could use this sample rubric in his or her classroom. By making the engineering design journal an assessed portion of the unit, you are forcing students to take it seriously and teaching them that engineers must keep careful records of developments, ideas, brainstorms, and discoveries.

Access to Engineering byDesign™ and I³

The EbD™ course curricula can be purchased by any individual, school, district, or state for a low price at www.iteea.org. However, schools can become a part of the EbD™

Table 10.2 Engineering Design Journal (EDJ) Rubric

Assessment Items	Below Target	At Target	Above Target
Sketch Entries	Sketches are incomplete, lack detail, or not present	Sketches are made as required but could contain additional details. Drawing not to scale.	All sketches are complete and include details to make it understandable and drawn to scale.
Annotations	Few if any annotations are given and the ones written provide incomplete information. There are few if any measurements given.	Annotations are provided but do not enhance the sketches. Some measurements are included with sketches.	Annotations and measurements are included with sketches.
Organization	EDJ is unorganized, missing key information, and messy.	EDJ contains most of the necessary information, mostly organized, and complete.	EDJ is very organized and complete. All information is included and accurate.

school network to access the full benefits of the entire EbD™ program and learning community. These benefits include

- online access to the curriculum and the latest updates;
- exclusive access to EbDonline to converse with online facilitators and teachers around the country who are also implementing the same courses; and
- online assessments for the students in their classes—access to real-time student performance data.

To become an EbD™ network school, you can download and complete a network agreement at www.iteea.org. Additionally, EbD™ has created a consortium of states to serve as leaders in collaborating for higher quality education. Any schools within a consortium state are provided with free access to the EbD™ program. The leaders in these states work together to create consistency in the advancement of STEM education. The state leaders implement the EbD™ curriculum in their school systems and together evaluate student achievement to make informed decisions in enhancing technological and engineering literacy for all through an integrative STEM study. These state members develop the necessary professional growth opportunities for teachers and propose any needed changes to the curricula. With the increase of states in the consortium, state decisions can become a powerful tool in shaping the future of education, and furthering students' technological and engineering literacy. The figure below illustrates the current consortium of states for EbD™.

The EbD™ network schools and consortium states have access to the curriculum through the EbD™ Portal. The EbD™ Portal is cloud-based solution for providing curriculum, assessment, and professional development. Though the portal, teachers can access the dynamic course curriculum and EbD™Online for ongoing professional development. Additionally, teachers can assign and mange student assessments through the portal to make data-driven decisions about their instruction.

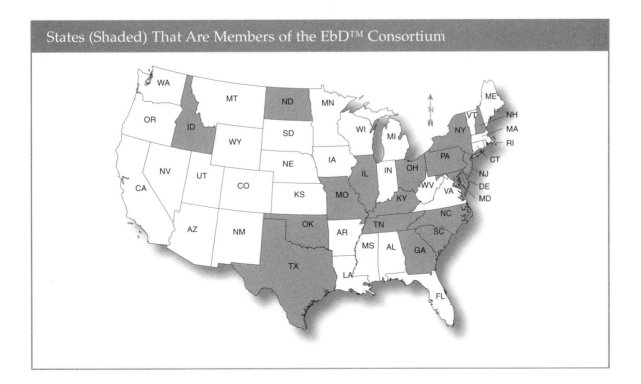

States (Shaded) That Are Members of the EbD™ Consortium

Conclusion

Why should I consider teaching one of the units in Invention, Innovation, and Inquiry? First, I³ was highly vetted and field-tested. It was developed with the assistance of an NSF grant, the resources of the ITEEA, and California University of Pennsylvania. These high-quality, inexpensive materials are aligned with the NGSS and the CCSS, and the units are teacher and student friendly. They were developed with the idea that *any* elementary teacher could implement them without major costs for supplies and materials. Give one a try and find out for yourself!

References

AAAS. (1993/2008). *Benchmarks for science literacy.* New York, NY: Oxford University Press.

International Technology and Engineering Educators Association. (2013). *Engineering byDesign: A standards based model program.* Reston, VA: Author. Retrieved from http://www.iteea.org/EbD™/EbD™.htm.

International Technology and Engineering Education Association. (2000, 2005, 2007). *Standards for technological literacy: Content for the study of technology.* Reston, VA: Author.

Millard, A. (1998). *A street through time: A 12,000-year walk through history.* New York, NY: Dorling Kindersley.

National Academy of Engineering. (1997–2010). *NAE Grand Challenges for engineering.* Washington, DC: The National Academies. Retrieved from http://www.engineeringchallenges.org/.

National Council of Teachers of Mathematics. (2000). *Principles and standards for school mathematics.* Reston, VA: Author. Retrieved from http://www.nctm.org/standards/default.aspx?id=58.

National Governors Association Center for Best Practices & Council of Chief State School Officers. (2010). *Common Core State Standards: Mathematics and English language arts.* Washington, DC: Authors.

NGSS Lead States. (2013). *Next Generation Science Standards: For states, by states.* Washington, DC: The National Academies Press.

11

Design It!

Design Engineering Projects for Afterschool

Charles Hutchison, Education Development
Center: Waltham, Massachusetts

Immersed in a Design It! Activity

Image by Burt Granofsky, courtesy of EDC.

A True Story[1]

> A child—about 7 years old—is deeply engaged with a set of bright yellow, remote-controlled trucks that carry cargo across a spaghetti junction of plastic tracks. Another child—a visitor, also about 7—sits to the side and watches. The "truck" child ignores his audience.
>
> After a while, the visitor picks up some of the spare tracks and starts fitting them together in ways that clearly have nothing to do with their intended use. His "sculptures" may or may not be dinosaurs. The two boys play silently and separately for some minutes. Eventually, the "truck" boy turns toward the "dinosaurs," picking each one up and studying it admiringly for a moment or two before returning to his trucks. Then, to no one in particular, he says, "You know, even when this thing is working right, it's not that interesting, actually!"

Overview

Design It! (Design Engineering Projects for Afterschool) is a hands-on, project-based after-school curriculum series designed to engage children in enjoyable, meaningful, and *interesting* engineering projects that promote the use of the *science and engineering practices* and build interest in future science, technology, engineering, and mathematics (STEM) study and careers.

The series was created for children from traditionally underserved communities who regularly attend afterschool and other nonacademic out-of-school programs: children who generally have little access to cultural institutions or high-quality out-of-school science enrichment programs. It takes a constructivist approach to learning and is designed for regular implementation within afterschool agencies *by the existing corps of youth workers and afterschool specialists.*

Design It! and the companion series Explore It! (Science Investigations for Afterschool) were developed by the Education Development Center (EDC) under the leadership of Bernie Zubrowski between 1999 and 2005,[i] with funding from the National Science Foundation (NSF) as part of its larger effort to rekindle interest in STEM study and careers—especially among children from populations that are chronically underrepresented in the STEM professions and trades. The popularity of Design It! and Explore It![2] as well as projects sponsored by the 4-H Extension community[3] and other agencies may preface a shift within the domain toward the integration of project-based science and engineering into the core afterschool programming in the place of occasional interventions by external volunteers and experts—as has previously been the norm.

Following the development and publication of the two curriculum series, NSF awarded further funding to EDC to develop a scalable professional development model that would enhance widespread implementation of high-quality afterschool science programming. The National Partnerships for AfterSchool Science (NPASS and NPASS2)[ii] have brought regular afterschool science programming to more than 1,000 large and small afterschool agencies in 15 states. In many cases, both statewide and local agencies have continued to provide NPASS training and programming beyond the period of NSF funding.

---

1. The author's son playing with a friend some years ago.

2. Between the 14 Design It! titles, nearly 25,000 copies have been sold to afterschool agencies, home schoolers, and some schoolteachers across the country.

3. The 4-H Extension community has produced many excellent out-of-school time science curricula. These vary in style and approach, but they cumulatively represent another very large presence of high-quality afterschool programming.

The theory of change upon which this model is based is that when afterschool staff master the best practices for teaching afterschool science and when students engage repeatedly in enjoyable, engaging, and well-run projects, they will gain confidence, skill, and self-efficacy in relation to "science," and thus be more prepared for (and interested in) further study in STEM topics that could lead to employment in the STEM workforce.

Engineering, Project-Based Learning, and Science Practices

Each Design It! project consists of a series of *challenges* that lead toward an engaging end-point—a rollercoaster, go-cart, bridge, crane, glider, string telephone, pinball machine, trebuchet, top, or yo-yo—made out of commonly available, expendable, and inexpensive materials. The choice of engineering and design (rather than "science") to begin the development of a new afterschool STEM curriculum portfolio placed the focus squarely on the *practices* of exploration and problem solving, rather than on *conceptual understanding* (or vocabulary) of physical science. To *engineer* is to make a device or structure do what you want it to do with the materials you have available. For young learners, it is best if the engineering objectives are fun and a little quirky but based in the familiar so that the learners can easily tell—and discuss—whether they have arrived at the objective or not. Design It! offers children the opportunity to tinker and build in a relaxed atmosphere, *but with a degree of structure, iterative problem solving, and reflection* that has hardly ever been characteristic of the afterschool domain at scale.

The companion series Explore It! is about science—focusing on interesting physical phenomena such as balance, buoyancy, heat transfer, baking, and electricity. But again the focus is not on understanding or explaining the science, but rather on observing and testing and reflecting on how the phenomenon behaves and presents itself. It is neither realistic nor appropriate to expect the afterschool domain to *teach* the scientific concepts that schools themselves struggle to convey. But afterschool *is* well poised to nurture the skills and habits (and joy) of careful and collaborative problem solving and investigation.

And therein lies the importance of the professional development. Having established the goal that these projects be led by frontline afterschool staff, it became essential to design the curriculum and a related professional development model in a way that would build the capacity of the afterschool workforce to lead and facilitate these projects *skillfully*—so that children reliably enjoy themselves, achieve the project goals most of the time, and increasingly use and understand the science and engineering *practices* that are central to the new NGSS.[4]

Essential Features of the Design It! Model

A number of *critical structural elements* were incorporated into the development of these curricula:

- **Focused**. A single "inherently interesting" and engaging device or toy per curriculum.
- **Project-Based**. Specific and sequenced *challenges* that build toward a final product.
- **Materials**. Inexpensive and commonly available, "nonscience" materials.

---

4. Next Generation Science Standards (NGSS Lead States, 2013).

- **Learning Outcomes**. Enjoyment of, and identification with, science. Use and understanding of science and engineering practices.
- **Science Content**. *Foundational experiences* with science content and concepts identified in state and national standards, including the National Science Education Standards (NRC, 1996), and the Next Generation Science Standards (NGSS) (NGSS Lead States, 2013).
- **Sense Making.** Frequent opportunities for verbal and representational sharing. Analysis and reflection on evidence and outcomes.
- **Collaboration.** Communities of practice among child and adult learners.
- **Facilitation**. Projects led by afterschool staff who receive regular training and support in the use of *Best Practices* for leading afterschool science.
- **Project guidebooks** include detailed materials lists, implementation coaching and trouble-shooting hints, extensions of most challenges as well as other professional development resources.

The Projects: Vivid Examples

In each Design It! project, teams of children work through a sequence of four to six related challenges over a period of several weeks. The objective of each challenge is narrow and well defined, and the materials are clearly prescribed. Each project begins with a somewhat open-ended challenge—to make a marble jump into a cup, make a glider *fly*, or make a trebuchet that can throw a cannonball—and then moves on through a progression of more structured challenges in which the children gradually discover a set of design principle that make the device perform its intended function more and more dependably. This process can span the course of a month and requires considerable commitment and persistence to complete.

Balls and Tracks

The best-known Design It! curriculum is the Balls and Tracks project in which children build and test progressively more daring and complex roller coasters made from 3/4-inch foam pipe insulation split lengthways down the middle to form a flexible half-track just wide enough to allow a marble to roll freely down. In the first challenge, children make a ramp or a "ski jump" using only a single 6-foot section of pipe, a paper cup, a small amount of tape and string, and the walls and furniture around them. The challenge is to make a freestanding structure that will launch a marble as far as possible and make it land in the cup on its first bounce.

This is a popular challenge. Children seem to enjoy rolling their marbles down the track over and over again, relying more on hope than planning to improve its range or accuracy. In the early stages, a really good jump is about 3 feet, and after all the children have had multiple turns lunching the marble about that far, they begin to ask for extra sections of pipe so they can add twists and turns to make their track more interesting and fun—and believing too that more tubing will make the marble jump farther.

More tubes *are* in store in the next few challenges, but the potential of this first challenge is far from exhausted. There is still plenty to discover about how the shape, slope, position, and stability of just this single piece of track can increase the jump to 4 feet and then to 5 and perhaps all the way to the current record of about 7 feet! Discovering the effect of adjusting these factors in the first challenge sets the stage

The Ski Jump Challenge

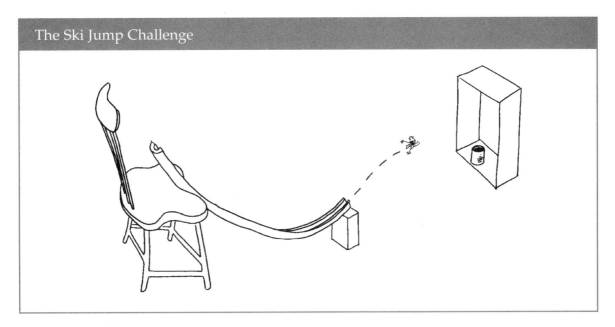

Image courtesy of EDC.

for the following challenges in which the children make all the loops, spirals, and horse-jumps that the materials (up to three sections of pipe), time, and their creativity will allow.

Spinning Toys

In Spinning Toys, the children are given several thick Chinette paper plates, a 1/4" × 8" dowel (or pencil), two rubber bumpers, and 3/4" binder clips: the challenge is to make a "top" that spins for 20 seconds. Most kids know immediately to push the dowel or pencil through the "middle" of plates and launch it on the table or floor with two fingers or two hands. Few of these prototypes spin for more than a couple of seconds, however, and many don't spin at all.

But as the teams work on their tops, and the whole group shares their results, they gradually establish several important design features: *really* accurate centering of the axle (dowel/pencil), fixing the axle tightly to the plates with the rubber bumpers or binder clips, finding the best

The ski jump challenge evolves with loops and spirals.

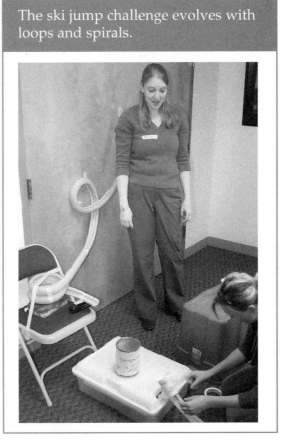

Image courtesy of EDC.

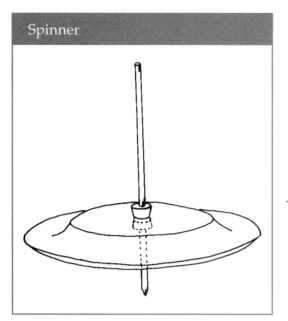

Spinner

Image courtesy of EDC.

height for the plates on the axle (quite low), and launching smoothly between the palms of both hands. With those factors settled, spin times of 20 or even 30 seconds can reliably be achieved.

In the later challenges, the children investigate how the weight and diameter of the top impact spin time, and they are allowed to substitute entirely new materials that are at hand (CDs, old LPs, Frisbees, or cardboard pizza bases). The final challenge is to make a string launcher or use a kitchen mixer to start the top spinning and to make it spin *for a full minute*—which it can.

Gliders

In the Gliders project, the opening challenge is to make a glider that can fly *straight and far* using just two 3 × 5 index cards, as many paper clips and 3/4" binder clips as desired, and as little masking tape as possible (up to 12 inches). The constraint is that the cards *may not be bent, folded, torn, rolled, or otherwise deformed!*

Not being allowed to fold and bend the cards rules out all the familiar paper airplane designs: it is a constraint that at first stumps (and annoys) many children and adults. In the face of this first roadblock, a common strategy is to load the cards with binder clips and paper clips on every side, making a "plane" that spins dangerously like a throwing star or drops like a stone. It soon becomes clear

Launching the Spinner

Image courtesy of EDC.

that the word "fly" needs a clearer definition. When someone eventually stumbles upon (or the project leader discreetly hints at) the design shown here there is much excitement. The movement is delightful, and eye-catching—swooping down and rising or turning one way or the other like a highly acrobatic or erratic bird.

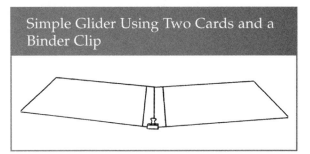

Simple Glider Using Two Cards and a Binder Clip

Image courtesy of EDC.

This "glider" rarely moves in a straight line and almost never beyond a few feet, but with just the right amount of weight (one binder clip), in just the right place (dead center, front), and launched with just the right thrust (very little), it moves in a way that is unquestionably *flying*—moving ON the air—in contrast to paper balls, throwing stars, and other missiles that move THROUGH it.

The wide flat wing shown above becomes the basis of all the remaining challenges. Retaining this double wing, the glider gets, by stages, a body and tail, larger wings and wing supports, and finally a catapult launcher, all with the addition of only drinking straws, more (and larger) index cards, paper clips, rubber bands, and a cardboard launch pad. With each modification, the glider looks more like a real plane and flies straighter and farther than before. Eventually, it can fly up to 30 feet or more in a perfectly straight path.

Facilitation and Pedagogy

In addition to choosing topics that would be appealing and playful, Design It! projects were designed around a number of key *pedagogical* elements.

- Projects consist of four to six *related* challenges that allow transfer of skills and results from one to another, offering interesting or rewarding new elements that build towards the final product.
- All the teams of children move through the sequence of challenges together so as to form a "community of learners" that shares findings and results among the whole group.
- After one or two challenges, some projects coalesce around a *standard model*—a basic and functional top, plane, or trebuchet that everyone uses as the basis for further modification and design.
- The facilitator provides just enough structure, help, and guidance to keep the energy, enthusiasm, and optimism alive while the children solve the problems *as a group.*

The Standard Model

Although most Design It! projects begin with a more or less open-ended challenge, by the second or third challenge, choices are deliberately narrowed toward a standardized version of the device—as in the flat, lateral wing glider design shown above. Funneling design choices toward this *standard model* does, of course, limit spontaneity and creativity to some extent, and the last thing we want is to give the students a set of "instructions" on how to make the glider fly straight. But keeping a group (class) of children on more or less the same design trajectory sets the stage for sharing of ideas and evidence and collective problem solving. This becomes much more difficult as design choices diverge and as individuals become less and less invested in (dependent upon) the success of others in the group.

Pacing and Extension Challenges

The prospect that some students will pronounce themselves "done" with an engineering challenge while others are still struggling to get started or are still working steadily can be an inexperienced facilitator's worst nightmare. Allowing some children to hurry ahead to the next challenge for the sake of maintaining their engagement is understandable enough, but it is also a lost opportunity. There is almost always more that individuals and the group can learn when they push beyond that early "success" and when the group moves forward with everyone more or less at the same stage of investigation.

When children personally overcome hurdles in the design process—and when they share or represent their success verbally and in other ways with the larger audience—they are likely to become more invested in the final outcome and more informed as successive problems arise. If the students get significantly out of sync with respect to critical discoveries or insights, then opportunities for group sharing and discussion will be lost and crucial "learnable moments" may be passed over unnoticed. Keeping the group more or less together through the multiple challenges of a project—although difficult for many facilitators—increases the chances that the group will engage in collaborative and reflective investigation, and become cognitively aware of the *science practices* they and each other are using (or not) to solve the challenges at hand.

To help facilitators overcome this problem, the Design It! curriculum guides suggest *extension* challenges to re-engage children who finish a task more quickly than their peers or who lose interest because of frustration. Extensions can be as simple as challenging a team to do the same thing but more so: make the marble/top/glider jump/spin/fly even farther or longer (or farther than your neighbors'!). Or it might offer a new material that changes the likely outcome in some interesting way or which is simply fun to experiment with. The point is to keep certain children engaged in productive, interesting, and *related* investigation while the rest of the pack catches up so that everyone can compare equivalent results before moving to the next stage of the project.

The Project Materials

Design It! curriculum materials are commonplace and inexpensive items that can be found in most classroom closets and recycling bins or purchased at any hardware and grocery store. The projects typically call for cardboard, string, paper plates, dowels, pipe insulation, rulers, scissors, rubber bands, balloons, rubber bumpers, index cards, 3/4" binder clips, plastic tubing, and so on in one combination or another. None of the materials for Design It! (or Explore It!) is produced specifically for these projects and none (except perhaps for batteries and "Hero" tubes) could be thought of as inherently "science" materials. The low cost of such materials is an obvious draw for resource-strapped afterschool agencies, and paradoxically, perhaps, for the children these materials are both more demanding and more rewarding than their shinier (and more expensive) counterparts. These "foraged" or repurposed materials seem to permit a wider scope for creativity than manufactured kits and toys, and being expendable (cheap to replace), they give permission for ample trial and error, experimentation, and restarts in the design process.

When children discover, for instance, that it wasn't a great idea to fold their paper plates into quarters to find the center of a wheel or top, there is every reason to let them start again with new plates. Or if their glider crashes and crumples, or if they speculate that larger or smaller marbles will jump farther, it is relatively easy to offer them whatever replacements or variants are available. Within the limits of common sense, safety and availability—and with caution not to reinvent the core of the design challenges—this category of materials opens doors to adaptation and constructive risk taking that more precious and highly defined materials may not.

But it is almost a given that these Rube Goldberg wheels or tracks or wings will wobble or fall apart or stick together in annoying and frustrating ways. Within reasonable limits, the struggle to master the unruly nature of the materials is one of the strengths of the projects. But these are not just any materials, pulled off the hardware store shelves at random. The developers sought far and wide for materials that are widely available and inexpensive and which (almost) ensure that with a reasonable amount of careful experimentation and reflection most children will be able to make a product that works reasonably well. There are a lot of risks in this approach, but the enduring popularity of these projects is a testament to the creativity and persistence that children bring to bear when the task or the goal at hand is truly enjoyable and rewarding.

Materials Purchase and Kit Assembly

For all the folksy look of the materials, the lists of items required for each Design It! project is surprisingly specific. The success of these projects depends not just on the developers having identified the best materials but also on implementers procuring *exactly* the materials prescribed. Ensuring that the right materials go into the kits for each project is no small logistical challenge.

Early on, it became apparent that it is not wise or efficient to ask the youth workers themselves to purchase materials or assemble kits. These are busy people who are not highly paid: the task of scouring the shelves of multiple stores for each new project kit would surely discourage all but the most determined. And for those who forge ahead anyway, there is still a strong chance they will inadvertently pick out the wrong items—seemingly equivalent, but different enough to sabotage the project. A lot can go wrong if you don't have exactly the right battery, or dowel, or tube and if you don't know how to pick out workable substitutes. Failure to pay close attention to these issues can crucially impact the quality of the experience for the children and the project leaders.[5]

So, despite the local availability of most of the materials, afterschool sites are always provided with a ready-made kit, assembled by their science trainer or by staff at the science trainers' overseeing agency. Kits contain almost all the supplies necessary for 15 students

---

5. Spinning Toys and Rubber Band Cars call for 6" and 9" Chinette paper plates and 1/4" wooden dowels. Cost-conscious or inattentive buyers might opt for less expensive paper or plastic plates or for a cheaper 3/16" dowel. Or, finding only 5" and 12" Chinette paper plates on the shelf, they might buy 6" and 9" of some other brand. In this case, the thickness and sturdiness of the Chinette plates matters far more than the exact sizes. And the thinner dowel is too weak and does not fit tightly inside the rubber bumpers that hold the disc or wheels respectively to their axles. Such well-meaning substitutions result in cars and tops that break or fall apart and for very unsatisfying experiences for the children.

to carry out that one curriculum project.[6] And to ensure that the kit assemblers themselves don't make inadvertent substitutions, they work from detailed lists that specify the brand, suppliers' product number, diameter (internal or external), length, thickness, and so on as well as the minimum quantity needed for every item. And for bulk buyers, links to online suppliers and Web catalogs are provided too. It is generally not until a trainer or a youth worker has led (and participated in) half a dozen or more of these projects that they fully appreciate how these seemingly minute details make all the difference to the success of the projects and until they begin to be able to make good judgments about which substitutions are benign and which are fatal.

Professional Development for Science in Afterschool

Until recently, "science" has rarely been included within the core mission of the afterschool domain. The National 4-H Council some years ago identified 4-H SET (Science, Engineering and Technology), and subsequently 4-H Science as a core component of its afterschool mission, but elsewhere science in afterschool has been sporadic and episodic— generally consisting of one-time activities or projects led by a staff member or volunteer, or of professional programs brought in from the outside. Prior to Design It!, systematic training of afterschool staff to lead regular science projects from the inside was virtually unheard of. The express intension in developing Design It! and its attendant professional development model was to build capacity *within* the domain to make high-quality project-based science a regular feature of afterschool programming.

Several hurdles stand in the way of such an ambitious objective. Traditionally, the afterschool realm has been relaxed and unpressured, where children find a safe and supportive environment in the hours between school and home. There is understandable resistance within the field to taking on an inherently "academic" role. Many in the field are reluctant to jeopardize this academic neutrality of their territory—fearing that the mere scent of school learning will scare away the children and overwhelm the staff.

But as science *does* become a more regular element of afterschool programming, the field must navigate the issue of "outcomes" carefully. When Design It! was conceived and developed more than a decade ago, there was a consensus among funders and supporters that children from underserved populations would benefit from increased access to high-quality afterschool STEM programming—notwithstanding the difficulties of measuring such benefits precisely. But with the recent increases in financial investment and political support for afterschool STEM programs has come increased demands for evidence of its impact on student "achievement" and ultimate career choice. There is a real danger that expectations for student outcomes will be set at unattainably high levels—mostly by constituencies outside the field—and that failure to meet these goals will result in a withdrawal of support before the more intangible benefits have had time to come to fruition.

Design It!, as well as other afterschool science programs, is premised on the belief that providing widespread opportunities for children to do serious science in a playful way—and thereby become self-aware and self-confident of their abilities and interests—is

---

6. Afterschool agencies/staff are responsible for supplying paper, pencils, markers, rulers, scissors and so on, as well as recycled paper, yogurt containers, tin cans, and cardboard boxes. These items are not included in the kits.

a valuable (and measurable) enough outcome that should not be jeopardized by overlaying the requirement to meet academic assessment standards as well.

Staff Training

Another *logistical* barrier to making high-quality afterschool science available at scale is the challenge of training large numbers of frontline facilitators to lead projects with children skillfully and on a regular basis. Generally, the people who work within the field have little confidence or experiences in this respect, and recruiting from outside the field presents its own set of challenges. But the afterschool workforce is quite large, and it includes plenty of intellectually curious people.

The clear finding of Design It! and its succeeding programs is that whatever youth workers lack in confidence and skill specific to science is more than compensated for in their knowledge of *youth development* and in their devotion to the well-being of children they serve. Youth development expertise, it turns out, strongly enhances informal science project leadership, especially when combined with open-mindedness, intelligence, and a willingness to take on new challenges.

Where scientists or formal science educators have participated in this project, however, science expertise, *per se*, has generally not enhanced the outcomes for children. Rather, it frequently gets in the way of adopting sound youth development practices. Simply put, we have found it easier to teach informal science to a youth worker than to teach youth development to a "scientist." Scientists and schoolteachers also tend to be less reliably available for training and programming over long periods of time. All in all, the choice of youth workers to lead these projects has worked out well.

Engaging Frontline Facilitators in a Hands-On Workshop

Image by Burt Granofsky, courtesy of EDC.

The staff training and support built into the Design It! project and refined at scale in the NPASS projects aims to identify and train large numbers of in-field youth workers and afterschool specialists who will integrate regular, high-quality project-based science and engineering into the fabric of afterschool programming *without relying on outside science professionals, volunteers, and experts.* The core of this training and support is the roughly monthly 3-Hour Afterschool Science Workshop.

The 3-Hour Afterschool Science Workshop

In late 1999, a remarkably talented group of educators at six U.S. science centers and children's museums[iii] each recruited five or six local afterschool agencies to attend a series of roughly monthly workshops over a period of three school years. Each month, the museum educators led a workshop at the museum on a new Design It! topic as it came off the development presses at EDC. With very little time to prepare or experience all aspects of each curriculum themselves, these educators led their recruits through each of the project challenges *as learners* before sending them home with a complete set of materials to lead the project with their students.

Out of that early experience has evolved a workshop format that has now been delivered more than 1,500 times in cities and towns across 16 states. About 1,000 afterschool agencies have received training (on average of about 1 years' duration), and it is estimated that several hundreds of thousands of children age roughly 7–12 (and some as old as 18) have experienced the Design It! and Explore It! projects one or more times as a result of these workshops. Evaluation data from all four Design It!–related projects[7] clearly indicate that the training and support provided for the frontline afterschool staff at these workshops has been crucial to the successful implementation of the projects with children.

Despite the financial and logistical burdens posed by the length and frequency of these workshops, participants overwhelmingly report that the intensity, frequency, and duration of training is crucial to building their confidence and skill. We still believe that three hours is the shortest possible amount of time necessary to prepare afterschool staff to lead the four or more challenges of a new curriculum and to build facilitation skills and pedagogical best practices.

Modeling Best Practices

A signature feature of the Design It! (NPASS) 3-Hour Workshops is that the afterschool staff spend the major portion of their time engaging with the project challenges as learners in *exactly the same way* the children will later do so at their afterschool sites—not reading or talking about them but actually struggling with each challenge as learners—and they are led in doing so by a trainer who models *exactly the way* the project should be led with the children.

The modeling of best teaching practice is itself one of the most fundamental best practices of afterschool science professional development—and it is vital that talking *about* teaching practice be separated from doing it. So long as the students or staff or trainers are immersed in the project, the role of the facilitator is only to encourage and validate and enrich that experience. Only during natural breaks or pauses between

---

7. Design It!, Explore It!, NPASS, NPASS2

extended bouts of exploration should the discussion switch to metacognitive analysis of teaching or learning strategies.

It is hard to do this consistently. Adult learners are often self-conscious about playing with the materials or are embarrassed to "fail." And they are prone to break out of the immediate and personal experience of the project to worry or query about implementation concerns as these come to mind. An inexperienced trainer might seize such teachable moments to engage in discussion on the spot. But this is a mistake: the two aspects of the training should be kept entirely distinct. Only when the adult learners have truly immersed themselves in each new section of the project should they be encouraged to switch to the role of potential project leader. This requires that the trainer stay clearly in character as the *activity facilitator* when leading the challenges themselves and that she or he "change hats" very deliberately and judiciously to discuss logistical or teaching practices.

In the early days, the overwhelming need of most afterschool staff is to leave the training with the right materials and with practical tips on making the project work *well* for their children. By far the best way to prepare them to *lead* a project is to have them *do* the project—from soup to nuts—or as many courses as time allows. One cannot really appreciate the nuances or anticipate problems until one has experienced them oneself. But trainers must also reserve time in every workshop to reflect on predictable implementation issues and to point out at least one pedagogical practice or teaching tip modeled by the trainer during the current workshop—thus gradually drawing attention to and building facilitation skills over the course of successive workshops.

Communities of Practice

A particularly important aspect of this capacity building professional development model has been the creation of communities of practice among afterschool agencies and staff and among the trainers who serve them. This requires commitment over time by participants at all levels. The science trainers who deliver the monthly workshops are generally professional educators and afterschool technical assistance providers within their city or state. They too generally enter the process lacking experience or confidence with science and science training. A commitment of two or more years seems to be the minimum that will allow individual skills and confidence to develop and to create a new cadre of mutually supportive afterschool science educators with professional development expertise within each state or region.

Throughout the whole 14-year period of development and dissemination of this curriculum series, many participating afterschool agencies have signed letters of commitment agreeing to assign one or more committed youth workers or program specialists to attend successive trainings for *at least one school year* and to dedicate a suitable physical space at their site and schedule the program at least once a week for the children. And the children too are asked to stay for at least a whole project at a time and may only join at the beginning of a new project. "Drop-ins" and intermittent implementation at any level undermine the strength of the communities of learners.

These requirements demand a degree of institutional or personal "readiness" that not all agencies or individuals possess. Afterschool staff and agencies, science trainers, and even state afterschool networks that could not achieve them have had to be passed over at the recruitment stage or replaced later on by others who *could* do so. The choice, then as now, has been to focus resources on sites with the highest likelihood of successful implementation while still remaining principally within communities with high needs and low resources.

Alignment With NSES and NGSS

The intellectual content of Design It! and Explore It! fits comfortably within state and national frameworks and standards for science and engineering learning in the elementary and middle school years. Experiences during Design It! projects *complement* and lay the foundations for formal learning in multiple area of physical science and engineering syllabus for those grades. But for philosophical and practical reasons, Design It! makes no attempt to *teach* children the particular conceptual content that arises within these projects. The curriculum does, however, have a near perfect match with the Science Practices identified in the NGSS.

- Asking questions and defining problems
- Developing and using models
- Planning and carrying out investigations
- Analyzing and interpreting data
- Using mathematics and computational thinking
- Constructing explanations and designing solutions
- Engaging in argument from evidence
- Obtaining, evaluating, and communicating information

Well-facilitated, project-based afterschool science and engineering programs offer significant opportunities for student to develop all the habits and skills described here. Much depends on the finesse and skills of the project leaders, however, to bring the students along with the practices. Students don't naturally talk precisely or accurately about what they see or what they plan to do or why they made such and such a choice. They rarely want to keep good records, and they can be circular and capricious in their reasoning. None of these practices develop quickly, and children will resist them mightily if they are promoted on the basis of future benefit or current virtue—"it will be good for you!" Practitioners must understand that the science practices are not just a set of ingredients in a recipe—in the way that the much-misused "scientific method" is so often invoked. The incentive for adopting these practices must always be practical and current—that they make the process of solving this particular set of problems more interesting, more effective, and more rewarding *right now.* Their primary selling point should be that they *work!*

Science Practices: *What Works*

It is a cliché of inquiry learning that there are no right answers. But the truth is that there usually *are* definitive patterns or features in a successful design! In Design It!—as in real engineering—a project is complete when the children discover the set of design features that work best for the current device and materials and when they *also* know *how they know* if their answers or findings are appropriate or accurate. Facilitating discourse of this kind is particularly difficult for inexperienced afterschool staff but is a vital element of critical thinking and problems solving.

As a first step in this direction, Design It! project leaders are trained to use the "What Works?" discussion technique to catalog the group's strategies, findings, methods, tests, and so on that appear to be working or not working in the current challenge. It is a brainstorm of empirical results with no judgment and no analysis: just a public record of the immediately observable relationships of cause and effect. "When we (added weight at the. . . .) it (crashed, spun longer, etc. . . . !.)" or "Wobbly wheels don't work!" and so on.

This sharing takes place away from the materials, should last only a few minutes, and should occur a couple of times during each working session. Children call out what has or has not worked, and the leader enters their contributions into two columns on a simple wall chart: WORKS/DOESN'T WORK. There is no comment or judgment or censorships by the teacher or other students beyond keeping contributions respectful and on topic. If a contribution contradicts an earlier one, it still goes into the proper column without comment. The group returns to this chart from time to time to confirm or eliminate previous findings and thus gradually catalogs the consensus finding of the whole group.

No theories or "explanations" are entered onto this chart—only observations and empirical conclusions. As they come up, "science words" like gravity, centrifugal force, or momentum[8] are added to a separate "Parking Lot" list without any attempt to define them or confirm their relevance. Interested children are invited to research or study these terms at another time. Most importantly, the facilitator must not allow his or her own expertise or confusion about these terms distract attention from the primary pedagogy here: to collect and assess empirical data in the light of the immediate and practical task at hand.

This rather formalized discussion format may appear at odds with the informal nature of afterschool science. But informal science should not necessarily be unstructured science. This format is one of a number of useful and relatively unobtrusive structures that guide and enable focused exploration, discourse and collaboration. It ensures sharing of evidence and respect for the views and findings of peers. It is a public record of data that can be revised by consensus as new evidence arises. And if kept short and used frequently, it is an effective classroom management technique—democratizing the sharing of ideas and grounding them firmly in personal rather than received wisdom.

Conclusion

Policy makers, educators, corporate leaders, and funders are increasingly looking to afterschool science to raise academic "achievement" and boost participation in the STEM professions among students from underserved and underrepresented groups. This new attention on STEM learning during the afterschool hours and associated increases in funding and infrastructural support is a move in the right direction for the nation and for the children served—up to a point!

Afterschool science must ever remember that its role is to *complement*—lay the foundations for—academic learning, by nurturing identification with science and increasing the use and understanding of the *science practices*. It is not the role of afterschool to fill in the gaps in "core content" learning left by formal K–8 science. The NGSS place the science practices firmly back in the center of the school science curriculum, but the sheer volume of core content in the new standards is no less daunting than in the old ones.

Only time will tell whether K–8 science will be able to deliver on the promises of NGSS for a more integrated and engaging approach to teaching and learning science

---

8. Some children use such terms freely whether they understand them or not. This tends to create the illusion of expertise that distracts from the vital goal of creating a safe and equitable learning environment for everyone. Afterschool staff should not be made to feel that they are falling short on their mandate if they cannot define or explain terms and concepts that they themselves do not understand well either.

in school. In the meantime, for a great many students, afterschool may be the only place where they experience science as a practical, enjoyable, and affirming enterprise. Imposing expectations for academic science learning on afterschool is tantamount to extending the school day by other means. It is unreasonable and unrealistic on a large scale, and it will drive away both the children and the staff, defeating the intended objectives in both domains.

Afterschool science must keep faith with its fundamental mission to support children's development and growth by nurturing their identity, self-confidence, and vision. Design It! and its attendant professional development model has shown that the capacity exists within the field to provide widespread programming that increases student confidence and identity and fills the one aspect of formal science learning that is appropriate to the afterschool mission—to nurture the use and understand of the *science practices* in the context of enjoyable, age-appropriate, and meaningful projects. Assessment efforts should therefore focus on the quality of the programming, the pedagogy and quality of facilitation, and on the impact on students' attitudes and subsequent study and career choices. The job of capitalizing on these renewed attitudes and interests, and turning them into "achievement," as measured by assessments of core scientific content knowledge, should be left to other domains.

References

NGSS Lead States. (2013). *Next Generation Science Standards: For states by states.* Washington, DC: National Academies Press.

National Research Council. (1996). *National science education standards.* Washington, DC: National Academies Press.

Endnotes

i Design It!: NSF grant ISE # 9814765 (1999–2002). Explore It!: NSF grant ISE # 0205883 (2002–2005), PI Bernie Zubrowski, EDC in Waltham, Mass.

ii NPASS[1]: NSF grant ISE # 0515549 (2005–2009). NPASS2 [Taking NPASS to Scale]: NSF grant ISE # 0917576 (2009–2013). PI Charlie Hutchison. Learn more at http://npass2.edc.org.

iii Margaret Leonard, Baltimore Museum of Science and Industry; Tim Porter, Boston Children's Museum, Maryanne Steiner, Science Museum of Minnesota; Paul Tatter, Science Center of Eastern Connecticut; Diane Miller, St. Louis Science Center; and Lois Winslow, Pittsburg Children's Museum.

12

Engineering for Everyone

4-H's Junk Drawer Robotics Curriculum

Steven M. Worker, 4-H Science, Engineering, and Technology Coordinator,
University of California Agriculture and Natural Resources
Richard L. Mahacek, 4-H Youth Development Advisor, Emeritus,
University of California Agriculture and Natural Resources
Tara D. M. Wheeler, Director, Learning Products, National 4-H Council
Saundra W. Frerichs, 4-H Science Education Specialist,
University of Nebraska-Lincoln

Are you wondering how to teach robotics? Are you looking for an inexpensive and fun engineering education curriculum for upper elementary and middle school youth? Then, 4-H's Junk Drawer Robotics (JDR) is for you. Using common household items such as paper clips, brass brads, toy motors, craft sticks, batteries, aluminum foil, binder clips, and many others, JDR engages youth in science inquiry, the engineering design process, and technology creation and building. Activities emphasize *design* as a pedagogical strategy, as educators engage youth, through design, with science, technology, engineering, and mathematics (STEM). This approach helps prepare young people to be creative problem solvers while developing dispositions as designers, which will serve them well in our digital society.

The key elements of JDR are scientific and engineering practices; facilitator instruction framed in the experiential learning cycle; and small-group collaborative learning. It also offers excellent opportunities for cross-age facilitation (teenagers-as-teachers). Published by National 4-H Council in 2011 as part of the 4-H Science Initiative, JDR is strengthening and reaffirming 4-H's legacy for high-quality science education in out-of-school time.

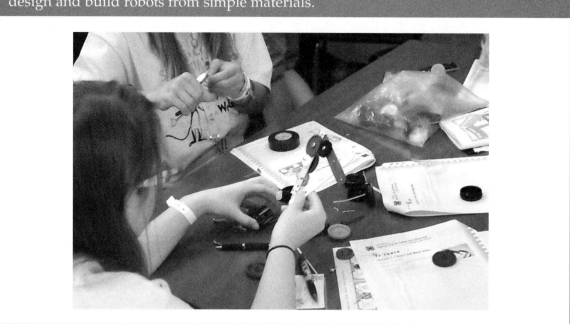

In Junk Drawer Robotics, teen mentors work with children, using hand tools to design and build robots from simple materials.

Image by R. Mahacek, courtesy of 4H National Council.

Educational robotics is emerging as a promising method to engage youth in STEM education. Educational robotics promotes an interdisciplinary approach, truly integrating STEM education while improving motivation for learning. In addition, educational robotics helps strengthen collaboration and fosters 21st century skills (Eguchi, 2012).

To download a sample activity and learn how to obtain all of the JDR materials, visit www.4-H.org/curriculum/robotics.

Big Ideas and Science Themes in Junk Drawer Robotics

The JDR curriculum consists of three levels in the form of facilitator guides. The first level is *Give Robots a Hand*, which focuses on robot arms and grippers. The second level is *Robots on the Move*, where youth learn about robot movement. The third level is *Mechatronics*, which emphasizes mechanical, electronic, and feedback systems and how these systems work together. A youth notebook has sections for each level and encourages youth to think like scientists and engineers, by recording data and ideas, drawing designs, and reflecting on their experiences. The notebook also provides specific information for the challenge activities. Following is a summary of the big ideas and science themes in each of the three levels.

Give Robots a Hand

Arms are flexible with joints—shoulders, elbows, and wrists—that allow us to place our arms in many positions. The hand with its fingers and thumb can grab, hold, and pick

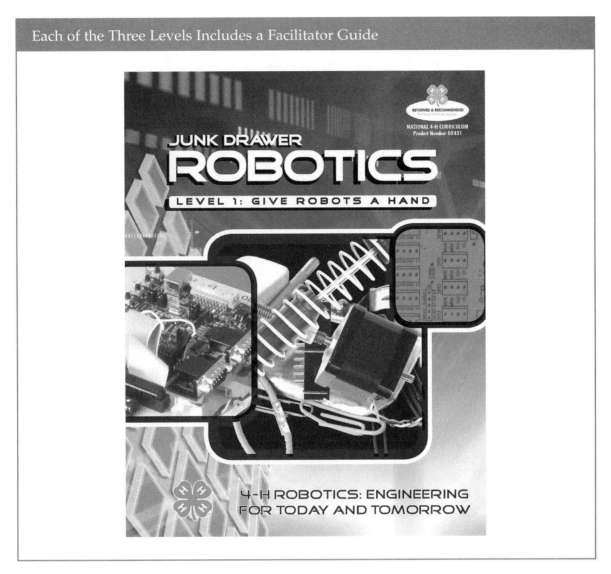

Each of the Three Levels Includes a Facilitator Guide

Image courtesy of 4-H National Council.

up items. Robot arms allow robots to grab, lift, move, or position items. Activities in *Give Robots a Hand* involve exploring the design and function of robotic arms, hands, and grippers and building a robotic arm that really moves!

The underlying science concepts in *Give Robots a Hand* include the crosscutting concept of structure and function. That is, the functioning of natural and built systems alike depends on the shapes and relationships of certain key parts as well as on the properties of the materials from which they are made. Robot designers often use simple machines (such as levers, gears, or wheels and axles) as tools to enable their robots to have certain functions. The fundamental ideas of simple machines can be thought of as special cases of structure and function. The activities in *Give Robots a Hand* also enable youth to explore the core physical science ideas that different materials have different properties, which make them better for some applications than others, and qualitative understanding of forces and interactions, including the idea of leverage.

Engineering and technology concepts in *Give Robots a Hand* include the core ideas of engineering at the upper elementary level—defining the problem to be solved, generating and comparing multiple solutions, and planning and carrying out fair tests (controlled experiments) to improve the design. Through their activities, youth learn that engineering design is a purposeful process of generating and evaluating ideas to develop and implement the best possible solution to a given problem.

Perhaps most important, by bringing the ideas of science and engineering together, youth learn that understanding physical science and mathematics concepts is necessary in making engineering design decisions. The enduring understandings about robots that youth develop are that the physical design (form) of a robot is based on its intended function, and it is often necessary to choose certain materials and design elements (e.g., pneumatics, levers) or otherwise constrain the design in order to achieve the goal. The robot's structure, components, and programming determine its potential behaviors and enable its function.

Robots on the Move

Mobility allows robots to complete tasks in locations and situations impossible for humans. Mobile robots can be used on land, in the air, on the surface, or underwater. A mobile robot can be controlled remotely using a cord or tether, radio control, or with programmed instructions. In *Robots on the Move*, youth design and build machines that roll, slide, draw, or move underwater and explore robot mobility—movement, power transfer, and locomotion.

The underlying science concepts in these activities include friction (energy and forces), basic electrical power and motors, gears systems, and buoyancy. Buoyancy is the force that causes an object to float in a fluid. An underwater remotely operated vehicle needs to be near neutral buoyancy so it can operate under water. Friction can slow down or limit the movement of objects, but friction is also a useful tool when we need traction or gripping power. A drive train directs the motion, speed, and direction of the movements from a motor. Gears, levers, and cams are components of a drive train.

Engineering and technology concepts emphasized in *Robots on the Move* include the role of constraints and the importance of iteration, which involves multiple trials to improve a design. As in the other units, understanding of underlying physical science and mathematics concepts is necessary in making engineering design decisions.

The crosscutting concept of cause-and-effect spans both science and engineering. In science the goal is to explain a phenomenon, usually by discovering its cause. In engineering the goal is to design a system to cause a desired effect, so cause-and-effect relationships are as much a part of engineering as of science. Indeed, the process of design is a good place to help youth begin to think in terms of cause-and-effect, because they must understand the underlying causal relationships in order to devise and explain a design that can achieve a specified objective.

Mechatronics

Robots are designed to perform a specific job better than it could be done by a person or another machine. They also provide an excellent example of the synergy that occurs when mechanical, electronic, and feedback systems are merged. Essential components include sensors that enable a robot to detect phenomena in the world around them, control systems that enable them to interpret the inputs they receive, and mechanical and electronic systems that enable them to carry out tasks. In this unit, youth explore sensors, computer science concepts, build circuits, and design their own robot.

The underlying science concepts include electronic circuits, sensing, and the binary number system. Youth have hands-on experiences, without computers, to learn important concepts in computer science, including programming that allows humans to control robot behavior. They learn how to use basic logic elements to predict outcomes and the essential ideas of Boolean logic, which forms the basis of all modern digital electronics. They also create flowcharts to help them design and clarify instructions for their robots.

Engineering and technology concepts guide the young peoples' applications of their growing knowledge of electronics and computers to compare different design ideas, to integrate the different systems into a working robot, and to troubleshoot their inventions in order to identify and repair failure points.

The crosscutting concept that spans science and engineering most appropriate for this unit is systems and system models. Just as scientists create simplified models to study complex interacting systems in the natural world, engineers also isolate a single system and construct a simplified model of it. This is especially important when designing a robot, which involves multiple complex interacting systems.

Flow of Activities

Each of the three books, or levels, contains three to five modules. Within a module there is a sequencing of activities in three stages: To Learn, To Do, and To Make. In this sequence, youth learn like scientists (To Learn), design like engineers (To Do), and build like technicians (To Make).

To Learn (Science Inquiry). These activities emphasize exploration and form the foundation upon which youth build conceptual understanding. Youth learn the underlying scientific concept through activities that contain minimal guidance or expectations of accomplishments. Through intentional debriefing, educators pose open-ended questions to help youth reflect individually and in groups.

To Do (Engineering Design). The design activity takes place after exploration of the scientific concepts in "To Learn" activities. Youth are presented with a design problem and work together to design and plan a solution. This phase promotes the engineering design concepts of problem identification, framing, and solving. Deeper learning happens because youth build upon the knowledge gained in the exploration phase and intellectually create a design without using the physical objects.

To Make (Technology Creation, Testing, and Rebuilding). After the design activity, youth build, construct, and test their solution. This stage often involves modifications to the original design. During this time, youth solidify their understanding of the scientific concepts as they enact a solution, build a prototype, and test the design. Through facilitated debriefing by the educator, youth compare their product to those constructed by the other groups.

This process allows youth to explore new knowledge using science inquiry, then build upon those budding concepts by applying them in designing, creating, and refining technologies. The curriculum captures the synergy between science, engineering, and technology by sequencing learning in such a way to allow each focus area to be addressed separately, yet highlights and reinforces the interconnections. In this manner, the curriculum supports the core idea that science, engineering, and technology continuously interact and move each other forward.

Get Things Rolling

Following is a vignette of a single activity from the first module of Level 2 Robots on the Move.

In order to extend the longevity of a robot's mechanical parts, it must be properly designed to minimize friction and reduce energy consumption. Get Things Rolling is a sequence of activities that help youth begin to understand friction, how friction depends on the properties of materials, and the application of these ideas in robotics.

Slip N Slide (To Learn—Science Inquiry). Youth begin by investigating how a box of paper clips slides down an angled cardboard ramp. The ramp consists of a number of surfaces with varying degrees of resistance. For example, some surfaces might be sandpaper, packaging tape, duct tape, and aluminum tape. Youth are asked to record the degree of incline required to overcome static friction—the angle at which the box begins to slide—for the various ramp surfaces.

Rolling Along (To Learn—Science Inquiry). Next, youth are challenged to modify their box of paper clips to reduce friction. Some youth may find that covering their box of paper clips with packaging tape works while others may add wheels (perhaps using paper clips and straws) so the box rolls down the ramp rather than slide.

The Clipmobile Challenge (To Do-Engineering Design; and To Make—Technology Creation, Testing, and Rebuilding). After the above investigations, youth are divided into teams and challenged to design and build a clipmobile—a vehicle that can overcome friction and travel down the ramp and continue traveling. The challenge incorporates the engineering aspect of "constraints" as each team has a certain amount of pretend money they can use to purchase parts for their clipmobile from the "Junk Drawer Supply Company." The company stocks parts, including craft sticks, paper clips, brass paper brads, binder clips, straws (drinking and coffee), rubber bands, wheels, and wood skewers. Free services include the use tools, such as pliers, wire cutters, saws, and hand-operated drills or punches. The first component of the activity (To Do) asks youth to work together to design a clipmobile and plan the type and number of parts their design

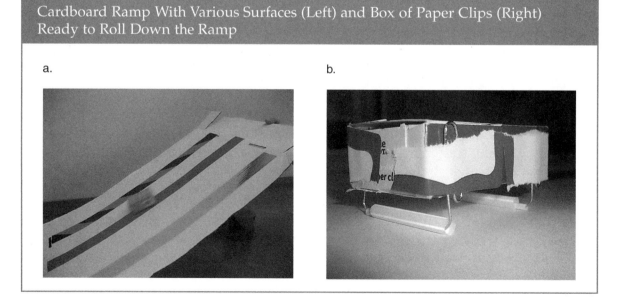

Cardboard Ramp With Various Surfaces (Left) and Box of Paper Clips (Right) Ready to Roll Down the Ramp

a.

b.

Image by R. Mahacek, courtesy of 4H National Council.

will require. The second component (To Make) invites youth to build their clipmobile, test it on the ramp, and rebuild it if necessary to improve performance.

Teams evaluate themselves on a number of factors, including weight capacity of their clipmobile, performance, and the cost effectiveness of their budget. Teams demonstrate their vehicle to the class along with an inventory sheet of parts and their budget. Even with the best performance (going the longest distance off the ramp), a team will not necessarily have the most effective clipmobile if they purchased a large number of parts. In the end, youth learn that the engineering design process often includes real-life constraints that impact the engineering design process. To conclude the activity, the educator helps youth reflect on their experience through sharing, processing, and generalizing. This includes posing questions for youth to reflect on individually and in groups.

Visit the 4-H Robotics page to download this sample activity: www.4-H.org/curriculum/robotics.

Junk Drawer Robotics Promotes Creativity and Problem Solving

JDR engages youth in learning science and engineering through the practices of science inquiry and engineering design. Our design-based learning approach fosters problem solving and critical thinking (Lee & Breitenberg, 2010), strengthens creativity (Doppelt, 2009), and is consistent with how youth naturally learn (Blumenfeld et al., 1991). Design-based learning is a special case of project-based learning, which helps youth develop skills in planning and construction, and testing, with frequent opportunities for reflection and metacognition. The end result is the creation of shareable artifacts that serve as external representations of the youths' growing knowledge and sense of accomplishment. An important part of the learning process involves reflection on the design and construction processes and the on the final artifact itself.

Elements of the Junk Drawer Robotics Curriculum

Focus on Scientific and Engineering Practices. The curriculum emphasizes scientific and engineering practices (although the curriculum uses the term "science processes" and "science, engineering, and technology abilities"). Through hands-on activities, youth identify, frame, and explore concepts and then apply their learning through design and construction. This approach helps youth develop critical thinking skills and scaffolds their ability to apply their knowledge to problem-solving activities. When extended over time, youth work toward advanced concepts. Engineering practices are enhanced when incorporated with communications, teamwork, and hands-on activities.

Hands-On Learning Through the Experiential Learning Cycle. The experiential learning cycle, which nurtures natural curiosity, contains three steps: (1) experiencing; (2) sharing and processing; and (3) generalizing and applying (e.g., Kolb, 1984). Each activity begins with an experience. After the experience, presenters help youth reflect on the activity by encouraging sharing and processing with open-ended questions. To complete the learning cycle, each activity contains a generalizing and applying section to help youth connect concepts to broader robotic concepts and to the real world. In addition, each module, which consists of several activities, also follows the learning cycle. Youth begin by exploring basic science concepts and processes, then apply what they have learned through designing and building activities.

Small-Group Collaborative Learning. Youth participants learn from each other by working in pairs or small groups. The opportunity for youth to collaborate, share, and work with each other promotes collaborative learning while also enhancing skills in teamwork, communication, and group decision making.

Engaging Teens as Mentors for Younger Children. JDR encourages teenagers to facilitate activities with younger youth. Older teens interact with younger learners and work together to explore the big ideas identified in each module. Allowing teens to teach younger youth has been shown to provide benefits for both the teens and younger participants (Lee & Murdock, 2001). Suggestions for helping teens become effective mentors can be found in the online facilitator guide.

Junk Drawer Robotics and the NGSS

Although JDR was developed before release of the Framework (NRC, 2012) and the Next Generation Science Standards (NGSS) (NGSS Lead States, 2013), it can be used to support all three dimensions of the NGSS.

Practices of Science and Engineering. JDR engages youth in all eight practices of science and engineering in the following ways:

1. **Asking questions (for science) and defining problems (for engineering).** Each three-part cycle begins with a scientific question. For example, in the above example,

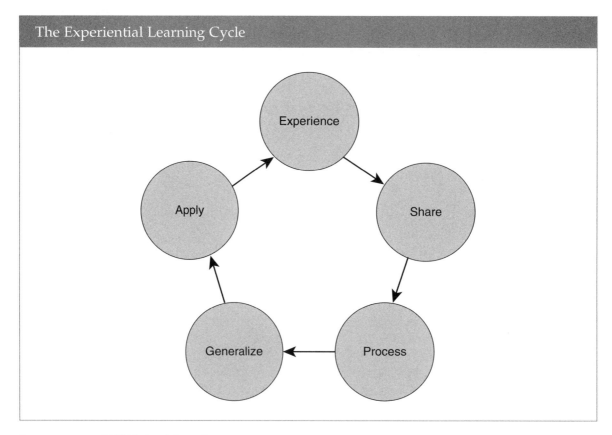

Image courtesy of 4-H National Council.

youth investigate how friction affects motion. Then, in the design challenges youth often need to clarify and define the problems that they are attempting to solve.

2. **Developing and using models.** Every level involves youth in developing and using models of robots, which are in turn models of various parts of the human body. For example, in the first-level activities, youth must model the ways that people use their hands and arms in various ways.

3. **Planning and carrying out investigations.** Youth control variables as they conduct investigations to answer scientific questions. This is evident in the friction activity above. Later, as they develop robotic systems, they carry out further investigations as engineers to see if their designs work in practice.

4. **Analyzing and interpreting data.** In both their science and engineering activities, youth collect and analyze data, aided by their youth notebook, which they then apply to their designs.

5. **Using mathematics and computational thinking.** Measurement is needed in each of the levels, while computational thinking is introduced primarily in level three: *Mechatronics*.

6. **Constructing explanations (for science) and designing solutions (for engineering).** As youth complete their inquiry activities, they are asked to reflect on what they've learned and explain concepts such as friction. Their designs and completed robots are their design solutions.

7. **Engaging in argument from evidence.** Facilitator guides urge educators to engage youth in frequent reflection and discussion, during which the youth discuss their current thinking based on their experiences. The friendly competitions facilitate arguments about the best solutions and provide evidence in support of some ideas over others.

8. **Obtaining, evaluating, and communicating information.** Youth are encouraged to go beyond these activities to learn more about robotics and related ideas from a variety of sources, aided by the Career Connections in the facilitator guides. Youth communicate their ideas through writing and drawing in their robotics notebook. They practice communicating their ideas verbally in the reflections and presentations at the end of each module.

Crosscutting Concepts. Each of the three levels emphasizes one of the seven crosscutting concepts from the Framework and NGSS:

Structure and Function is a key idea in *Give Robots a Hand*, since youth must consider both the materials and shape of the parts that they use to construct a robotic hand such that it functions as intended.

Cause and Effect is an essential idea in *Robots on the Move*. The investigations conducted by youth lead to causal principles, which they then apply in their design efforts to create effects that they want.

Systems and System Models is a perfect fit for *Mechatronics*, in which youth synthesize the mechanical and electronic systems to design and create robots of their own design.

Core Ideas. JDR provides opportunities for youth to learn about core ideas at the fourth and fifth grade levels in both the physical sciences and engineering design. For example, consider the following performance expectations from the NGSS (the first number indicates grade level):

4-PS3–2. Make observations to provide evidence that energy can be transferred from place to place by sound, light, heat, and electric currents. (Transfer of energy from place to place is woven into each level.)

4-PS3–4. Apply scientific ideas to design, test, and refine a device that converts energy from one form to another. (Conversion of energy from one form to another—from electrical energy to kinetic energy—is emphasized in all levels.)

4-PS4–3. Generate and compare multiple solutions that use patterns to transfer information. (In the third level, youth learn to use patterns to simulate the process of programming to give instructions to their robots.)

4-LS1–2. Use a model to describe that animals receive different types of information through their senses, process the information in their brain, and respond to the information in different ways. (Robots provide an excellent model for using nature, to inspire engineering designs, for example, how animals sense their environment, interprets the information, and responds.)

5-PS1–3. Make observations and measurements to identify materials based on their properties. (Material properties is emphasized in the first level, but continues to be important as youth select materials based on their properties in each level.)

3–5-ETS1–1. Define a simple design problem reflecting a need or a want that includes specified criteria for success and constraints on materials, time, or cost. (Each challenge involves problem clarification and definition, as well as specification of criteria and constraints.)

3–5-ETS1–2. Generate and compare multiple possible solutions to a problem based on how well each is likely to meet the criteria and constraints of the problem. (Each of the levels engage youth to generate and consider multiple possible solutions to problems.)

3–5-ETS1–3. Plan and carry out fair tests in which variables are controlled and failure points are considered to identify aspects of a model or prototype that can be improved. (Youth conduct a number of investigations involving the control of variables both to answer scientific questions and to improve their designs.)

Contrasting Junk Drawer Robotics to Other Robotics Programs

The JDR curriculum differs from many other educational robotics programs in several ways. First, the JDR emphasis on "learning through messing about," supported by activities that require common household items (e.g., paper clips, rubber bands, craft sticks, straws), contrasts with other robotics platform kits that require predesigned, prepackaged, and often expensive robotics kits. Avoiding predesign kits and having youth repurpose common items offer more opportunities for creativity. The open-ended approach promotes a materials engineering perspective, which Bennett and Monahan (2013) describe as promoting *materials literacy,* helping children become comfortable with exploring the affordances of different objects, reusability, and repurposeability.

Second, computers are not needed in JDR. While the third level has youth simulating computer programming concepts through group games (e.g., loops, logic statements), there is no actual computer programming taking place. In a traditional educational robotics program, youth build a device (often using predesigned pieces), connect sensors, and program a controller for actions mediated by the sensor input. In contrast, JDR focuses on the scientific and engineering concepts behind robotics but does not extend as far as a specific computer programming language.

Evaluation

JDR was evaluated using three primary methods, including expert review of content, formative evaluations with youth, and an external evaluation field test, described in Mahacek and Worker (2011). These evaluations demonstrated gains in content knowledge around engineering and robotics as well as high levels of engagement and motivation of youth through the curricular activities. We look forward to the continued momentum for engineering education and believe that JDR is a welcome resource for educators interested in science and engineering education.

More About 4-H Science

The 4-H Youth Development Program is administered by Cooperative Extension, a system composed of the U.S. Department of Agriculture, respective state Land-Grant Universities, and county governments. 4-H has a mission to provide school enrichment and out-of-school time community-based youth programs that engage youth in reaching their fullest potential while advancing the field of youth development. The vision of 4-H is to help young people become healthy, happy, thriving people who make a positive difference in their communities.

Since its inception in 1902, the 4-H Youth Development program has created hands-on experiences for youth (ages 5–18) to learn about the natural world, technology, and their communities. In 2011, young people enrolled in 5.3 million science-related 4-H projects. At the core of 4-H's work is a commitment to high-quality positive youth development. This approach requires that young people have access to a long-term relationship with a caring adult, leadership and service experiences, and the opportunity to acquire and use meaningful skills. 4-H programs contribute to youth development and educational outcomes including the Six C's of Positive Youth Development—caring, contribution, confidence, competence, character, connection—and improved science, engineering, and technological literacy, health literacy, and civic engagement.

As the youth development program of the nation's land-grant universities, 4-H is uniquely positioned to address the challenges of increasing STEM (science, technology, engineering, and math) engagement, interests, skills, knowledge, and aspirations among youth. In support of this mission, 4-H has developed a comprehensive 4-H curriculum system that includes standards, professional development, peer review, and diverse learning products in the STEM fields. These learning products are available to all via the 4-H Mall, where more than 50 curricula are offered on topics ranging from aerospace to robotics and more. Learn more at www.4-Hmall.org/curriculum.

In 2008, 4-H launched a bold goal to engage one million new young scientists. To achieve this goal, 4-H built a comprehensive science initiative, with high-quality learning products at its core. This includes a rubric, training, and tools to enhance existing 4-H science curricula and develop new resources. These "Science Ready" standards have helped the 4-H system (1) identify science-focused programs; (2) improve the quality and quantity of programs; and (3) track youth participation in programs that are aligned with these quality standards. In 2012, 4-H achieved its goal of engaging one million new young scientists, with 1.33 million 4-H youth enrolled in 4-H Science Ready programs.

A 4-H Science Checklist serves as a guide for high-quality Science Ready programs. Specifically, Science Ready 4-H experiences (1) are based on the NGSS; (2) develop participants' scientific and engineering practices; (3) ground learning environments in a positive youth development foundation; (4) are facilitated by educators who are well-trained in youth development and educational practices; (5) use an experiential approach to learning; (6) foster creativity and curiosity among participants; and (7) attend to frequency and duration in nurturing youth outcomes.

References

Bennett, D., & Monahan, P. (2013). NYSCI design lab: No bored kids! In M. Honey & D. E. Kanter (Eds.), *Design. Make. Play. Growing the next generation of STEM innovators* (pp. 34–49). New York, NY: Routledge.

Blumenfeld, P. C., Soloway, E., Marx, R. W., Krajcik, J. S., Guzdial, M., Palincsar, A. (1991). Motivating project-based learning: Sustaining the doing, supporting the learning. *Educational Psychologist, 26*(3 & 4), 369–398.

Doppelt, Y. (2009). Assessing creative thinking in design-based learning. *International Journal of Technology and Design Education, 19*(1), 55–65.

Eguchi, A. (2012). Educational robotics theories and practice: Tips for how to do it right. In B. S. Barker, G. Nugent, N. Grandgenett, & V. I. Adamchuck (Eds.), *Robots in K–12 education: A new technology for learning* (pp. 1–30). Hershey, PA: IGI Global.

Kolb, D. A. (1984). *Experiential learning: Experience as the source of learning and development.* Upper Saddle River, NJ: Prentice Hall.

Lee, H. K., & Breitenberg, M. (2010). Education in the new millennium: The case for design-based learning. *The International Journal of Art & Design Education, 29*(1), 54–60.

Lee, F. C. H., & Murdock, S. (2001). Teenagers as teachers programs: Teen essential elements. *Journal of Extension, 39*(1). [Article 1RIB1]. Retrieved from http://www.joe.org/joe/2001february/rb1.php.

Mahacek, R., & Worker, S. (2011). Extending science education with engineering and technology: *Junk Drawer Robotics* curriculum. In A. Subramaniam, K. Heck, R. Carlos, & S. Junge (Eds.), *Advances in youth development: Research and evaluation from the University of California Cooperative Extension 2001–2010* (pp. 46–57). Davis, CA: University of California Agriculture and Natural Resources.

National Research Council. (2012). *A framework for K–12 science education: Practices, crosscutting concepts, and core ideas.* Washington, DC: The National Academies Press.

NGSS Lead States. (2013). *Next Generation Science Standards: For states, by states.* Washington, DC: The National Academies Press.

13

PictureSTEM

Tamara J. Moore, Institute for P -12 Engineering Research & Learning (INSPIRE),
Purdue University: West Lafayette, Indiana
Kristina M. Tank, STEM Education Center,
University of Minnesota: St. Paul, Minnesot

Kindergarten Students Working on Their Design in PictureSTEM: Designing Hamster Habitats

Image courtesy of Kristina Tank and Tamara Moore.

PictureSTEM is an integrated curriculum that employs engineering design and literacy contexts to connect science, mathematics, and technology content in meaningful and significant ways. PictureSTEM consists of six curricular modules for students in Grades K–5 that were developed to meet elementary teachers' needs for instructional materials to teach essential core content and cross-disciplinary concepts in STEM disciplines called for by the Next Generation Science Standards (NGSS) (NGSS Lead States, 2013) and the Common Core State Standards (NGA & CCSSO, 2010).

PictureSTEM modules engage students in STEM learning through the use of high-quality picture books, STEM activities, and engineering design challenges. The modules are flexible so teachers can implement either one or two activities each day, depending on what works best for their schedules and their students.

Engineering Design as the Interdisciplinary Glue

The focus on engineering allows for a real-world context in which students experience the interdisciplinary nature of learning science and mathematics and develop engineering habits of mind. As described below and illustrated on the next page, the engineering design process in PictureSTEM has six components clustered in three main stages:

Problem and Background: A design process begins by defining a problem and identifying criteria for a successful solution. This stage also includes researching the problem, participating in learning activities (often science and mathematics activities) to gain the necessary background knowledge to develop a viable solution, and identifying constraints.

Plan and Implement: As students engage in engineering design, they must develop a plan for their design solution. This includes brainstorming, proposing multiple potential solutions, and evaluating the pros and cons of competing solutions. In doing so, they must judge the relative importance of different constraints and trade-offs. Students implement their design by creating a prototype, model, or other product.

Test and Evaluate: Once a prototype or model is created, it must be tested and evaluated. This likely involves generating testable hypotheses or questions and designing experiments. Students may conduct experiments and collect data (and/or be provided with data) to analyze and display in graphs or tables in order to evaluate the prototype or solution. Students use the results to identify strengths and weaknesses and redesign their solution. Students are encouraged to redesign and test their solution multiple times until it meets the design criteria.

In PictureSTEM curricular modules, engineering design is "(1) highly iterative; (2) open to the idea that a problem may have many possible solutions; (3) a meaningful context for learning scientific, mathematical, and technological concepts; and (4) a stimulus to systems thinking, modeling, and analysis" (NAE and NRC, 2009, p. 4). Additionally, the engineering experiences encourage students to begin developing engineering *habits of mind*—the developmentally appropriate values, attitudes, and thinking skills associated with engineering, including systems thinking, creativity, optimism, collaboration, communication, and ethical considerations.

High-Quality Literature to Promote Engagement

The use of high-quality trade books in PictureSTEM is based on the idea that story and context engage student interest and provide a means to integrate learning across disciplines. Trade books have an advantage over the typical science textbook in that they can provide up-to-date content with a deeper focus that is more relevant to students' lives, and they tend to be more engaging due to excellent visual features and high-quality writing. Additionally, when English language arts and STEM are taught together, student learning can be deeper and more meaningful in all areas. The PictureSTEM modules provide opportunities to cross the discipline-specific boundaries by meaningfully integrating across all four STEM disciplines and literacy to foster the interconnectedness of real-world problems.

This chapter will focus on one of the early elementary PictureSTEM modules, *Designing Hamster Habitats*, to describe how the literacy integration, STEM activities, and engineering design challenges work together for a STEM integration experience for students. For more information on the PictureSTEM project or to download the modules, visit http://sites .google.com/a/umn.edu/picturestem/.

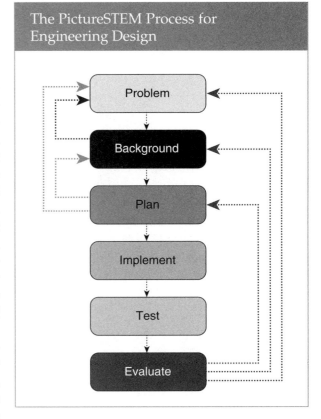

Image courtesy of Kristina Tank and Tamara Moore.

Designing Hamster Habitats

This module is geared toward the early elementary grades (K–2) and consists of five pairs of literacy and STEM integration activities, each of which requires approximately 30 minutes of class time. In the *Designing Hamster Habitats* module, students are introduced to the science concepts of animal characteristics and basic needs, and the mathematics concepts of basic two-dimensional (2-D) and three-dimensional (3-D) shapes and spatial reasoning skills. They then apply what they have learned to an engineering design challenge.

Animals and their homes are a high-interest topic for younger children, and this unit allows children the opportunity to think like engineers as they use their science and mathematics learning to design a habitat for an imaginary pet hamster. Constraints are put on their design, including requiring the students to use exactly 20 connected 3-D shapes to form an exercise habitat trail that would meet the hamster's need for food, water, shelter, space, exercise, and fresh air. To read about the implementation of *Designing Hamster Habitats* in a kindergarten setting, see Tank, Pettis, Moore, and Fehr (2013).

Lesson 1: Animals begins with a whole-class reading of the first chapter of the book *Is My Hamster Wild? The Secret Lives of Hamsters, Gerbils, and Guinea Pigs* (Newcomb & McLarney, 2008), which sets the context for the final design challenge. This informational text introduces students to the lives and habitats of hamsters in nature and describes similarities between how the animals may act when observed as pets to how they act in the wild. In addition to introducing the context and building background knowledge about hamsters, the literacy lesson teaches students about identifying big ideas in informational text by having them identify physical characteristics about hamsters and what they need to survive.

After each literacy lesson, there is a related STEM lesson that reinforces the content from the literacy lesson and builds important math and/or science skills. This STEM lesson consists of two different sorting activities using cards, each of which has information about a different animal (below). In the first activity, students sort the cards into groups based on the animals' physical characteristics, such as fur, wings, scaly skin, and fins. In the second activity, students sort the cards into different groups based on the animals' basic needs. In a discussion following the sorting activity, students apply what they learned about hamsters to identify where other animals get their food, water, and shelter. This lesson lays the foundation for the Day 2 lessons, when students learn that animals' habitats provide for their basic needs.

Lesson 2: Help Me Find My Home uses the book *The Magic School Bus Hops Home* (Relf, 1995) to introduce students to the concept of animal habitats and how these habitats provide animals with food and other basic needs. In this story, students follow Mrs. Frizzle on a "field trip" as they look for a pet frog that has escaped. Mrs. Frizzle suggests that they look for the pet frog in the place where it will be most happy—the pond, its natural habitat, which introduces students to the idea of animal habitats. While students are learning about animal habitats, they are also practicing the reading comprehension skill of making connections to prior knowledge as they identify and share connections between human and animal homes.

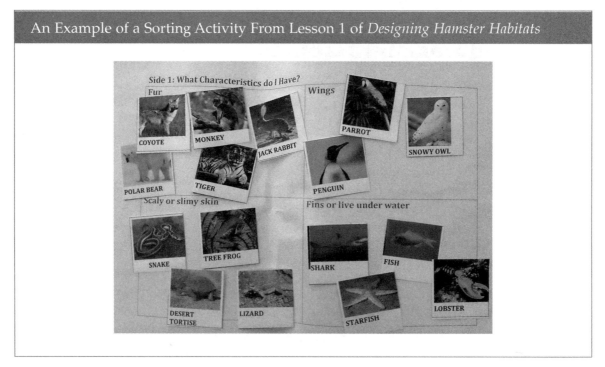

An Example of a Sorting Activity From Lesson 1 of *Designing Hamster Habitats*

Image courtesy of Kristina Tank and Tamara Moore.

The corresponding STEM lesson has students using the same animal cards from the previous lesson, but this time they are sorting animals according to the habitat in which they live. Once students have identified the correct habitats for their animals, then they will select one animal and identify places in that habitat that meet the selected animal's basic needs. This lesson helps to build students' understanding of the physical characteristics and basic needs of animals, as well as how these relate to animal habitats. This prepares students for the final engineering challenge, where they need to design a habitat that keeps their hamster happy and healthy by providing for its basic needs.

Lesson 3: Shapes and Animals focuses on developing the mathematics concepts of shape recognition and spatial reasoning, which the students will need to complete the design challenge. The literacy lesson for this day builds on students' understanding of basic two-dimensional shapes through the story of *The Greedy Triangle* (Burns, 1994) in which a triangle visits a shape shifter to add sides and angles in order to become different shapes.

The STEM activity provides a foundation for the idea of shape rotation, leading to the idea that shapes fit together in different ways. After a whole-class reading of the book *Three Pigs, One Wolf, and Seven Magic Shapes* (Maccarone & Neuhaus, 1998), students use tangram pieces to recreate the animal shapes shown in the story. Tangrams are dissection puzzles that have students use seven basic geometric shapes to make larger shapes. Students learn the names of the different shapes and work individually or in pairs to arrange the tangram pieces to make the target shapes. The teacher can vary the level of difficulty of the puzzle by providing different mats to guide the students' efforts (full size or small size, with or without tangram shape divisions). The figure above shows kindergarten students working on a full-size mat without tangram shape divisions.

Students Working on Their Spatial Reasoning Skills Through the Tangrams Activity

Image courtesy of Kristina Tank and Tamara Moore.

Lesson 4: The Importance of Testing introduces the next part of the engineering design cycle. The story for this day, *Leo Cockroach . . . Toy Tester* (O'Malley, 1999), features a fictional cockroach who takes it upon himself to test toys for a toy company. Throughout the story, he models why testing is an important component of engineering design, helping students see the need for testing their materials before creating their habitat trail designs. Students are reminded of the final design challenge of creating a model of an exercise habitat trail for their hamster using exactly 20 3-D shapes. The shapes may be laid next to one another or stacked in order to create a habitat trail that meets their hamsters' need for running and tunneling.

To prepare for this design challenge, students are asked to think like engineers (and Leo Cockroach) while they test these three-dimensional solids for "flickability" and "stackability." The flickability test has students observing what happens when they (gently!)

flick the different shapes, particularly noting which shapes roll away and which shapes do not based on their orientation. The stackability test has students stacking different combinations of the shapes to determine which shapes may be easily stacked and whether orientation of those shapes affects their stackability.

After testing the different shapes, students start working on the engineering challenge of designing a hamster habitat trail by reviewing and completing the first three steps of the engineering design process, which include defining the problem, identifying necessary background information (and recalling the work they have done in the earlier lessons), and individual brainstorming and group planning (below).

Lesson 5: *Designing a Hamster Habitat* is the culminating lesson of the unit. The picture book *The Perfect Pet* (Palatini & Whatley, 2003) tells the fictional story of a young girl who tries to persuade her parents to buy her several different pets. Her parents respond by pointing out how each animal has needs that make it a poor choice for her as a pet. This sets up a discussion with the students about the needs of different pets and allows the students to revisit the needs of their imaginary pet hamster and how successful habitats must meet the needs of the animals living there.

During the related STEM lesson, students work in pairs to implement the group plan that they created for their hamster habitat. To ensure that their new habitat design is meeting their hamster's basic needs, students use the shapes from Lesson 2 to indicate where the hamster would find food, water, and a safe place to sleep. Once they have completed their habitat design, students test their models by counting out loud the number of shapes they used to ensure that that they met the 20 shape constraint. They also test their models by moving pictures of a hamster along the trail pretending to let the hamster escape

Students Working on the Individual Brainstorming Step of Designing Their Hamster Habitats

Image courtesy of Kristina Tank and Tamara Moore.

Students testing their hamster habitats by moving their imaginary hamster around their trail and looking for places to eat, drink, rest, and escape.

Image courtesy of Kristina Tank and Tamara Moore.

through any holes or gaps in the trail and pretending to let the hamster eat, drink, and rest at the appropriate places as a way of checking that the habitat trail meets all of the hamster's basic needs (shown above).

After sharing their designs with their classmates, students are given the opportunity to redesign their trails, fixing any areas in which the original design challenge requirements were not met, and testing their new designs as before. The final redesign and test phase takes only a short time but provides a critical learning opportunity for students to experience the iterative nature of engineering design.

PictureSTEM Connections to Standards

The PictureSTEM modules are designed to address multiple areas within the NGSS and the Common Core State Standards for mathematics and English language arts. The *Designing Hamster Habitats* module will be used in the following tables to illustrate how these modules help students meet specific standards. Table 13.1 shows disciplinary content standard connections in English language arts and mathematics.

Tables 13.2, 13.3, and 13.4 illustrate how the *PictureSTEM* curriculum can help students achieve standards in all three dimensions described in *A Framework for K–12 Science Education* (NRC, 2012) and embedded in the NGSS (NGSS Lead States, 2013)—core ideas,

Table 13.1 Common Core State Standards in the *Designing Hamster Habitats* Module

Common Core State Standards	Instructional Activities
CCSS: English Language Arts 1.1.2.2—Retell stories, including key details. 1.2.1.1—Identify main topic and key details of a text. 1.2.8.8—Identify the reasons an author gives to support points in a text.	Students recall details from informational text, express the main idea, make connections with prior knowledge, discuss the authors' purpose, and develop vocabulary and questioning abilities.
CCSS: Mathematics 1.0A—Operations: Add and subtract within 20 1.G—Geometry: Reason with shapes and their attributes	Students learn the names and attributes of basic shapes, have experience in composing and decomposing objects using smaller objects, express their reasoning in using 20 shapes to construct an exercise pathway for hamsters.

Table 13.2 NGSS Disciplinary Core Ideas in the *Designing Hamster Habitats* Module

Disciplinary Core Ideas from the Framework	Addressed in Designing Hamster Habitats
ETS1.A: Defining and Delimiting Engineering Problems A situation that people want to change or create can be approached as a problem to be solved through engineering. Asking questions, making observations, and gathering information are helpful in thinking about problems. Before beginning to design a solution, it is important to clearly understand the problem.	Students are introduced to the problem situation of needing a habitat for their imaginary pet hamster and learn that they will be solving this problem using an engineering design process. Throughout the module, students gather background information to help them to think about how to best design their habitat. Before starting the actual design of their habitat, students are asked to explain the problem and criteria and constraints of the design challenge.
ETS1.B: Developing Possible Solutions Designs can be conveyed through sketches, drawings, or physical models. These representations are useful in communicating ideas for a problem's solutions to other people.	Students individually sketch multiple design ideas that are used to communicate their ideas to group members prior to deciding on a group design. Students also use physical models of their habitats to communicate their design ideas to classmates.
ETS1.C: Optimizing the Design Solution Because there is always more than one possible solution to a problem, it is useful to compare and test designs.	In the final lesson, students test and share their designs before having the opportunity to redesign and retest their habitats.

Table 13.3 NGSS Engineering Practices in the *Designing Hamster Habitats* Module

Engineering Practices	Addressed in *Designing Hamster Habitats*
Defining Problems	The first lesson begins with the presentation of the need for a hamster habitat and the subsequent learning is related back to the problem of creating a hamster habitat. Additionally, before starting their design, students are introduced to the constraints and the criteria that need to be met to ensure a successful solution.
Developing and Using Models	Students create physical models of their hamster habitats and use these models to test and share their proposed solutions.
Analyzing and Interpreting data	The fourth lesson focuses on the importance of testing their materials before designing. The students use the collected data to determine which shapes best meet their stacking and building design criteria.
Using Mathematics and Computational Thinking	The integration of mathematics concepts throughout the module and the application in the design challenge helps students to see the integral role of mathematics in engineering.
Designing Solutions	In the fourth and fifth lessons, students follow a systematic process in which they design a habitat for their hamster. While there is not a single best solution, students' proposed solutions result from a process of balancing the criteria and constraints.
Engaging in Argument from Evidence	Students learn to defend their ideas and consider the ideas of others as they work to select the most promising group design from their individual brainstorms. Additionally, students learn to evaluate their own ideas and the ideas of others as they work to revise and improve their own designs.

Table 13.4 NGSS Crosscutting Concepts in the *Designing Hamster Habitats* Module

Crosscutting Concepts	Addressed in *Designing Hamster Habitats*
Patterns	The first two STEM lessons ask students to sort animals according to different criteria. As they are sorting, students identify patterns that help with the organization of these different animals and their habitats.
Cause and Effect	In the fourth lesson, students test the 3-D shapes that they will use in the design challenge, and the testing of these shapes represents a cause-and-effect relationship. For example, through the "flickability" test, students gather evidence about curved edges that supports ideas about how shapes resting on their curved sides will roll when lightly pushed.
Systems and System models	During the design challenge, students create their proposed solutions by using 3-D shapes to create a model of the system of a hamster habitat. This habitat model is the system that students use to test their solutions, and the identification of basic needs within their habitat demonstrates students' understanding of the boundaries of the system.
Stability and Change	Students perform the flickability and stackability tests on their 3-D shapes to learn about the characteristics of these shapes and which shapes are beneficial to the structure and stability of their designed model system.

practices of science and engineering, and crosscutting concepts. As before, the *Designing Hamster Habitats* provides the examples, but similar connections can be found in all six PictureSTEM modules. Table 13.2 lists disciplinary core ideas from the Framework to illustrate how the module helps students develop core ideas. Table 13.3 shows science and engineering practices that students develop. While all eight of the science and engineering practices are addressed through this module, six practices were chosen to show strong connections. Table 13.4 lists the crosscutting concepts addressed in this module.

Characteristics of Quality STEM Integration in the Elementary Classroom

The PictureSTEM modules were based on six tenets, which are described below. We believe that these tenets would be beneficial to any curriculum that attempts to integrate the STEM fields and connect with other important parts of the elementary school curriculum. Examples from *Designing Hamster Habitats* have been added to provide clarity.

1. Context. High-quality STEM integration modules should have a personally meaningful, motivating, and engaging context. Students need to have various personally meaningful contexts that provide them with access into the activity. *Designing Hamster Habitats* provides this in several ways. For example, the engineering design is for a pet, which will interest some students, while other students will enjoy the play aspect of recreating a hamster cage with geometric shapes. Some students will be motivated by the theme of animals throughout the module. The trade books engage the students in learning STEM in a meaningful context about hamsters, animals, and pets and telling stories about testing products and changing geometrical shapes.

2. Engineering Design. It is important for learners to participate in engineering design of relevant technologies for a compelling purpose that involves problem-solving skills, ties to the context, and requires science and mathematics for a successful design. *Designing Hamster Habitats* has students design the habitat trail to meet hamsters' physical needs (food, water, space, air, exercise, and shelter) through the use of 3-D geometrical shapes as a model of the trail.

3. Learn From Failure and Redesign. Students should be allowed to learn from initial failure and then have the opportunity to be successful by redesigning their solution. In *Designing Hamster Habitats*, students test their hamster habitat trail by looking for areas where the hamster can escape and justifying where the hamsters' food, water, space, air, and shelter will be located in their design. The students are given opportunities to redesign based on their test in order to improve their design for the hamsters.

4. Standards-Based Content. Activities should include appropriate, standards-based science, mathematics, engineering, or English language arts content that is relevant to the overall activity. *Designing Hamster Habitats* meets several of the content standards for both the NGSS and the Common Core State Standards for mathematics, as well as standards from the Common Core State Standards for English language arts.

5. Student-Centered Pedagogies. STEM subjects should be taught using student-centered pedagogies, such as inquiry, argumentation, discovery, and so on, that help students develop their scientific or mathematical knowledge in a manner that engages their interest as it deepens conceptual understanding. Student-centered pedagogies are used throughout the *Designing Hamster Habitats* module. For example, Lesson 1 has students sort animals by their characteristics from their own background knowledge, prior experiences, and observations, leading to generalizations about the animal types. Lesson 3 has students solve dissection puzzles with tangrams to develop their spatial reasoning abilities with 2-D shapes and provides opportunities for the teacher to employ differentiated instruction to meet students at their current skill level. Throughout the module, students are given opportunities to develop the STEM knowledge and skills that they will need to need to succeed in solving the major challenge.

6. Teamwork and Communication. Provide many opportunities for students to work together and present their work in order to develop their teamwork and communication skills. *Designing Hamster Habitats* emphasizes teamwork throughout the module and communication through students' sharing and defending their designs to their teacher and classmates.

Conclusion

PictureSTEM presents activities and ideas as interdisciplinary and integrated across STEM content areas and beyond. Through the implementation of PictureSTEM modules, elementary students are able to make connections between the disciplines and gain a deeper understanding of the content ideas. Additionally, students are able to apply what they have learned in other contexts. Teachers find that the picture books provide a realistic and engaging context in which to situate their students' learning of STEM concepts. STEM integration modules tied to literacy instruction from the PictureSTEM project have the potential to provide a new model for STEM learning environments, meaningfully addressing standards from NGSS and Common Core State Standards for mathematics and English language arts.

Acknowledgment

This material is based upon work supported by the National Science Foundation under Grant No. 1055382 through the Early Faculty Career program from the EEC division. Any opinions, findings, and conclusions or recommendations are those of the authors and do not necessarily reflect the views of the National Science Foundation.

References

Burns, M. (1994). *The greedy triangle*. New York, NY: Scholastic.
Maccarone, G., & Neuhaus, D. (1998). *Three pigs, one wolf, and seven magic shapes*. New York, NY: Scholastic.
National Academy of Engineering & National Research Council. (2009). *Engineering in K–12 education: Understanding the status and improving the prospects*. Washington DC: National Academy Press.

National Governors Association Center for Best Practices and Council of Chief State School Officers. (2010). *Common Core State Standards: Mathematics and English language arts.* Washington, DC: Authors.

National Research Council. (2012). *A framework for K–12 science education: Practices, crosscutting concepts, and core ideas.* Washington, DC: The National Academies Press.

Newcomb, R., & McLarney, R. (2008). *Is my hamster wild? The secret lives of hamsters, gerbils and guinea pigs.* New York, NY: Lark Books.

NGSS Lead States. (2013). *Next Generation Science Standards: For states, by states.* Washington, DC: The National Academies Press.

O'Malley, K. (1999). *Leo Cockroach . . . toy tester.* New York, NY: Walker & Company.

Palatini, M., & Whatley, B. (2003). *The perfect pet.* New York, NY: Harper Collins.

Relf, P. (1995). *The magic school bus hops home: A book about animal habitats.* New York, NY: Scholastic.

Tank, K. M., Pettis, C., Moore, T. J., & Fehr, A. (2013). Designing animal habitats with kindergartners: Hamsters, picture books, and engineering design. *Science and Children, 50*(9), 39–43.

14

STEM in Action

Solar House Design

Elizabeth Gajdzik, Purdue University
Johannes Strobel, Texas A&M University
Barbara diSioudi, ETA hand2mind

Students Collaborating on Their Model House

Image courtesy of ETA hand2mind.

Hands-On Standards STEM in Action is an activity-based integrated science, technology, engineering, and mathematics (STEM) enrichment program for students in Grades preK–5. The suite of modules focuses on developing students' critical problem-solving skills through age-appropriate collaborative engineering activities. Each topic is organized as a compact module that includes mathematics, science, and English language arts (ELA) content, centered on a real-world engineering challenge. The modules are designed to meet the new elementary-level Next Generation Science Standards (NGSS) engineering standards and Common Core State Standards in mathematics and ELA in an easy, approachable, and time-efficient format. The program is composed of three types of modules, including the following:

Adventure Series (Grades PreK–K)

- *Ron's Ramp Adventure*
- *Pam's Camping Adventure*
- *Bee-Bot's Space Adventure*
- *Pam and Ava's Mapping Adventure*
- *Shaking Adventure*

Exploration Series (Grades K–2)

- *Helicopter Hang Time Exploration*
- *Sunny Sandbox Exploration*
- *Wild Feet Exploration*
- *Muddy Mats Exploration*

Challenge Series (Grades 3–5)

- *Silly Straw Challenge*
- *Farmer Grady's Challenge*
- *Solar House Design Challenge*
- *The Great Toy Design Challenge*

Each of the modules is described at the following website: www.hand2mind.com/hos/stem/index.jsp.

Our decision to start as early as prekindergarten is grounded in existing research, which emphasizes the importance of developing interest as early as possible. Engaging early student interest is important, especially for girls and underrepresented minorities who turn away from STEM fields at an early age. Girls do so as early as third and fourth grade. Although the NGSS do not address the preK level, the modules in the Adventure Series target readiness for the NGSS standards by foreshadowing content and practices. preK modules require a modest instructional time investment—four 20-minute sessions. The lessons in the Exploration Series and Challenge Series are longer, requiring between 30 and 60 minutes per session.

Most modules contain four to six lessons that build on each other. The modules are designed to be flexible, so they can be used individually or in a coherent sequence. To further describe the modules from Hands-On Standards STEM in Action, the following paragraphs describe the *Solar House Design Challenge*, a Challenge Series module that targets fourth-grade standards.

Solar House Design Challenge

In the *Solar House Design Challenge*, students engage in an authentic integrated STEM module. Their charge as engineers is to help a client determine how to best use the sun to heat homes. This module, which includes mathematics, science, and engineering activities, builds students' understanding of energy conversion, passive solar energy, and budgeting while sharpening their critical thinking skills. Following is an overview of the module and an explanation on how the module's activities address the NGSS (NGSS Lead States, 2013) and Common Core State Standards for mathematics and ELA (NGA & CCSSO, 2010).

Get Ready to Engineer. In the first activity, students investigate three types of flooring being considered for use in their homes. Students examine flooring materials and predict which type will warm up most quickly and retain heat best. Next, the materials are placed under lights at testing stations, and the students observe and record the temperature just before the light is turned on and at the end of a measured time interval. Students calculate the difference in temperature and use their data to decide which material would keep the floor warmest.

Define the Problem. Once students have some experience working with the heat retention of flooring materials, the teacher introduces the engineering design problem and prompts students to consider how they will know if their design is successful. The teacher uses visuals and an interactive tool to think about how energy will move through the house.

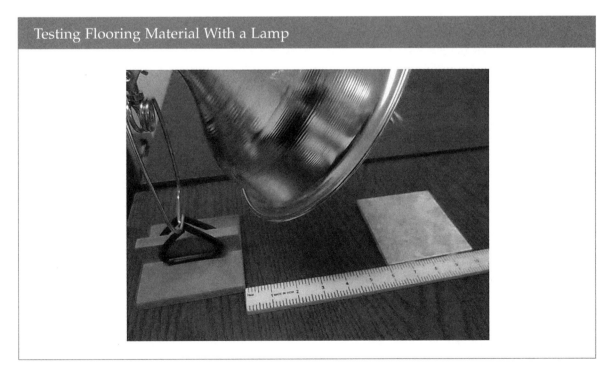

Testing Flooring Material With a Lamp

Image courtesy of ETA hand2mind.

Plan Solutions. Students work independently to use what they have learned about passive solar heating to create two house designs. Each student shares individual plans within a small team. The team members combine their best ideas to create a single team design plan.

Within a single team, students divide into pairs to develop a materials budget. The pairs first estimate how much area each window or skylight covers. Students measure and calculate the actual area of the windows and skylight. Based on a list of materials costs, they then calculate the cost of each type of window or skylight and then add up the components to determine the final cost of their house design. Once each pair has determined the total cost of their house, they return to their team to compare calculations. If they do not have the same solution, teammates work together to reach a single answer.

Make a Model. The students are given a budget and asked to redesign their model houses if their current plans exceed the budget. Once a team has created an acceptable budget, they collect a house kit, window coverings, and flooring to construct the team's model house. The teacher walks around ensuring that teams are building their models in accordance with their design plans.

Test the Model. The teacher sets up three testing stations to allow students to test their models. The teacher encourages analysis by asking students to consider the following: Which part of the testing stations represents south? Are the flooring materials in a position where the sun can shine on them? Why is this important? Which side of the house should the thermometer cord come out of? What difference might that make?

Teams place their models the same distance from the lamp to help ensure a fair test. When all of the models are in place, the teams record the temperature inside their houses. The teacher then gives the signal to turn on the lamp. The teacher announces the time at

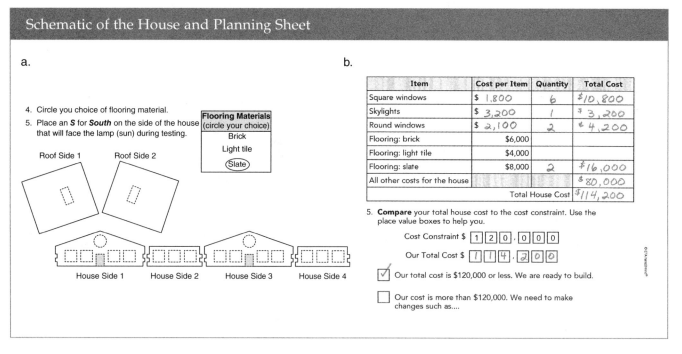

Image courtesy of ETA hand2mind.

10-minute intervals so that the teams can record the temperature readings inside their houses. At 20 minutes, the teacher signals to turn off the lamp so that the students can measure the rate at which their houses cool. After 40 minutes, the test is complete.

While waiting for their houses to heat up and cool down, students calculate the total open area on each side of the house and roof.

Student teams use their design plans and test results to analyze their findings using "Reflect On It" sheets as a guide. Teams prepare presentations about the effectiveness of their designs. The teacher encourages students to include pertinent data and draw conclusions by using prompts such as *We claim that the design of our house was successful because . . .*

Teams present their findings. The teacher assists the class in comparing their house designs by creating a class chart and graph. The teacher fills in the data as students provide it in their presentations.

Reflect and Redesign. The teacher introduces what it means to reflect and optimize. The teacher reviews the engineering design process and explains that engineers conduct numerous tests on their designs. Each test gives engineers information about how to make designs better.

One Team's Completed House

Image courtesy of ETA hand2mind.

Student Table With Temperature Data

Starting Temperature: __26.6__°C

Temperature Inside with Lamp On (Sun)			Temperature Inside with Lamp Off (No Sun)		
Time (minutes)	Temperature (°C)	Degrees above Starting Temperature	Time (minutes)	Temperature (°C)	Degrees above Starting Temperature
10	27.4	0.8	10	26.6	0
20	28.2	1.6	20	26.6	0

6. **Evaluate** the success of your design plan. Recall that a successful design must:

☐ Increase the inside temperature of the house by at least 4°C above the starting temperature in 20 minutes with the lamp on.

How successful was your design? Explain. _____

_____

☐ After 20 minutes with the lamp off, have a final temperature of at least 1° C

© ETA hand2mind

Image courtesy of ETA hand2mind.

Students Completing "Reflect On It" Sheets

Image courtesy of ETA hand2mind.

Next, the teacher leads the students to think about the results of testing their model houses. What was successful? What did not work well? The teacher also encourages students to consider the results of the models developed by other teams. Can students find similarities in the number and placement of windows among the successful designs? Are the same flooring materials used in all of the successful designs? Teams can revise their design plans and rebuild their model houses.

The teacher prompts students to discuss ways they can apply what they have learned about passive solar homes to keep their own homes warm in the winter and cool in the summer. *Sunlight comes in through windows, so in winter we should . . . To keep our house cool in summer, we could . . .*

Design Features

All STEM in Action units share certain design features:

1. **Each unit integrates different STEM disciplines.** The mathematics, science, technology, and engineering lessons are all needed for the students to solve the problem.

2. **There are several different ways to solve the problem.** The challenge is to rely on optimization and trade-off thinking to find the best possible solution (Purzer, Duncan-Wiles, & Strobel, 2013).

3. **The projects are story-based** and either connected to a personalized character (*preK*) or to a customer or company that has asked for their assistance (*K–5*).

4. **The problems students are asked to solve are authentic.** Each task emphasizes different forms of authenticity, including *task authenticity* in which students are

engaged in tasks similar to scientists and engineers; *impact authenticity* so students see that their work has meaning outside the classroom; and *context authenticity* in the form of a real project (Strobel, Wang, Weber, & Dyehouse, 2013).

5. **The units lead from concrete experiences to abstract thinking.** Each unit comes with its own manipulatives, which are tested in conjunction with the learning outcomes to enhance the experience of the students.

6. **Hands-on activities alternate with content enrichment** to deepen and strengthen the connection between content and practice.

7. **Unit designs are based on landmark reports** such as the National Academy of Engineering's *Changing the Conversation* (NAE, 2008) and research on engineering as an empathetic and caring discipline (Strobel, Hess, Pan, & Wachter Morris, 2013), emphasizing the role of engineering as contributing to the social good, the importance of diversity of people and ideas, and the balance of individual and team contributions and achievement.

8. **The units are broken up by phases of communication, presentation, and reflection**, emphasizing language to engage students in scientific reasoning and argumentation, the integration of mathematical reasoning, and the stimulation of engineering thinking.

9. **The units are field tested** throughout the design process, and the design team employs engineering processes for the design of the units.

10. **The teacher materials are clearly written** to avoid the need for extensive teacher professional development and preparation.

Connections to the Next Generation Science Standards and Common Core State Standards

Although it is a relatively short module with just four to six class sessions, *Solar House Design Challenge* can be used to help students achieve the NGSS and Common Core State Standards for mathematics and ELA.

Next Generation Science Standards

4-PS3 Energy

4-PS3–2 Make observations to provide evidence that energy can be transferred from place to place by sound, light, heat, and electric current.

> *Students observe, record, and draw inferences about energy transferred from electrical energy to light energy to heat energy.*

4-PS3–4 Apply scientific ideas to design, test, and refine a device that converts energy from one form to another.

> *Students investigate the properties of materials, then apply the scientific ideas they gained from that investigation to designing, testing, and refining a model house that heats up quickly and retains heat as long as possible.*

3–5-ETS1 Engineering Design

3–5-ETS1–1 Define a simple design problem reflecting a need or want that includes specified criteria for success and constraints on materials, time, or cost.

Although the teacher provides the scenario and constraints of materials, time, and costs, the students help to define the problem and criteria for success.

3–5-ETS1–2 Generate and compare multiple possible solutions to a problem based on how well each is likely to meet the criteria and constraints of the problem.

The students are challenged to brainstorm several solutions, then they meet as a team to compare ideas and decide on a single design. Later they are asked to compare their work to the designs made by their classmates.

3–5-ETS1–3 Plan and carry out fair tests in which variables are controlled and failure points are considered to identify aspects of a model or prototype that can be improved.

Students first conduct simple controlled experiments with different flooring materials, and later they conduct more complex experiments with model houses.

Science and Engineering Practices

The Solar House Design Challenge module engages students in six of the eight pracitces from the NGSS:

Practice 2: Developing and Using Models

Develop a diagram or simple physical prototype to convey a proposed object, tool, or process.

The students sketch, plan, and build physical models of their houses. They then use the models to test their ideas about how to design an efficient solar house. Finally, they build on what they learned with the models to consider how to keep their own homes warm in winter and cool in summer.

Practice 3: Planning and Carrying Out Investigations

Test two different models of the same proposed object, tool, or process to determine which better meets criteria for success.

Although each team builds just one house, it is compared with all of the other houses in the class. Students discuss the idea of a controlled experiment, keeping the intensity of the light equal in each trial.

Practice 4: Analyzing and Interpreting Data

Compare and contrast data collected by different groups in order to discuss similarities and differences in their findings.

Analyze data to refine a problem statement or the design of a proposed object, tool, or process.

Use data to evaluate and refine design solutions.

Students collect and analyze the data about how quickly their houses heat up and how long it takes them to cool down. They analyze the data by subtracting starting temperature from the temperature at different points in time. They graph the data and compare and contrast the data from different model houses, and they use that data to think about how to redesign their model houses.

Practice 5: Using Mathematics and Computational Thinking

Describe, measure, estimate, and/or graph quantities (e.g., area, volume, weight, time) to address scientific and engineering questions and problems.

In addition to the data analysis and graphing mentioned earlier, the students also quantify the elements of the house that may affect its energy efficiency, estimate and calculate the cost of materials, and redesign as necessary to stay within a given budget.

Practice 6: Constructing Explanations and Designing Solutions

Use evidence (e.g., measurements, observations, patterns) to construct or support an explanation or design a solution to a problem.

Apply scientific ideas to solve design problems.

During the presentation of the data from their houses, the students reference the data they have collected and offer explanations for the performance of their models based on their understanding of how different materials transfer energy.

Practice 7: Engaging in Argument From Evidence

Respectfully provide and receive critiques from peers about a proposed procedure, explanation, or model by citing relevant evidence and posing specific questions.

Make a claim about the merit of a solution to a problem by citing relevant evidence about how it meets the criteria and constraints of the problem.

Students are encouraged to ask questions and critique each others' models, appealing to evidence to determine which variables were most important.

Common Core State Standards Mathematics

Grade 4

4.MD.A.2 Use the four operations to solve word problems involving distances, intervals of time, liquid volumes, masses of objects, and money, including problems involving simple fractions or decimals, and problems that require expressing measurements given in a larger unit in terms of a smaller unit. Represent measurement quantities using diagrams such as number line diagrams that feature a measurement scale.

4. MD. A.3 Apply the area and perimeter formulas for rectangles in real world and mathematical problems.

Students engage in all of these operations as they investigate flooring, measure the dimensions of their plans and model houses, and collect and analyze data on the performance of their model houses.

Common Core State Standards English Language Arts

Grade 4

SL.4.1 Engage effectively in a range of collaborative discussions (one-on-one, in groups, and teacher-led) with diverse partners on *grade 4 topics and texts,* building on others' ideas and expressing their own ideas clearly.

SL.4.4 Report on a topic or text, tell a story, or recount an experience in an organized manner, using appropriate facts and relevant, descriptive details to support main ideas or themes; speak clearly at an understandable pace.

W.4.1 Write opinion pieces on topics or texts, supporting a point of view with reasons and information.

W.4.2 Write informative/explanatory texts to examine a topic and convey ideas and information clearly.

The lessons were designed to engage students in a number of conversations in pairs, small groups, and as a whole class. Students also record information and their ideas in journals. In addition, the students are asked to develop a plan to present their data and their ideas about why their model houses functioned as they did.

Conclusion

The unit presented here is part of a larger suite of modules provided for preK–5 STEM education. The other modules are comparable in the extent to which they can be used to support learning of the NGSS and CCSS in mathematics and ELA.

STEM in Action was developed though a collaborative effort of ETA hand2mind, which has provided hands-on learning supplemental solutions for more than 40 years; Purdue University's Institute for P–12 Engineering Research and Learning in the School of Engineering Education, which conducts basic and applied research in precollege engineering education; and Texas A&M's Institute for Engineering Education and Innovation with its *Foundations in Engineering Think & Make Tank.*

This joint project translates research in areas of STEM learning progressions, children's natural way of STEM thinking and acting, and age- and developmentally appropriate language to introduce engineering into practice.

Acknowledgment

The authorship team wants to acknowledge the pedagogy and production team members at ETA hand2mind and the brainstorm and design team members at Purdue University.

References

National Academy of Engineering. (2008). *Changing the conversation: Messages for improving public understanding of engineering.* Washington DC: National Academies Press.

National Governors Association Center for Best Practices and Council of Chief State School Officers. (2010). *Common Core State Standards: English language arts and mathematics.* Washington, DC: Authors.

NGSS Lead States. (2013). *Next Generation Science Standards: For states, by states.* Washington, DC: The National Academies Press.

Purzer, S., Duncan-Wiles, D., & Strobel, J. (2013). Teaching about engineering optimization and trade-offs to fourth and fifth graders. *Science and Children, Special Issue on Engineering and Science, 50*(5), 34–39.

Strobel, J., Hess, J., Pan, R., & Wachter Morris, C. A. (2013). Empathy and care within engineering: Qualitative perspectives from engineering faculty and practicing engineers. *Engineering Studies, 5*(2), 137–159.

Strobel, J., Wang, J., Dyehouse, M., & Weber, N. (2013). Conceptualizing authenticity in engineering education: A systematic literature review. Invited paper for special issue for David Jonassen. *Computers and Education, 64,* 143–152.

Index

CORWIN
A SAGE Company

Corwin is committed to improving education for all learners by publishing books and other professional development resources for those serving the field of PreK–12 education. By providing practical, hands-on materials, Corwin continues to carry out the promise of its motto: **"Helping Educators Do Their Work Better."**